Law of the C
Agricultural Policy

Law of the Common Agricultural Policy

JOSEPH A. McMAHON

Professor in Law at the
Queen's University of Belfast

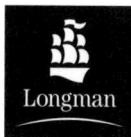

Longman

An imprint of **Pearson Education**

Harlow, England · London · New York · Reading, Massachusetts · San Francisco
Toronto · Don Mills, Ontario · Sydney · Tokyo · Singapore · Hong Kong · Seoul
Taipei · Cape Town · Madrid · Mexico City · Amsterdam · Munich · Paris · Milan

Pearson Education Limited
Edinburgh Gate
Harlow
Essex CM20 2JE
England

and Associated Companies throughout the world

Visit us on the World Wide Web at:
www.pearsoneduc.com

First published 2000

© Pearson Education Limited 2000

ISBN 0-582-30294-3 PPR

British Library Cataloguing-in-Publication Data
A catalogue record for this book is available from the British Library

Set by 7 in 10/12.5 pt Sabon
Printed in Malaysia

Contents

Series Preface

The Longman European Law Series is the first comprehensive series of topic-based books on EC Law aimed primarily at a student readership, though I have no doubt that they will also be found useful by academic colleagues and interested practitioners. It has become more and more difficult for a single course or a single book to deal comprehensively with all the major topics of Community law, and the intention of this series is to enable students and teachers to 'mix and match' topics which they find to be of interest: it may also be hoped that the publication of this Series will encourage the study of areas of Community law which have historically been neglected in degree courses. However, while the Series may have a student readership in mind, the authors have been encouraged to take an academic and critical approach, placing each topic in its overall Community context, and also in its socio-economic and political context where relevant.

The fundamental importance of the law of the Common Agricultural Policy is undeniable, yet, as Professor McMahon points out, it has not been a popular topic for inclusion in European Law courses. Perhaps this is due to the popularly held view that this is an area of forbidding complexity. If so, it may be hoped that the present book will help change that view. It is in fact a particularly appropriate time for a book on the law of the Common Agricultural Policy to appear, following the introduction of major changes to the structure of the common organisations of agricultural markets influenced by a combination of the Community's own budgetary concerns, the WTO agreements resulting from the Uruguay Round negotiations, and the anticipation of enlargement to Central and Eastern Europe. Professor McMahon analyses and describes his subject with admirable clarity, and his book will make the law of the Common Agricultural Policy a more approachable subject for study.

John A. Usher

Author's Preface

The Common Agricultural Policy is not a popular topic for inclusion within any European Law course as a distinct area of study, yet the principles emerging from cases under the policy are an integral part of every European Law course. These include principles dealing with the institutional structure of the Community, the use of Article 234 and the general principles of law, including human rights.

The study of the Common Agricultural Policy, however, deserves to be accorded a higher profile in the years to come. This is not only because of the reforms agreed to the policy at the Berlin European Council, but also because of the prospects for the enlargement of the Community from the middle of the next decade. The profile of the policy will be further increased as a result of the continuing process of ensuring a more equitable and market orientated international trade regime in agriculture. The negotiations for a new set of reforms will begin next year, and for the Community such negotiations will mark the beginning of efforts to agree international standards in the areas of social standards, consumer protection and the environment.

The Community has already started to incorporate environmental concerns within the scope of the Common Agricultural Policy, a process given added impetus by the 1992 MacSharry reforms and further impetus by the conclusions of the Berlin European Council. However, the process will have to go much further if the Community is to receive appropriate international recognition and credit for its activities. The mechanism to achieve this has been provided by the Treaty of Amsterdam with its demand that environmental concerns be incorporated into all policies of the Community. Similar pressures have or will emerge in the areas of regional and social cohesion, development cooperation, consumer protection and animal welfare. The next few years will be interesting times for the Common Agricultural Policy as it seeks to evolve to meet the challenges facing it.

The Articles of the EC Treaty have been renumbered by the Treaty of

Amsterdam with effect from May 1999. The new Article numbers have been used throughout this book, but a Table of Equivalence is provided at p. xxii so that readers may compare the old and new numbering.

Lastly, I would like to thank a number of people. Professor Usher for his invitation to contribute to this series, John Knowles and all the staff of the Law Library and the Official Publications section here at the Queen's University of Belfast, and Brian Willan, Pat Root and Patrick Bond at Longman. Special thanks also go to Catherine Minahan for all her work on the manuscript. Of course, the final word must go to the two people who make it all worthwhile.

Joseph A McMahon
October 1999

Table of Cases

Table of Legislation

Table of Equivalence

Treaty Establishing the European Community

Previous Numbering	*New Numbering*
Article 3	Article 3
Article 5	Article 10
Article 12	Article 25
Article 18	repealed
Article 28	Article 26
Article 30	Article 28
Article 36	Article 30
Article 37	Article 31
Article 38	Article 32
Article 39	Article 33
Article 40	Article 34
Article 41	Article 35
Article 42	Article 36
Article 43	Article 37
Article 44	repealed
Article 45	repealed
Article 46	Article 38
Article 85	Article 81
Article 86	Article 82

Previous Numbering	*New Numbering*
Article 92	Article 87
Article 93	Article 88
Article 94	Article 89
Article 100	Article 94
Article 100a	Article 95
Article 103	Article 99
Article 103a	Article 100
Article 105	Article 105
Article 110	Article 131
Article 113	Article 133
Article 130a	Article 158
Article 130r	Article 174
Article 130s	Article 175
Article 130u	Article 177
Article 130v	Article 178
Article 155	Article 211
Article 201	Article 269
Article 215	Article 288
Article 226	repealed
Article 228	Article 300
Article 235	Article 308

List of Abbreviations

ACP   African, Caribbean and Pacific

ACP	African, Caribbean and Pacific
AMS	Aggregate Measurement of Support
BFA	Banana Framework Agreement
BSE	Bovine Spongiform Encephalopathy
CAP	Common Agricultural Policy
CARPE	Common Agricultural and Rural Policy for Europe
CCT	Common Customs Tariff
EAGGF	European Agricultural Guidance and Guarantee Fund
ECU	European Currency Unit
GATS	General Agreement on Trade in Services
GATT	General Agreement on Tariffs and Trade
GDP	Gross Domestic Product
GNP	Gross National Product
GSP	Generalized System of Preferences
SPS	Sanitary and Phytosanitary Measures
UCLAF	Unité de Coordination de la Lutte Anti-Fraude
WTO	World Trade Organization

CHAPTER ONE

The role of agriculture in the Treaty

1.1 Introduction

On ne peut conceivoir l'établissement d'un marché commun général en Europe sans que l'agriculture s'y trouve incluse. C'est un des secteurs où les progrés de productivité qui résulteront du marché commun, c'est-à-dire de la spécialization progressive des productions et de l'élargissement des débouchés, peuvent avoir des effets les plus importantes sur le niveau de vie des producteurs aussi bien que les consommateurs. En outre, cette inclusion de l'agriculture dans le marché commun est une condition de l'équilibre des échanges entre les différentes économies des Etats membres.[1]

This was how the Spaak Report argued that the move to greater European integration which they advocated should include agriculture. It recognized that such inclusion was necessary to achieve equality between the Member States and would bring benefits to both producers and consumers. The Report was ambiguous on the type of policy to be followed, merely indicating that barriers to trade were to be gradually reduced during a transitional period in which a common policy was to be negotiated. It did not specify what type of agricultural policy was to be followed, although it did recognize that agriculture held a very special position in all the Member States.[2]

The likely future agricultural policy of the Community would be shaped by this 'special position' and by previous attempts to promote integration. One such attempt had been made as a result of a study initiated by the Consultative Assembly of the Council of Europe, the aim of which was to decide how western European countries could commonly

---

[1] Spaak Report (Bruxelles, 1956) p. 50. See Neville-Rolfe, E., *The Politics of Agriculture in the European Community* (European Centre for Political Studies, London, 1984), p. 185.

[2] For a discussion of this point see Tracy, M., *Agriculture in Western Europe: Challenge and Response (1880–1980)* (2nd edn) (Granada, London, 1982).

organize their agricultural markets. One of the resulting plans, referred to as the Charpentier plan after the French delegate who drafted it, would have created a High Authority with power to control production through the fixing of prices. Provision was also to be made for the elimination of all restrictions on the free flow of agricultural products between members and the harmonization of production costs through a series of compensatory taxes to be paid to members with high costs of production. As alternatives to this, building on the Charpentier plan, the Dutch proposed a common market for agricultural products and the British suggested inter-governmental cooperation to eliminate the disparities in members' agricultural policies. The plans, referred to as the Green Pool proposals, were never accepted, in part due to the then existing structural diversity of European agriculture and the varying methods of agricultural support used by different states.[3]

At this time all governments were intervening, to some extent, in the agricultural sector. The goal of such intervention was to achieve increased production through the provision of income guarantees to farmers, either through internal price support measures or through deficiency payments schemes. The primary purpose of such intervention was to ensure adequate food supplies for their populations in the immediate aftermath of the Second World War. However, Tracy concludes that:[4]

> From about 1953 there was a change in emphasis as agricultural production caught up with demand. The aim was no longer to raise production at all costs but to achieve selective expansion and to raise agricultural efficiency. At the same time concern with the relatively low level of farm incomes was increasingly felt and governments were placed in a quandary as the price guarantees they offered farmers tended to stimulate excess production.

Given the political and economic commitment of the western European countries to their farming communities, the diversity of structural problems within and between these countries and an inability to agree on the most appropriate mechanisms for European cooperation in agriculture, it is not surprising that the Spaak Report was ambiguous as to the type of agricultural policy to be adopted. This ambiguity was to be reflected in the Treaty of Rome provisions on agriculture.

[3] For a discussion of the Green Pool proposals see Tracy, pp. 261–66, Mansholt, S., 'Towards European Integration, Beginnings in Agriculture' (1952) 31 *Foreign Affairs* 112, Camps, M., *Britain and the European Community 1955–63* (OUP, London, 1964) and Griffiths, R. and Girvin, B. (eds), *The Green Pool and the Origins of the Common Agricultural Policy* (Lothian Press, Bloomsbury, 1995).

[4] Above n. 2, p. 240.

1.2 The Treaty provisions

Article 32(1) of the Treaty of Rome confirms that the common market extends to agricultural and trade in agricultural products, and Article 32(2) provides that the rules laid down for the establishment of that market are to apply to agricultural products 'save as otherwise provided in Articles 33 to 38'. However, unlike industrial products, the establishment of the common market, in the words of Article 32(4), must be accompanied by 'the establishment of a common agricultural policy among the Member States' thus confirming Article 3(e). An important link is therefore made between a common market for agricultural products and a policy to regulate this market; a link which is further confirmed by Article 37(3)(b), under which common organizations of the market must ensure 'conditions for trade within the Community similar to those existing in a national market'. In essence one cannot exist without the other. This link is of legal significance.

One aspect of the legal significance of this link is that the general rules of the Treaty must give way to any stricter rules laid down in agricultural legislation, and such legislation is to have precedence over national provisions. This principle was clearly established in the first reference by a Northern Ireland court to the European Court of Justice (hereafter, the Court), the case of *Pigs Marketing Board v Redmond*.[5] The case concerned the operation of the Board which was a state monopoly governing the marketing of pigs in Northern Ireland. By virtue of Article 60 of the Act of Accession of the United Kingdom, the common organization of the market in pigs was applicable as from 1 February 1973 and so the restrictions imposed by the Board were contrary to that legislation. The United Kingdom argued that as the Board was a state monopoly, Article 44 of the Act of Accession allowed it until 31 December 1977 to comply with the requirements of Article 31 of the Treaty on state monopolies. Using Article 32(2), the Court held that provisions relating to the common agricultural policy had precedence over the other rules relating to the establishment of the Common Market. So Article 44 of the Act of Accession was irrelevant. As the Court concluded:[6]

> ... any provisions or national practices which might alter the pattern of imports or exports or influence the formation of market prices by preventing producers from buying or selling freely within the State in which they are established, or in any other Member State, in conditions laid down by Community rules and from taking advantage directly of intervention

---

[5] Case 83/78 [1978] ECR 2347.   [6] *Ibid.*, p. 2371.

measures or any other measures regulating the market laid down by the common organization are incompatible with the principles of such organization of the market.

The ruling was repeated the following year in another case dealing with the common organization of the market in pigmeat, this time from the Republic of Ireland, where the issue was not the free movement of goods but the rules on competition, particularly the state aids provisions. The Court stated that 'recourse to the provisions of Articles 92 to 94 of the Treaty [now Articles 87–89] cannot modify the requirements flowing, for the Member States, from observance of the rules relating to the common organization'.[7] Such a consequence, for the Court, was necessitated by Article 32(2) of the Treaty which give priority to the specific provisions adopted in the context of the Common Agricultural Policy (CAP) over the general provisions of the Treaty relating to the establishment of the Common Market.

1.2.1 Scope of the Common Agricultural Policy

Before continuing the discussion of the significance of the link between the establishment of the Common Market on the one hand and that of the CAP on the other, it is necessary to discuss briefly the scope of the CAP. Article 32(1) refers to agricultural products as meaning 'the products of the soil, of stockfarming and of fisheries and products of first-stage processing directly related to these products'. Further guidance is also provided by Article 32(3), which notes that the products which are to be the subject of the CAP are listed in Annex II of the Treaty.[8] Analysis of Annex II reveals a number of products, such as cheese, margarine and processed fruits, which do not come within the definition offered by Article 32(1), and excludes a number of products, such as cotton, wool and wood, which do come within the scope of that paragraph.[9] For cotton, Protocol 4 of the Greek Treaty of Accession effectively amended Annex II to include this product, and a Community regime for cotton was established by Regulation 2169/81.[10]

---

[7] Case 177/78 *Pigs and Bacon Commission v McCarren* [1979] ECR 2161, p. 2191.

[8] Annex II of the Treaty is still based on the 1950 Customs Cooperation Council Nomenclature despite the fact that since 1988, the Common Customs Tariff is based on the International Convention on the Harmonized Commodity Description and Coding System. Alignment of Annex II to the Harmonized System would require a Treaty amendment, and so could be an opportunity to revise the coverage of Annex II.

[9] Community regulations in these areas are thus based on Article 308. For a discussion of wool, see Case 77/83 *CILFIT* [1984] ECR 1257.

[10] OJ 1981 L 211/12.

In the event of a conflict between the two definitions of agricultural products, the Court has determined that Article 32(3) has priority.[11] The final sentence of this paragraph allowed the Council to decide, within two years of the entry into force of the Treaty, on the inclusion of new products in Annex II. Regulation 7a/59 added certain products to this list, but this Regulation was not published in the *Official Journal* until January 1961.[12] One of the products so added was ethyl alcohol, and this addition, as well as the late publication of the Regulation, was challenged in the case of *König*.[13] After declaring that the late publication of the Regulation did not affect its validity, the Court went on to interpret the definitions of agricultural products offered in Article 32(1) and (3). It concluded:[14]

> The definition of agricultural products, placed at the head of the Title devoted to agriculture, would be devoid of practical meaning if it were not to be interpreted, as regards the power of the Council to fill in the gaps with which Article 38(3) [now Article 32(3)] is concerned, in the light of the aims of the common agricultural policy and with reference to the products with which the authors of the Treaty considered that policy to be concerned.

With specific reference to ethyl alcohol, the Court continued:

> The concept of 'products of first-stage processing directly related' to basic products must, accordingly, be interpreted as implying a clear economic interdependence between basic products resulting from a productive process, irrespective of the number of operations involved therein.

As ethyl alcohol had not undergone such processing as to render the price of the agricultural raw materials a marginal cost, it was legitimately included within the scope of Annex II by Regulation 7a.

The definition offered by the Court in *König* sets the limits for the application of the CAP, as the Court made clear in 1962 that the list provided by Annex II as supplemented by Regulation 7a was exhaustive.[15] New products can be added only through interpretation of Annex II, and as there are no Community provisions interpreting Annex II, reference may be made to the Explanatory Notes to the 1950 Brussels Nomenclature.[16] For those products which fall outside the scope of Annex II, as amended – for example, products of secondary processing – the Community has enacted a parallel system for what are referred to as

[11] See, for example, Case 77/83 *CILFIT* (above n. 9).
[12] JO 1961, p. 71.   [13] Case 185/73 [1974] ECR 607.   [14] *Ibid.*, p. 618.
[15] Cases 2 & 3/62 *Commission v Belgium and Luxembourg* [1962] ECR 425.
[16] Case 61/80 *Stremsel* [1981] ECR 851.

'non-Annex II products'.[17] Measures affecting such products cannot be taken on the basis of Article 37, which provides the legislative mechanism for the implementation of the CAP, unless the inclusion of such products is necessary to ensure the common organization of the market in the related Annex II product.[18] So, for example, the Court has upheld the use of Article 37 as the legal basis for the administration of hormones to farm animals, even though the hormones were not listed in Annex II.[19]

Although the Treaty offers a definition of agricultural products, no definition is offered for persons engaged in agriculture (Article 33(1)(b)) or producers (Article 37(3)(b)); and, likewise, no definition is offered for an agricultural holding. With respect to the first, differing definitions emerge from secondary legislation. One of the clearest definitions is found in the context of structural policy, where Article 2(1) of Regulation 797/85 provides that aid should be granted to agricultural holdings when the 'farmer' practises farming as his main occupation.[20] Further definition of 'farmer' under the Regulation is left to the discretion of the Member States, with the proviso that the 'farmer' should earn more than 50% of his income from farming and not devote more than 50% of total working time to work unconnected with the agricultural holding. Judicial interpretation of the Directive which this Regulation replaced revealed that part-time farmers not falling within this definition might still be entitled to assistance. So in *Lee v Minister of Agriculture*, in which the applicant was an office worker as well as a part-time farmer, the Court left it to the national court to decide whether the work undertaken by Lee was for the purpose of farm modernization.[21] Subsequent to the Regulation the Court ruled that the concept of farmers extended beyond human beings to include a legal person carrying on a farming activity.[22]

One consequence of no definition being offered of an 'agricultural producer' in the Treaty is that a discretion is vested with the Community

---

[17] See Regulation 3033/80 OJ 1980 L 323/1 establishing a general trade arrangement for the importation of certain industrial products resulting from the processing of Annex II products. See also Regulation 3448/93 OJ 1993 L 100/1.

[18] See Case 123/83 *BNIC v Clair* [1985] ECR 391.

[19] Case 69/86 *UK v Council (Hormones)* [1988] ECR 855.

[20] OJ 1985 L 93/1.

[21] Case 152/79 [1980] ECR 1495. See also Case 107/80 *Adorno* [1981] ECR 1469, where the applicant was a producer *and* a processor of wine; the Court did not consider the latter as a reason for excluding Adorno from the scope of Regulation 355/77 giving assistance to processors.

[22] Case 312/85 *Villa Banfi* [1986] ECR 4039 and Case C-162/91 *Tenuta* [1992] ECR I-5279. See also for a different decision Case 121/78 *Bardi* [1979] ECR 221.

institutions and the Member States in this area.[23] For example, in the case of *Denkavit* the Court noted:[24] '... for the purposes of the agricultural rules derived from the Treaty it is for the competent authorities where necessary to define the scope of such rules in relation to person and in relation to subject-matter.'

A similar approach to the question of the definition of 'agricultural holding' has been taken by the Court. The question arrived before the Court in the case of *Santa Anna*, where the plaintiff company were seeking a declaration that their business, raising poultry and laying hens, should be classified as agricultural, not industrial, for the purposes of social security contributions.[25] Apparently building on its decision in *Denkavit*, the Court noted:[26]

> Although the words 'agricultural holding' are used in various places in the Community rules ..., adopted by the Council or in certain cases by the Commission, in the sphere of agriculture, the definition of these words is far from being uniform throughout these rules which are, in any case, heterogeneous, but on the contrary varies according to the specific purpose pursued by the Community rules in question.

Given this heterogeneity, there was no general definition of 'agricultural holdings' in Community law. So, in the specific case of *Santa Anna*, the Member States were not obliged to employ the concepts used in the Treaty and the secondary legislation in the identification of agricultural holdings for the purposes of social security law.

1.2.2 The agricultural provisions and the free movement of goods

Returning to the significance of the link between the establishment of the Common Market and that of the CAP in the case of *Ramel*, the Court pointed out that 'the objectives of free movement and of the common agricultural policy should not be set against the other nor in order of precedence but on the contrary combined'.[27] In this particular case,

---

[23] In Case C-164/96 *Siagricola* [1997] ECR I-6129 the Court concluded (at p. 6129): 'Community legislation does not permit Member States, which are required to define the precise scope of the expression "farmer practising farming as a main occupation" to limit its scope to natural persons alone'.

[24] Case 139/77 [1978] ECR 1317, p. 1332. [25] Case 85/77 [1978] ECR 527.

[26] *Ibid.*, p. 540. The Court noted in an almost verbatim repeat of its decision in *Denkavit* that '... since the Treaty contains no precise definition of agriculture and still less of agricultural holding, it is for the Community institutions to work out, where appropriate for the purposes of the rules deriving from the Treaty such a definition of agricultural holding'.

[27] Cases 80 & 81/77 [1978] ECR 927, p. 944.

which concerned the common organization of the market for wine, France imposed levies on imports of Italian wine. The levies were permissible under Regulation 816/70, which created a derogation from the obligation not to impose charges having equivalent effect to customs duties. Under Article 31(2) of the Regulation, producer Member States were allowed to impose levies so as to limit imports where a disturbance of their market was threatened 'so long as all the administrative mechanisms necessary for the management of the market in wine are not in application'. France claimed that the necessary administrative mechanisms had not been put in place by Italy and, furthermore, that Article 32(2) of the Treaty constituted a general derogation from the free movement of goods rules. The question for the Court to answer was therefore whether Article 31(2) of the Regulation was consistent with the general Treaty rules on the free movement of goods.

Using Article 32(2), the view of the Court was that an express provision had to be found in Articles 33 to 38 of the Treaty which would justify, either expressly or by implication, a departure from the general free movement of goods rules. The Court concentrated on Article 44 (of the original Treaty but now repealed) which, during the transitional period, allowed Member States to introduce a system of non-discriminatory minimum prices if the abolition of customs duties and quantitative restrictions resulted in prices likely to jeopardize the attainment of the objectives of the CAP. As the use of this provision was subject to a number of strict conditions, and was limited to the transitional period, the Court considered that it could not justify the imposition of greater restrictions such as those allowed by Article 31(2) of Regulation 816/70. So, as the Court could not find such a provision, Article 31(2) was incompatible with Articles 13(2) (now repealed) and 32 to 38 of the Treaty and was declared invalid. The Court concluded:[28]

> Any prejudice to what the Community has achieved in relation to the unity of the market moreover risks opening the way to mechanisms which would lead to disintegration contrary to the objective of the progressive approximation of the economic policies of the Member States set out in Article 2 of the Treaty.

Priority must be given to the free movement of goods rules.[29]

In some respects the ruling in *Ramel* was to be expected. As early as 1964, in *Commission v Luxembourg and Belgium*, the Court had made it clear that the standstill provision in Article 25 of the Treaty prohibited

---

[28] *Ibid.*, p. 947.
[29] Case 68/76 *Commission v France* [1977] ECR 515, p. 523.

the imposition of new customs barriers to agricultural trade, irrespective of the fact that there was a special chapter of the treaty dealing with agricultural products.[30] Although this case and *Ramel* concerned customs duties and charges having equivalent effect, the principle that priority is to be given, unless there are exceptional circumstances, to all of the free movement of goods rules has been confirmed by the Court in subsequent cases. For example, in *Riviora* the Court concluded that a clause allowing for restrictions to be imposed by the Member States on the import of Spanish grapes had to be interpreted as applying only to direct imports, as otherwise it would impose restrictions on products already in free circulation within the Community.[31]

The priority given to the free movement of goods rules was acknowledged by the Commission in 1976 in the case of *Commission v France* (above), where it argued that:

> ... the special rules on agriculture cannot, in principle, affect the rules of the Treaty governing the free movement of goods. These rules are binding upon the Community legislator in relation to the setting-up of the common agricultural policy. ... Apart from the case of quite exceptional circumstances, the agricultural provisions of the Treaty do not allow the Community institutions the possibility of drawing up measures which do not conform to these rules.

The necessary conclusion from this is that the Community institutions cannot interfere with the free movement of goods within the Community. However, the priority accorded to the free movement of goods rules must be qualified. Various measures taken by the Community institutions to implement the CAP, such as price-fixing, subsidies and levies, could be declared to be an interference with trade. Given the economic nature of such measures, it is unlikely that they would be covered by either Article 30 (see below) or the list of mandatory requirements emerging from *Cassis de Dijon*.[32]

Whenever the Community takes action in the implementation of the CAP, it cannot be treated in the same way as action by the Member

---

[30] Cases 90 and 91/63 [1964] ECR 625.

[31] Case 179/78 [1979] ECR 1147. See also, as examples, Case 288/83 *Commission v Ireland* [1985] ECR 1761, Case 199/84 *Migliorini* [1985] ECR 3317, Case 216/84 *Commission v France* [1988] ECR 793.

[32] Case 120/78 *Rewe-Zentrale v Bundesmonopolverwaltung für Branntwein* [1979] ECR 649. The Court in this case held that a measure may be recognized as being necessary in order to satisfy the following mandatory requirements: (i) the effectiveness of fiscal supervision; (ii) the protection of public health; (iii) the fairness of commercial transactions; and (iv) the defence of the consumer.

States. This conclusion is obvious given the difference between action by a Member State, which is necessarily limited to its national territory, and action by the Community, which relates to a single regime applicable in all the Member States.[33] As the Court concluded in *Ramel*:[34]

> Many mechanisms of the organization of the market, such as price fixing and intervention systems, by organizing and regulating trade involve limitations on free movement and such limitations are not therefore of a temporary nature or justified by exceptional circumstances but are characteristic of the common agricultural policy.

So, for example, while production restrictions imposed by a Member State will constitute a breach of the free movement of goods provisions,[35] similar restrictions imposed by the Community will be acceptable despite the fact that they interfere with the free flow of goods between Member States and distort competition in the Common Market.[36] Likewise, while a Member State may not unilaterally extend the production and marketing rules of producer organizations to non-members,[37] a Community measure authorizing or obliging such an extension will be acceptable.[38] However, the Court's acceptance of such restrictions is not unlimited, as in *Commission v Ireland* the Court overturned Commission authorization for Ireland to maintain measures

---

[33] The obvious example here is the extensive case law of the Court on the legality of monetary compensatory amounts which operate in a manner similar to charges having the equivalent effect to customs duties. This case law is discussed in further detail in Chapter 4. In Case 216/84 *Commission v France (Milk Substitutes)* [1988] ECR 793, the Court held French measures prohibiting the sale of substitute milk powder to be contrary to the Treaty, for although they supported the CAP they ran counter to the principles of the free movement of goods.

[34] Above n. 27, p. 944.

[35] See for example, Case 190/73 *van Haaster* [1974] ECR 1123, where the Court stated (at p. 1134): 'It thus follows from the general pattern of the regulation that as regards trade within the Community the organization of the market in question is based on the freedom of commercial transactions, in conditions of fair competition, thanks to the stabilization of the quality of the products. Such a system excludes any national regulatory system capable of impeding intra-Community trade, directly or indirectly, actually or potentially.' See, however, Case 148/85 *Forest* [1986] ECR 3449.

[36] See for example, Case 139/79 *Maizena* [1980] ECR 3393, Case 37/83 *Rewe-Zentrale* [1984] ECR 1229 and, more recently, Cases C-157/96 *R v Ministry of Agriculture ex parte National Farmers' Union* [1998] ECR I-2211 and Case C-180/96 *United Kingdom v Commission* [1998] ECR I-2265.

[37] See for examples, Case 94/79 *Vriend* [1980] ECR 327, Case 29/82 *van Luipen* [1983] ECR 151 and Case 218/85 *Cerafel* [1986] ECR 3513. Producers of a product subject to a common organization may however be required by national law to affiliate with a national body provided the aims and activities of that body are compatible with Community law, see Case 222/82 *Apple and Pear Development Council* [1983] ECR 4083 and Case 237/82 *Kaas* [1984] ECR 483.

[38] See for example, Case 212/87 *Unilec* [1988] ECR 5075.

which it had unilaterally adopted and which were contrary to Community law.[39]

One final area of discussion is in relation to the interpretation of the exception to the free movement of goods relating to the protection of human and animal health laid down in Article 30. It is obvious that this exception to the free movement of goods will be particularly relevant given the wide scope of the measures adopted by the Community institutions in the implementation of the CAP. It is worth noting here that although public health forms one of the mandatory requirements identified by the Court in *Cassis de Dijon*, the Court seems to consider the validity of such measures under Article 30 even if they are equally applicable to both domestic and imported products.[40] In the case of *De Peijper* the Court concluded that:[41]

> Health and the life of humans rank first among the property or interests protected by Article 36 [now Article 30] and it is for the Member States, within the limits imposed by the Treaty, to decide what degree of protection they intend to assure, and in particular how strict the checks to guard against a risk of this kind, however slight, so long as that risk is genuine.

However, it must be pointed out that the discretion of the Member States in this area is limited. For example, inspections and the composition of feeding stuffs are governed by Community law, so national measures will be justifiable only where the matter is not governed by such laws or where such laws permit such measures.

In cases where there is some doubt as to the exact scope of Community legislation, a distinction has been drawn between legislation which is intended to regulate a particular matter comprehensively, in which case a Member State may not invoke its national measures, and those cases where the legislation is either irrelevant or incomplete, so allowing for the possible use of national measures. So, for example, in two cases dealing with a Directive on the composition and preparation of animal foodstuffs, the Court held that Germany could not use national provisions on minimum and maximum levels of certain ingredients in such foodstuffs as the Directive was comprehensive in this area,

---

[39] Case 288/83 [1985] ECR 1761. The case concerned preventing the import of potatoes originating in Cyprus which were in free circulation in the United Kingdom. See also Case C-128/89 *Commission v Italy* [1990] ECR I-3239 where the Court held that the Community institutions could not authorize a Member State to take measures which could not be justified under Article 30.
[40] See for example, Case 97/83 *Melkunie* [1984] ECR 2367.
[41] Case 104/75 [1976] ECR 613, p. 635.

but national health inspections under the Directive were permissible as it did not regulate these matters.[42]

Assuming that the Member States are allowed to carry out inspections, the Court has imposed various restraints on the powers of the Member States. For example, in *Commission v France*, the Court held that excessively frequent inspections, in this case of Italian wine, would lead to such inspections falling outside the scope of Article 30.[43] In this case the French government admitted that inspections of 10% of all consignments would be reasonable, but it had conducted inspections which at times reached 75% of Italian consignments of wine.[44] Such inspections were in addition to the checks conducted by the Italian authorities prior to the export of the wine. Indeed, the Court has confirmed that systematic inspections of imported goods along with a requirement of an export certificate from the exporting Member State confirming inspection may go beyond what is justifiable under Article 30.[45] Assuming that the inspection is carried out as a result of the requirements of Community law, according to the Court in *Bauhuis* a reasonable charge may be imposed by the Member State only where it constitutes payment for a service rendered to the economic operator.[46] In the event that there is no service rendered, for example if the inspection is carried out in the general interest, or the charge is imposed for an inspection conducted under the provisions of national law, this case confirms that such a charge constitutes a charge having an equivalent effect to a customs duty.[47] These principles do not apply, however, to inspections carried out at the external borders of the Community.[48]

To come within the scope of Article 30, the measures adopted by the Member States must be part of a seriously considered health policy. One case showing the need for such policy is *Commission v United Kingdom*, which involved a challenge to the imposition by the United Kingdom of

---

[42] Respectively Case 28/84 *Commission v Germany* [1985] ECR 3097 and Case 73/84 *Denkavit Futtermittel* [1985] ECR 1019. See also Case C-52/92 *Commission v Portugal* [1993] ECR I-2961.

[43] Case 42/82 *Commission v France* [1983] ECR 1013.

[44] In an order for interim measures in this case, the Court set the maximum percentage of 15% of consignments to be inspected, Case 42/82R *Commission v France* [1982] ECR 841. In a later case the Court accepted a percentage of 33% as it had been laid down in the relevant Directive, Case 37/83 *Rewe-Zentral* [1984] ECR 1229.

[45] Case 251/78 *Denkavit Futtermittel* [1979] ECR 3369.

[46] Case 46/76 [1977] ECR 5. See also Case 89/76 *Commission v Netherlands* [1977] ECR 1355, where the Court accepted the legitimacy of a charge imposed under the International Plant Protection Convention of 1951.

[47] See also Case 87/75 *Bresciani* [1976] ECR 129. The principle also applies where the inspections are carried out at a regional or municipal level, see Cases C-1/90 & C-176/90 *APESA v DSSC* [1991] ECR I-4179 and Joined Cases C-277/91, C-318/91 & C-319/91 *Ligur Carni* [1993] ECR 6621.

[48] See Case 70/77 *Simmenthal* [1978] ECR 1453 and Case 30/79 *Wigei* [1980] ECR 15.

an import prohibition on poultrymeat and eggs for all Member States with the exception of Denmark and Ireland.[49] The justification for this measure was to prevent the spread of Newcastle disease, a disease affecting poultry. Denmark and Ireland were excluded from the scope of the ban because they were totally free from the disease, indeed Ireland had a policy of prohibiting vaccinations and a requirement to slaughter flocks whenever infections broke out. The Irish policy was adopted by the United Kingdom which had previously operated a policy of vaccinations. The Court considered that this abrupt change of policy could not be characterized as a seriously considered health policy. As for their reasoning, it was pointed out that previous changes in United Kingdom policy had been preceded by studies and reports. The real aim of the change of policy seemed to be a response to domestic pressures to limit imports, in particular French imports, ahead of the Christmas period.[50]

In a subsequent case, the Irish ban on imports of poultry adopted as part of the policy of preventing Newcastle disease was also held not to be justified under Article 30.[51] Although the Court did not question the existence of a seriously considered health policy, they found that the complete ban on imports from countries operating the vaccination policy was out of proportion with the aim pursued by the ban, especially as outbreaks of the disease within the Community had been steadily declining for years. So, for a measure to be justifiable under Article 30 once the obstacle of a seriously considered health policy has been overcome, it must also be proportionate to the objectives pursued and not involve arbitrary discrimination. As for the element of proportionality, the Court held that the United Kingdom requirement that imports of UHT milk needed a licence and that such milk be re-treated, which had the effect of rendering imports prohibitively expensive, could not be justified under Article 30; import declarations and a policy of sampling imports could have achieved the same goals.[52] In relation to the discrimination requirement, the Court has held that a French measure imposing restrictions on the advertising of certain alcoholic drinks, which the French government claimed was part of their campaign against alcoholism, fell outside Article 30 as equivalent restrictions were not imposed on similar domestic products.[53]

---

[49] Case 40/82 [1982] ECR 2793.
[50] French producers would later bring an action against the UK Ministry of Agriculture, see *Bourguoin* [1984] 3 All ER 585.
[51] Case 79/82 *Commission v Ireland* [1984] ECR 317.
[52] Case 124/81 *Commission v United Kingdom (UHT Milk)* [1983] ECR 203.
[53] Case 152/78 *Commission v France* [1978] ECR 2299. See also Cases C-1/90 & C-176/90 [1991] ECR I-4179, where the Court upheld a similar ban imposed on all products on the basis of the mandatory requirement of consumer protection.

Once a seriously considered health policy has been established, there is no need to demonstrate unanimity of scientific opinion on the matter at issue, serious doubt will be sufficient. The approach of the Court in this area is that:[54]

> ... in so far as there are uncertainties at the present state of scientific research it is for the Member State, in the absence of harmonization, to decide what degree of protection of the health and life of humans they intend to assure, having regard however for the requirement of the free movement of goods within the Community.

Using this test the Court has held that a Dutch ban on the use of nisin in processed cheese intended for the domestic market was justified under Article 30, even though other Member States allowed the use of this additive.[55]

Despite the discretion given to Member States in the absence of scientific unanimity on the safety of a particular additive or pesticide, the Court has stated that such a discretion is not unlimited. In *Commission v Germany (Beer Purity)*, the Court considered that where an additive had been approved in one (or more) Member State, an importing Member State must authorize that additive if certain conditions are met.[56] Such conditions included if international scientific data showed the additive to be harmless to individuals given the dietary habits of the population, and if the additive met a genuine need, either technical or some other need. In this particular case the Court considered that the blanket prohibition imposed by Germany on the use of all additives in beer was not justified under Article 30 as it had been imposed without regard to the dietary habits of its population and the additives in question had been permitted in other foodstuffs.[57]

1.2.3 The agricultural provisions and the rules on competition

As the above discussion has illustrated, agricultural products are subject to the application of the general rules on the free movement of goods. No provision is made in Articles 33 to 38 for the contrary position. This is not the case with the rules on competition. Article 36 provides: 'The

---

[54] Case 174/82 *Sandoz* [1983] ECR 2445, p. 2463.
[55] Case 53/80 *Eyssen* [1981] ECR 409. See also Case 272/80 *Maatschappij* [1981] ECR 3277, Case 94/83 *Heijn* [1984] ECR 3263, Case 247/84 *Motte* [1985] ECR 3887 and Case 54/85 *Mirepoix* [1986] ECR 1067.
[56] Case 178/84 [1987] ECR 1227.
[57] The ruling in this case casts some doubt on the decisions of the Court in *Heijn*, *Motte* and *Mirepoix* (above n. 55).

provisions of the Chapter relating to rules on competition shall apply to production of and trade in agricultural products only to the extent determined by the Council ..., account being taken of the objectives set out in Article 33.'

According to the Court in 1994, Article 36 was a recognition of the priority given to agricultural policy over the objectives of the Treaty in the competition area, for although Article 3 provides for the institution of a system of undistorted competition, it also provided for the establishment of the CAP.[58] Recognizing that the simultaneous pursuit of these objectives might prove difficult, Article 36 gives the Council the power to determine the extent to which the competition rules should apply to agriculture.

The Council made the determination provided for in Article 36 through the enactment of Regulation 26/62, Article 1 of which provided for the application of Articles 81 to 86 of the Treaty to the production of or trade in agricultural products.[59] Article 2(1) is an immediate exception to this, providing for the non-application of Article 81(1) to agreements, decisions or concerted practices which are either an integral part of a national market organization or necessary to attain the objectives of the CAP.[60] A third, and final, exception relates to the activities of producer associations concerned with the production or sale of agricultural products or the use of joint facilities for the storage, treatment or processing of agricultural products, and under which there is no obligation to charge identical prices. The Commission has the power under this provision to determine whether or not competition is excluded or the objectives of the CAP are being jeopardized by the activities of the producer associations. In the event that a national court considers an agreement to fall within the second sentence of Article 2, the national court may stay proceedings to allow itself or the parties to seek a decision from the Commission or to refer the matter to the Court.[61]

As an exception, Article 2 has been strictly construed.[62] For example, the Court has held that it applies only to Annex II products. In *BNIC v Clair*, the Court held that cognac was an industrial product and rejected an argument for special treatment based on the regional economic importance of the product.[63] Similarly, in *BNIC v Aubert* the Court

---

[58] Case C-280/93 *Germany v Council* [1994] ECR I-4973.
[59] JO 1962, p. 993.
[60] See Joined Cases C-319/93, C-40/94 and C-224/94 *Dijkstra* [1995] ECR I-4471, where the Court laid down rules for the application of Regulation 26 by the national courts.
[61] *Ibid.*, pp. 4510–11.
[62] See for example, Case C-399/93 *Oude Luttikhuis* [1995] ECR I-4515.
[63] Case 123/83 (above n. 18). In 1976 the Commission had decided that armagnac was an industrial product, *Pabst and Richarz/BNIA* OJ 1976 L 231/24.

found brandy to be an industrial product and it did not matter that the levies collected by BNIC were in part used to finance measures to support wine, an Annex II product.[64] In relation to national market organizations, a similar strict approach to interpretation has been adopted. In its decision in *New Potatoes* the Commission, confirming the jurisprudence of the Court,[65] held that the objectives of the national market organization must be equivalent to those pursued by common organizations of the market.[66] As the decisions and agreement between the various groups of producers did form an integral part of the French national market organization, negative clearance was granted.[67]

Equally, for an agreement to come within the scope of the exception it must promote all of the objectives of the CAP, not just some of them. Hence, a Commission decision declaring an agreement concluded between Dutch fruit importers and fruit wholesalers outside the scope of Article 2 of Regulation 26/62 was upheld by the Court even though it met the objectives of Article 33(1)(c) to (e) of stabilizing the market, assuring availability of supplies and ensuring that supplies reached consumers at reasonable prices.[68] For the Court, the applicants had not shown how their agreement was necessary to 'increase agricultural productivity' or to 'ensure a fair standard of living for the agricultural community', objectives for the CAP in Article 33(1)(a) and (b).[69] For the Court, it was essential that in their decisions the Commission should explain how the agreement satisfies (or fails to satisfy) each of the objectives in Article 33.[70] Finally, in *Suiker Unie* the Commission argued, and the Court accepted the argument, that the exception in Regulation 26/62

---

[64] Case 136/86 [1987] ECR 4789. See also *Stremsel* (above n. 16), where the Court concluded that rennet, an enzyme used in the manufacture of cheese, was not included in Annex II, so Regulation 26/62 could not be used to excuse an exclusive purchasing obligation. See also Case T-61/89 *Dansk Pelsdyravlerforening* [1992] II-ECR 1931, where the Court of First Instance rejected the argument that animal furs came within the scope of Annex II, and Case C-250/92 *Gottrup-Klim* [1994] ECR I-5641, where the Court rejected the argument that fertilizers and plant protection products, products not listed in Annex II and for which Community rules had been adopted using Article 37, came within the scope of Regulation 26/62.

[65] See Case 48/74 *Charmasson* [1974] ECR 1383 which is discussed further in Chapter 2.

[66] OJ 1988 L 59/35.

[67] This was the first decision granting negative clearance under this part of Article 2(1). See also *Bloemenveilingen Aalsmeer* OJ 1988 L 262/27 and the subsequent changes to this arrangement, Joined Cases T-70/92 and T-71/92 *Florimex and VGB* [1997] ECR II-693 and Case T-77/94 *VGB* [1997] ECR II-759.

[68] Case 71/74 *Frubo* [1975] ECR 563.

[69] For further decisions on this point, see *Preserved Mushrooms* OJ 1975 L 29/26 and *Cauliflowers* OJ 1978 L 21/23.

[70] See also Case C-399/93 *Oude Luttikhuis* (above n. 62) and Joined Cases T-70/92 and T-71/92 *Florimex and VGB* (above n. 67).

applies only when the competition rules jeopardize the implementation of the CAP.[71]

The exception in Article 2 relates only to Article 81; Article 82 applies with full force to the production of or trade in agricultural products. With respect to the remaining rules on competition, in particular those on state aids, Article 4 of Regulation 26/62 provides for the application to Annex II products of Article 88(1) and the first sentence of Article 88(3). Therefore, the Commission, in cooperation with the Member States, is to keep all existing aid granted by the Member States under review, and is to be informed of plans to grant or alter aid, in time for it to make comments. If there is no common organization of the market, the Member States have a duty to notify the Commission of their plans to grant or alter aid.[72] In practice, most common organizations of the market provide for the application of the Treaty's rules on state aids. It is clear, however, that the application of these general rules are subordinate to the rules laid down for the common organization of the market.[73] In the case of *McCarren*, the Irish Pigs and Bacon Commission used part of the proceeds of a levy it raised to grant export bonuses, and the Court concluded:[74]

> A Member State cannot therefore, either directly or through the intermediary of an agency on which it confers powers to that intent, pay bonuses in whatever form for products intended to be marketed within the Common Market.

The national state aid, provided by the export bonuses, although allowable under the general rules on state aids, was prohibited under the more specialized rules governing the common organization of the market in pigmeat. However, a general aid granted by a Member State may fall outside the scope of Article 4 and so be subject to the Treaty rules on state aids.[75]

---

[71] Commission Decision, OJ 1973 L 140/17 and the Court decision, Cases 40–48, 50, 54–56, 111, 113–114/73 [1975] ECR 1663. See also *Milchförderungsfonds* OJ 1985 L 35/25.

[72] Case 337/82 *St Nikolaus Brennerei* [1984] ECR 1051.

[73] However, see Case C-122/94 *Commission v Council* [1996] ECR I-881, where the Court dismissed the Commission's argument that aid granted by the Council to France and Italy undermined the common organization of the market in wine.

[74] Case 177/78 [1979] ECR 2161, p. 2188.

[75] Case 290/83 *Commission v France* [1985] ECR 439.

1.2.4 *The agricultural provisions and the Common Commercial Policy*

In common with the free movement of goods, no provision in Articles 33 to 38 refers to the specific relationship between the agricultural provisions and the provisions on the Common Commercial Policy. This is a matter which has not been the subject of much debate within the Community, but its importance cannot be denied, especially as international efforts to reform agricultural policies have become increasingly important.

The Preamble to the Treaty recognized the desire of the Member States to create improved social and economic development by 'deciding to contribute, by means of a common commercial policy, to the progressive abolition of restrictions on international trade'. This was reaffirmed in Articles 3(b), 18 and 131. Before its deletion by the Treaty of Amsterdam, Article 18 on the setting of the Common Customs Tariff (CCT) stated:

> The Member States declare their readiness to contribute to the development of international trade and the lowering of barriers to trade by entering into agreement designed on a basis of reciprocity and mutual advantage, to reduce customs duties below the general level of which they could avail themselves as a result of the establishment of a customs union between them.

Article 131 provides:

> By establishing a customs union between themselves Member States aim to contribute, in the common interest, to the harmonious development of world trade, the progressive abolition of restrictions on international trade and the lowering of customs barriers.

As a result of the Treaty on European Union, an international aspect has been added to the Community's profile. For example, Article 177 requires a Community contribution to the economic and social development of developing countries through promoting, *inter alia*, their gradual integration into the world economy.[76]

What, therefore, is the relationship between these provisions and the provisions on agriculture? According to Article 34(3), common organization of the market for agricultural products established to realize the

---

[76] Case C-280/93 *Germany v Council* (above n. 58), where the Court rejected the German argument that the regulation establishing the common organization of the market in bananas was part of a development policy for the ACP and so could not be based on Article 37.

objectives of Article 33 may include machinery for the stabilizing of imports. The necessary implication here is that customs duties and other more restrictive measures may be chosen to achieve this goal. According to the Court in *Redmond*, the more specific provisions of agricultural legislation will prevail over the more general provisions on the free movement of goods, so the goal promoted by the original Article 18 would have to give way to the more specific objective of stabilizing imports.[77] Indeed, in the case of *Neumann* the Court had made it clear that although import levies imposed under the common organization of the market bore a resemblance to customs duties, the levy did not constitute a customs duty but rather was a charge regulating external trade connected with the common price policy.[78] As such, external protection for agricultural products would be guaranteed through this system, in contrast to other products where protection would be offered through the CCT. Although it is true that the Treaty provisions on customs duties and charges having equivalent effect must give way to more specific agricultural legislation, it is also true that such legislation anticipated developments in commercial policy. For example, in *Daimantarbeiders v Indiamex* the Court concluded that after the entry into force of the CCT, Member States were no longer free unilaterally to change the level of external protection afforded by the CCT. A similar prohibition had already been included in the agricultural legislation establishing the common organizations of the market which had been established throughout the transitional period.

As for the relationship between the provisions on agriculture and Article 131 and the Common Commercial Policy, it must be assumed that by virtue of Article 32(2) the latter provisions are applicable to the CAP. It could be argued that the objective of assuring availability of supplies in Article 33(1)(c) points to a policy which is reasonably open to international trade. This was at issue in the case of *Dürbeck*, which involved a challenge to the validity of various Commission regulations which had suspended the release into free circulation of Chilean dessert apples.[79] In response to the allegation that the measures infringed Article 131, the Court noted that:[80]

> Article 110 of the Treaty [now Article 131] ... cannot be interpreted as prohibiting the Community from enacting, upon pain of committing an

---

[77] Case 83/78 [1978] ECR 2347.
[78] Case 17/67 *Neumann* [1967] ECR 441, see also discussion in Chapter 5.
[79] Case 112/80 [1981] ECR 1095. See also Case C-152/88 *Sofrimport* [1990] ECR I-2477 and Case T-489/93 *Unifruit Hellas* [1994] ECR II-1201.
[80] *Ibid.*, pp. 1119–20.

infringement of the Treaty, any measure liable to affect trade with non-member countries even where the adoption of such a measure is required in this case, by the risk of a serious disturbance which might endanger the objectives set out in Article 39 of the Treaty [now Article 33] and where the measure is legally justified by provisions of Community law.

This confirms similar statements made by the Court in the earlier case of *Balkan*.[81] The fact that Chile had complained to the GATT about this measure was not, in the opinion of the Court, capable of putting the validity of the Regulations in question.[82] While the Court upheld the validity of the Regulations in the GATT complaint, the panel ruled that there had been a breach of various aspects of Articles XI and XIII GATT.[83]

Dürbeck also confirms that when the normal mechanisms used within the common organization are not sufficient to deal with the situation where the Community market experiences, or is threatened with, serious disturbances endangering the objectives of Article 33, safeguard measures may be adopted. In adopting such measures the Community can discriminate between third countries.[84] Finally, and with respect to export subsidies, their purpose was characterized by the Court in *Westzücker* as a means of ensuring the proper functioning of the market by allowing for the export of agricultural products, and thus to help to achieve the objectives of the CAP.[85] The subsidy system was designed to allow Community products to compete fairly on the world market, so in a situation where the exporter had been overcompensated for the difference between the Community and world market price, the Court has declared such subsidies illegal.[86]

Further guidance on the relationship between Articles 32 to 38 and

---

[81] Case 5/73 [1973] ECR 1091. In this case the Court noted that the measure at issue did contravene Article 131 as it had not been established that 'by adopting such measures the Council had overstepped the boundaries of the wide power of assessment' conferred by Article 34 in matters of commercial policy.

[82] The Court had decided in Cases 21–24/72 *International Fruit Company* [1972] ECR 1219 that the Community had assumed the powers previously exercised by the Member States under the GATT and thus the provisions of that agreement were binding on the Community but did not allow individuals to use GATT provisions to challenge the lawfulness of Community measures. See also Cases 267 & 269/81 *SPI and SAMI* [1983] ECR 801 and Case C-280/93 *Germany v Council* (above, n. 58).

[83] Basic Instruments and Selected Documents (BISD) 27th Supplement (1981) 98. As the measure was abolished before the panel met, no further action was taken on the complaint. It is worth noting that subsequent complaints led to much more critical rulings, BISD 36/S (1990) 93 and 135.

[84] See, for example, Case 245/81 *Edeka* [1982] ECR 2745. For further discussion of safeguard mechanisms see Chapter 5.

[85] Case 57/72 [1973] ECR 231. For further discussion of export subsidies see Chapter 5.

[86] Case 167/82 *Nordgetreide* [1983] ECR 1149.

Article 131 would emerge from a series of cases from the late 1980s and early 1990s. In the case of *Commission v Council (Glands)*, which concerned a directive to facilitate trade in glands for pharmaceutical manufacturing purposes, the Court delivered its opinion on the relationship between these two sets of provisions.[87] The particular measure had been adopted using Articles 37, 94 and 133, and the Commission argued that Article 37 by itself was sufficient. The Court concluded that Article 37 was the most appropriate legal basis for this measure. As for the Council's recourse to Article 133, the Court stated:[88]

> It must further be pointed out that the mere fact that the contested directive concerns imports into the Community does not suffice to make Article 113 [now Article 133] applicable. It is apparent from Article 40(3) [now Article 34(3)] that measures taken in the context of the Common Agricultural Policy may also affect importation and exportation of the products concerned.

The conclusion to be drawn is that the provisions on agriculture have precedence over those on the Common Commercial Policy. It must be pointed out, however, that the contested measure also concerned the marketing of these products within the Community, so the regulation of trade may not have been the primary purpose of the measure. So, measures which have as their primary purpose the regulation of trade in agricultural products may be based on Article 133, in addition to Article 37.[89]

Further guidance on this issue emerged as a result of the Court's response to a request by the Commission under Article 300(6) for an opinion on the competence of the Community to conclude various aspects of the overall Uruguay Round Agreement.[90] The Court drew a distinction between the directive which was at issue in the case of *Commission v Council (Glands)*, which was properly based on Article 37, as it pursued one or more of the objectives listed in Article 33, and the Agreement on Agriculture the purpose of which was to establish a 'fair and market-oriented agricultural trading system'. The Court continued:[91]

> The fact that the commitments entered into under the Agreement require internal measures to be adopted on the basis of Article 43 of the Treaty

---

[87] Case 131/87 [1989] ECR 3473.   [88] *Ibid.*, p. 3771.

[89] In Case 52/81 *Faust* [1982] ECR 3745, the Court rejected the argument that Article 34(3) limits a common organization of the market to the pursuit of Article 33 objectives. In its opinion, objectives of external commercial policy can also be pursued by the organization.

[90] Opinion 1/94 [1994] ECR I-5276.   [91] *Ibid.*, pp. 5397–98.

[now Article 37] does not prevent the international commitments themselves from being entered into pursuant to Article 113 [now Article 133]
alone.

The Court thus rejected the argument of the Council, which was supported by the European Parliament and the United Kingdom, that
Article 37 should have been used to adopt the Agreement on Agriculture
as it would affect Community products subject to common organizations of the market.[92] The Court went on to reject the argument that
Article 37 should have been used as the legal basis for the conclusion of
the Agreement on the Application of Sanitary and Phytosanitary
Measures. Like the Agreement on Agriculture, the purpose of this agreement was to establish a multilateral framework of rules and disciplines
in this area, so Article 133, by itself, was a sufficient legal basis.

Opinion 1/94 confirms that measures which have as their primary
purpose the regulation of international trade in agricultural products
may be based on Article 133. The Court would later go on to confirm,
however, that measures which pursued one or more of the objectives
listed in Article 33 were properly based on Article 37. In a case concerning the export ban imposed on British beef as a result of the BSE crisis,
the Court stated that:[93]

> It is settled case-law that Article 43 of the Treaty [now Article 37] is the
> appropriate legal basis for any legislation concerning the production and
> marketing of agricultural products listed in Annex II to the Treaty which
> contributes to the achievement of one or more of the objectives of the com-
> mon agricultural policy set out in Article 39 of the Treaty [now Article 33].

The export ban, based on Article 37 and Directives 89/662 and
90/425,[94] was challenged on the basis that the ban should not have been
adopted under measures aimed at the internal market but rather under
more specific measures governing trade with third countries. Article 37,
the Court maintained, was an appropriate and sufficient legal basis in
relation to trade in agricultural products with third countries.

Having examined the relationship between the agricultural provisions
and various other sets of Treaty provisions, it is now time to turn to a
detailed consideration of Articles 33 to 38.

[92] *Ibid.*, 5287.
[93] Case C-180/96 *United Kingdom v Commission* [1998] ECR I-2265, pp. 2305–06.
[94] This will be discussed further in Chapter 3.

CHAPTER TWO

The Common Agricultural Policy and the Treaty

2.1 Introduction

The previous chapter concentrated on the relationship between the general provisions of the Treaty and the more specific provisions of the CAP and, in particular, Article 32. This chapter will examine the objectives set for the policy in Article 33, both individually and collectively. Thereafter the mechanisms chosen to implement these objectives are discussed, in particular the nature of common organizations of the market and the position of national market organizations. The legislative power granted to the Community institutions under Article 37 to implement the CAP is also examined. The chapter ends with a brief discussion of the evolution of the CAP from the first set of decisions taken on it to the recent efforts to promote further reform of the policy.

2.2 The objectives of the CAP

The objectives set for the CAP in Article 33 are:

1. (a) to increase agricultural productivity by promoting technical progress and by ensuring the rational development of agricultural production and the optimum utilization of the factors of production, in particular labour;

(b) thus to ensure a fair standard of living for the agricultural community, in particular by increasing the individual earnings of persons engaged in agriculture;

(c) to stabilize markets;

(d) to assure availability of supplies;

(e) to ensure supplies reach consumers at reasonable prices.

2. In working out the common agricultural policy and the special methods of its application, account shall be taken of:

(a) the particular nature of agricultural activity, which results from the social structure of agriculture and from structural and natural disparities between the various agricultural regions;

(b) the need to effect the appropriate adjustments by degrees;

(c) the fact that in the Member States agriculture constitutes a sector closely linked with the economy as a whole.

The objectives are a reflection of the three factors which have always been used to justify governmental intervention in the agricultural sectors.[1] Firstly, the politico-economic factor, to contribute to overall economic growth of the Member States, both individually and collectively, which is reflected in Article 3(e), Article 33(1)(a) and (c) and Article 33(2)(c). Secondly, the socio-political factor, a concern with the welfare of the rural population, reflected in Article 33(1)(a) and, more significantly, (b) and in Article 33(2)(a) and (b). Thirdly, and lastly, the socio-economic factor, a concern with adequate food supplies for consumers, which is reflected in Article 33(1)(d) and (e).

Looking more closely at the objectives, the first objective in Article 33(1), an increase in agricultural productivity, is to be pursued by promoting technical progress and a rational development and optimum use of agricultural production factors. This implies a type of regional structural policy; an implication which is given added weight by Article 33(2)(a), which requires the particular nature of agricultural activity to be taken into account in the working out of the policy. Through the use of the word 'thus' in paragraph (b), it appears that both objectives are connected. So, it could be argued that the regional structural policy must lead to an achievement of a fair standard of living for the agricultural community. However, some doubt can be cast on this interpretation as a result of the second part of paragraph (b), which sets as an objective an increase in the individual earnings of persons engaged in agriculture. This may mean that the most important aspect of the objectives is to increase the earnings of agricultural producers so that they have a fair standard of living, thus making paragraph (b) a type of income guarantee. As such it would have to be achieved over the longer term. In contrast paragraph (c) is more interested in the short-term effects of fluctuations in prices, demand and supply. The policy must therefore include mechanisms designed to smooth out these fluctuations, thereby connecting paragraph (c) with paragraph (d), although no reference is made to techniques which would ensure such availability of supplies or to the

---

[1] See El-Agraa, A., *The Economics of the Common Market* (4th edn) (Harvester Wheatsheaf, London, 1994), pp. 211–12 and Marsh, J. and Swanney, P., *Agriculture and the European Community* (Allen & Unwin, London, 1980), pp. 12–16.

scope of Community activity in this area. Lastly, paragraph (e) confirms that the scope of the CAP is not to be limited to producers and processors but is to extend to consumers. Prices for them are to be 'reasonable', as opposed to the standard of living of farmers which is to be 'fair'.

Turning from the literal approach to Article 33(1) to the jurisprudence of the Court on the separate objectives of the CAP, the range of possible approaches to the future development of the policy are identified. For example, in the *Danske Landboforeninger* case, the Court pointed out that:[2] '... the very wording of Article 39(1) [now Article 33] shows that the increase in the individual earnings of persons engaged in agriculture is envisaged by being primarily the result of the structural measures described in sub-paragraph (a).' The Court has also declared that Article 33(1)(b) does not constitute an income guarantee for farmers.[3]

With respect to the remaining objectives of Article 33(1), the Court has held that a range of measures may be used to stabilize markets.[4] Measures to effect such stability which impact adversely on individuals do not give that individual the right to complain.[5] In relation to the safeguarding of supplies, as the above discussion has illustrated, there are no fixed mechanisms to achieve this. The Court has made it clear that this objective covers all aspects of agricultural production, from trade agreements through public health and consumer protection to animal welfare issues.[6] Such interpretations by the Court allow the scope of the CAP to expand to embrace new policy goals identified within the Treaty, such as environmental regulation in Article 174 or development cooperation in Article 177.[7] Lastly, with respect to paragraph (e), the Court made it clear in the case of *Germany v Commission* that reasonable prices did not mean the lowest possible prices but had to be considered in the light

---

[2] Case 297/82 [1983] ECR 3299, p. 3317. See also Cases 36 and 71/80 *Irish Creamery Milk Suppliers Association* [1981] ECR 735.

[3] See for example, Case 2/75 *Mackprang* [1975] ECR 607 and Case 281/84 *Bedburg* [1987] ECR 49.

[4] Case 250/84 *Eridania* [1986] ECR 117 and Case 46/86 *Romkes* [1987] ECR 2687.

[5] Cases 63–69/72 *Wehrhahn* [1973] ECR 1229.

[6] On public health and consumer protection, see for example Case 11/88 *Commission v Council (Pesticides)* [1989] ECR 379, Case C-146/91 *KYDEP* [1994] ECR I-4199 and Case C-180/96 *United Kingdom v Commission* [1998] ECR I-2265; on animal welfare see Case 131/86 *UK v Council (Battery Hens)* [1988] ECR 905 and Case C-27/95 *Woodspring* [1997] ECR I-1847.

[7] See Case C-280/93 *Germany v Council* [1994] ECR I-4973, where the Court rejected the German argument that the regulation establishing the common organization of the market in bananas was part of a development policy for the ACP and so could not be based on Article 37.

of the CAP.[8] In a later case, the Court would rule that Article 33 would be breached only if a measure led to consumer prices which were obviously unreasonable.[9]

No hierarchy of objectives is indicated in Article 33(1), but it is obvious that the CAP is to have a series of objectives which are both conflicting and not capable of reconciliation. Despite the fact that this has been recognized for a long time, Article 33 has never been considered as an article in need of reform at the various Inter-Governmental Conferences. As early as 1968, the Court recognized that the Community institutions would have to balance the competing demands of Article 33(1).[10] The classic formulation of this balancing act occurred in the case of *Balkan*, where the Court stated:[11]

> In pursuing these objectives the Community institutions must secure the permanent harmonization made necessary by any conflict between these aims taken individually and, where necessary, allow one of them temporary priority in order to satisfy the demands of the economic factors or conditions in view of which their decisions are made.

The formulation has been repeated by the Court on several occasions with the Court limiting itself to an examination of whether the measure in question contains a manifest error, constitutes a misuse of power or whether the discretion enjoyed by the Community institutions has been exceeded.[12]

With respect to the *Balkan* formula, it must be pointed out that it is in conflict with the Court's approach to the interpretation of Article 2 of Regulation 26/62, where an agreement hoping for exemption must satisfy all the objectives of the CAP, as demonstrated by the decision in *FRUBO*.[13] Secondly, the statement suggests that at some stage the Court may overrule a measure of the institutions if the situation of 'temporary priority' is continued for a substantial period of time, thus jeopardizing the achievement of the other objectives of the CAP. The possibility that the Court could adopt such an approach was highlighted in its decision

---

[8] Case 34/62 [1963] ECR 131.   [9] Case 5/73 *Balkan* [1973] ECR 1091.

[10] Case 5/67 *Beus* [1968] ECR 83, where the Court stated that: 'As those objectives are for the protection of agricultural producers as well as of consumers, they cannot all be realized simultaneously and in full.'

[11] Above n. 9, p. 1112.

[12] See for example, Case 29/77 *Roquette Frères* [1977] ECR 1835; Case 203/86 *Spain v Council* [1988] ECR 4563, Case C-311/90 *Hierl* [1992] ECR I-2061 and Case C-280/93 *Germany v Commission* (above n. 7). See also the repetition of the *Balkan* formula by the Court of First Instance, Case T-489/93 *Unifruit Hellas* [1994] ECR II-1201.

[13] Case 71/74 [1975] ECR 563. For further discussion see 1.2.3.

in *Behla-Mühle*.[14] The Court in this case declared a regulation on the compulsory purchase of skimmed milk powder, which was designed to reduce stocks of this product which had increased significantly, to be null and void. In doing so the Court used the objectives in Article 33(1), the rule on non-discrimination contained in Article 34(3) and the general principle of proportionality to rule that the obligations imposed by the regulation were discriminatory and not necessary to attain the objectives of the CAP. One further interesting feature of the case, arising from the current reforms of the CAP, was the suggestion by Advocate General Capotorti that a strict interpretation of Article 33(1) might[15]:

> ... justify the conclusion that the whole of the market policy so far followed by the Community is illegal in view of the fact that ... its essential basis is the fixing of prices to suit agricultural products in order to assure farmers an adequate income, whereas the policy favouring the modernization and structural improvements and, in consequence, the rational development of agricultural production has been late in gathering momentum and is now evolving slowly and with considerable difficulty.

While the Community institutions enjoy considerable discretion in the implementation of a policy to achieve the objectives of Article 33(1), both individually and collectively, it is important to conclude that the discretion is not unlimited. Considerable latitude has been given to the institutions by the *Balkan* formula, but as *Behla-Mühle* indicated there are limits to that latitude. The limits were hinted at in *Crispoltoni II* where, after repeating the *Balkan* formula, the Court continued: 'That harmonization must preclude the isolation of any one of those objectives in such a way as to render impossible the realization of other objectives.'[16]

2.3 Attaining the objectives of the CAP

As to how these objectives were to be attained, so that a common policy could be brought into force by the latest at the end of the transitional

---

[14] Cases 114, 116 and 119–20/76 [1977] ECR 1211.

[15] *Ibid.*, p. 1229. See also Case C-353/92 *Greece v Council* [1994] ECR I-3411 involving a challenge to Regulation 1765/92 (OJ 1992 L 181/12) where the Court accepted that stabilizing markets can take precedence over a fair income for farmers in certain circumstances.

[16] Joined Cases C-133/93, C-300/93 and C-362/93 [1994] ECR I-4863, p. 4903. See also Joined Cases 197–200, 243, 245 and 247/80 *Ludwigshafner Walzmühle* [1981] ECR 3211 for a similar statement.

period, guidance was provided in Articles 34 to 36 of the Treaty. According to Article 34(2), a common organization of agricultural markets was to be established which could take one of three forms: (a) common rules on competition; (b) compulsory coordination of the various national market organizations; or (c) a European market organization. The choice of form would depend on the particular product concerned. Further detail on the common organizations, which are to be limited to the pursuit of the objectives set out in Article 33 and exclude discrimination between producers and consumers within the Community, is provided in Article 34(3), which states that it may:

> ... include all measures required to attain the objectives set out in Article 39 [now Article 33], in particular regulation of prices, aids for the production and marketing of various products, storage and carrying over arrangements and common machinery for stabilizing imports or exports.

Article 34 concludes by stating that any common price policy should be based on common criteria and uniform calculation methods, and that one or more agricultural guidance and guarantee funds may be set up to allow the common organization to attain its objectives.

Article 34 confirms the special position enjoyed by agriculture in the Treaty by requiring a choice to be made in establishing a common organization of the market. As for the options, it seems clear that the special position of agriculture would not be guaranteed if option (a), common rules on competition, were chosen, as this would treat agricultural products in the same way as the Treaty treats industrial products. Indeed, if it had been chosen, the end of the transitional period would have led to the full application of the competition rules to this sector. The special position of agriculture therefore demanded a choice between options (b) and (c). The reference to a 'market organization' in both these options also dictated that some form of interference with the market would be required, as adoption of a policy of *laissez-faire* would not have involved any 'organization' of the market. As for the contents of the 'organization', some indication is given in Article 34(3)(a) with the list of measures which can be adopted to regulate the market, Article 34(3)(b) with the endorsement of the general principles of proportionality and non-discrimination, Article 34(4) with provision for the financing of the measures adopted under Article 34(3)(a) and the choice of the applicable competition regime under Article 36. These provisions set the scope of, and limits to, the common organizations of the market for the agricultural products listed in Annex II.

2.3.1 *Common organizations of the market*

In making the choice demanded by Article 34(2), the Community has opted for (c), the establishment of a European market organization, whose objective is to establish a single market for that product for the Community. After making this point in *Galli*, the Court noted:[17]

> So as to ensure the freedom of internal trade the regulation comprises a set of rules intended to eliminate both the obstacles to the free movement of goods and all distortions in intra-Community trade due to market intervention by Member States other than that authorized by the regulation itself.

At issue in *Galli* was the power of the Member States, in this case Italy, to impose price controls. In the opinion of the Court, in sectors covered by a common organization of the market, unilateral measures interfering with the mechanisms of price formation within the common organization were no longer possible. Interference by the Member States with the formation of prices at other stages in the marketing process may, however, be acceptable.[18] More generally on the powers of the Member States once a common organization of the market has been established, the Court pointed out in *Van den Hazel*:[19]

> Once the Community has, pursuant to Article 40 of the Treaty [now Article 34], legislated for the establishment of the common organization of the market in a given sector, Member States are under an obligation to refrain from taking any measure which might undermine or create exceptions to it.

Subsequent cases have confirmed this principle and, indeed, extended it to include the principles underlying the common organization as well as the provisions establishing that organization.[20]

---

[17] Case 31/74 [1975] ECR 47, p. 61. See also Case 4/79 *Providence Agricole v ONIC* [1980] ECR 2823.

[18] See Case 66/75 *Tasca* [1976] ECR 291, where the Court left the question of the compatibility of maximum prices with a common organization of the market (in this case sugar) to the national courts to decide on the basis of whether or not they make it difficult or impossible for producers to obtain Community prices. See also Case 10/79 *Toffoli* [1979] ECR 3301 and Cases 16–20/79 *Danis* [1979] ECR 3327.

[19] Case 111/76 [1977] ECR 901, p. 909. See also Case 50/76 *Amsterdam Bulb* [1977] ECR 137, Cases 36 and 71/80 *Irish Creamery Milk Suppliers Association* (above n. 2), Case 218/85 *Cerafel* [1986] ECR 3513 and Case C-132/95 *Jensen* [1998] ECR I-2975.

[20] See for example, Case C-32/89 *Greece v Commission* [1991] ECR I-1321 and the principle also applies even if the unilateral measures were to support the common policy, Case 90/86 *Zoni* [1988] ECR 4285. As for the powers of the Member States in the area of structural policy, see Case C-190/91 *Lante* [1993] ECR I-67 and Case C-255/95 *Agri and Agricola Venta* [1997] ECR I-25.

National legislation which is either anticipated by the common organization of the market, or which is pursuing objectives different from those of the common organization may still be permissible.[21] So, for example, in the case of *Holdijk* the Court held that:[22]

> ... the establishment of such an organization pursuant to Article 40 of the Treaty [now Article 34] does not have the effect of exempting agricultural producers from any national provisions intended to attain objectives other than those covered by the common organization, even though such provisions may, by affecting the conditions of production, have an impact on the volume or the cost of national production and therefore the operation of the Common Market in the sector concerned.

Given the absence at that time of Community legislation on the protection of animals, and pending the adoption of such legislation, the Court upheld the validity of Dutch measures laying down minimum requirements for keeping fatting calves in enclosures. In *Pluimveeslachterij Midden-Nederland,* the Court rejected the argument that Dutch legislation on the packaging and slaughtering of poultry was not permissible under the common organization of the market, especially as the Regulation establishing that organization had anticipated such legislation.[23] Such legislation had been proposed but never enacted, and with regard to the nature of the national measures pending the enactment of Community measures, the Court stated:[24]

> ... such measures may not be regarded as involving the exercise of the Member State's own power, but as the fulfilment of the duty to cooperate in achieving the aims of the common organization of the market which, in a situation characterized by the inaction of the Community legislature, Article 5 of the Treaty [now Article 10] imposes on them.

The legislation, which the Court characterized as temporary and provisional in nature, would cease to apply once the Community legislated in the particular area.

The Court has also upheld a system of national production quotas in

---

[21] See Case 16/83 *Prantl* [1984] ECR 1299 and Case 48/85 *Commission v Germany* [1986] ECR 2549.

[22] Cases 141–143/81 [1982] ECR 1299, pp. 1313–14.

[23] Cases 47 and 48/83 [1984] ECR 1721. See also Case C-134/92 *Morlins* [1993] ECR 6017, where the issue involved the continuing application of German competition and company law pending Community legislation anticipated under the common organization of the market in sugar.

[24] *Ibid.*, p. 1738. In Case 804/79 *Commission v United Kingdom* [1981] ECR 1045 the Court considered the Member States to be the 'trustees of the common interest' in this situation.

the cereals sector as it did not affect trade between Member States.[25] One of the reasons given by the Court for this decision was that the quotas allocated exceeded demand within France. However, the plaintiff in this case was prosecuted for exceeding its quota, which can be taken as evidence that the quotas acted as a restriction of trade between Member States. Although the common organization of the market in cereals does not extend to flour, given the close connection between the products, restrictions on the production of flour would have an impact on the common organization. More usually, the Court has held national measures which interfere with the operation of a common organization to be unacceptable. So, in *Apple and Pear Development Council*, the Council could not lay down quality standards for fruit, a matter covered by the common organization of the market in fruit and vegetables, but it could give advice on quality, a matter not covered by that organization.[26] Likewise in *Commission v France (Milk Substitutes)*, the Court held French measures prohibiting the sale of substitute milk powder to be contrary to the Treaty, for although they supported the CAP they ran counter to the principles of the free movement of goods.[27] An attempt to justify the measures by pointing to the then surplus of this product in the Community was rejected by the Court who pointed out that the elimination of surpluses was a Community responsibility.

2.3.2 National organizations of the market

For most products by the end of the transitional period common organizations had been established. There were, of course, some notable exceptions (alcohol, potatoes, sheepmeat and bananas). One question raised at this time was the status of national organizations after the end of the transitional period. It was argued that such organizations would be protected until replaced by common organizations. Support for this argument could be found in Article 37(3)(a), which provides that the Council may replace a national market organization with a common organization if two conditions are met:

(a) the common organization offers Member States which are opposed to this measure and which have an organization of their own for the production in question, equivalent safeguards for the employment and standard of living of the producers concerned, account being

---

[25] Case 148/85 *Forest* [1986] ECR 3449.
[26] Case 222/82 *Apple and Pear Development Council* [1983] ECR 4083.
[27] Case 216/84 [1988] ECR 793.

taken of the adjustments that will be possible and the specialization that will be needed with the passage of time;

(b) such an organization ensures conditions for trade within the Community similar to those existing in a national market.

The argument about the effect of the end of the transitional period on national market organizations would eventually come before the Court.

In *Charmasson* the plaintiff argued that France had violated the provisions of the Treaty (and the Yaoundé Convention) by applying a quota system for the importation of bananas into France. The starting point for the Court was to offer the following definition of a national market organization, as being:[28]

> ... a totality of legal devices placing the regulation of the market in the products in question under the control of the public authority, with a view to ensuring, by means of an increase in productivity and of optimum utilization of the factors of production, in particular manpower, a fair standard of living for producers, the stabilization of markets, the assurance of supplies and reasonable prices to the consumers.

National market organizations were therefore to have objectives equivalent to those of the CAP.[29] A simple quota system, such as existed in this case, could not amount to a national market organization. Turning to the question of the impact of the end of the transitional period on such organizations, after analyzing the original Articles 43 to 46 of the Treaty, the Court concluded that before the end of that period the national organization must adapt itself to the fullest extent possible to the requirements of the Common Market. It continued:[30]

> Accordingly, the derogations which a national organization may effect from the general rules of the Treaty are only permissible provisionally, to the extent necessary to ensure its functioning, without however impeding the adaptations which are involved in the establishment of the common agricultural policy.

---

[28] Case 48/74 [1974] ECR 1383, p. 1396. This mirrors the definition offered by the Court in 1964 when it stated: 'a market organization is a combination of legal institutions and measures on the basis of which appropriate authorities seek to control and regulate the market' (Cases 90 & 91/63 *Commission v Luxembourg and Belgium* [1964] ECR 625, p. 635).

[29] In Case 237/82 *Kaas* [1984] ECR 483 the Court noted that in those areas where the Member States remain competent, the exercise of their powers must respect the objectives of Article 33(1).

[30] Above n. 28, p. 1395. For a discussion of the decision, see Paulin, B. and Forman, J., 'The French Banana Story and its Implications' (1975) 12 CMLRev 399.

As that policy was to enter into force at the end of the transitional period, any national market organizations in existence after that time would become subject to the general rules of the Treaty.

The ruling of the Court in *Charmasson* was confirmed in *Commission v France*, a case concerning restrictions on the export of potatoes from France.[31] Indeed, a similar ruling was given with respect to the expiration of the transitional period in the UK Act of Accession, in the case of *Commission v UK*, which concerned the maintenance of restrictions on the import of potatoes after 1977.[32] This was despite the existence of Article 60(2) of the Act of Accession which provided for the non-application of the rules on the free movement of goods in respect of products not covered by a common organization of the market on the date of accession but for which a national market organization existed at that time. No time limit had been set in the Act of Accession for the expiration of this provision.[33]

The principles of *Charmasson* were also forcefully restated in *Commission v Ireland* where the Court said:[34]

> ... agricultural products in respect of which a common organization of the market has not been established are subject to the general rules of the common market with regard to importation, exportation and movement within the Community.

Although this makes it clear that the free movement of goods rules apply to national market organizations, problems arose in the area of competition policy. These problems were recognized in the case of *Commission v France*, where the Court suggested that there was nothing to prevent France from implementing a scheme of national aids in the sheepmeat sector pending the establishment of a common organization of the market in that product.[35] State aid for potatoes, for which there is still no common organization of the market, was specifically endorsed in the decision of the Court in *SICA*.[36]

---

[31] Case 68/76 [1977] ECR 515.

[32] Case 231/78 [1979] ECR 1447. For a discussion of the decision see Wyatt, D. 'British Import Controls on Main Crop Potatoes' (1979) 4 ELRev 359. See also Case 118/78 *Meijer* [1979] ECR 1387, in which the plaintiff sought a declaration that the United Kingdom was not entitled to maintain these restrictions.

[33] As a result of this ruling, the equivalent provision in the Greek Act of Accession, Article 65(2) and subsequent Acts of Accession set dates at which time the provision would cease to apply. See Cases 194 and 241/85 *Commission v Greece (Bananas)* [1988] ECR 1037 for discussion of Article 65(2).

[34] Case 288/83 [1985] ECR 1761, p. 1774.

[35] Case 232/78 [1979] ECR 2729, an action concerning French measures restricting imports of UK sheepmeat on the basis that the UK system of support for this product constituted a state aid.

[36] Case 114/83 [1984] ECR 2589.

A solution to problems relating to the continued existence of national market organizations is to be found in the continuing use of Article 38. Under this provision, where a national market organization exists for an agricultural product, the competitive positions of similar production in other Member States can be maintained through the imposition of a countervailing charge. The use of Article 38 was upheld by the Court in the case of *St Nikolaus Brennerei*.[37] The plaintiff in the case challenged the validity of Regulation 851/76, which allowed for the imposition of countervailing charges on imports of ethyl alcohol of agricultural origin from France into West Germany and the Benelux countries. One of the questions referred to the Court asked whether Article 38 could still be applied after the end of the transitional period. The response of the Court was positive.[38] The Court acknowledged, as it had in *Charmasson*, that national market organizations pursued objectives comparable to those of the CAP, and provided the measures adopted by a Member State did not prejudice the pursuit of these objectives by other Member States then there would be no breach of the Treaty given the absence of a common organization.

For the Court Article 38 was therefore still useful, even after the end of the transitional period, as it allowed distortions of competition created by a Member State to be remedied by the Commission. However, the Court did impose conditions on the use of the Article: the measure must be adopted in the general interest of the Community; the amount must be fixed by the Commission; the charge must have the effect of promoting, rather than hindering, trade; and the charge should be proportionate. It was recognized that Article 38 countervailing charges were not the cause of distortions of competition, but rather a mechanism to remove the effects of such distortions. Rather than rely on the mechanisms of Article 38, it would be preferable for the Community to attack the sources of such distortions of competition, through the application of state aid rules to all agricultural products and completion of the process of developing common organizations as required by Article 34.

2.4 The legislative power of the Community institutions

By virtue of Article 37(2), the Council is given the power to implement the CAP through regulations, directives, decisions and recommenda-

---

[37] Case 337/82 [1984] ECR 1051. For a comment on the Case see Shaw, J., 'The effect of Article 46 EEC' (1984) 9 ELRev 284.

[38] This was despite the fact that in Cases 80–81/77 *Ramel* [1978] ECR 927, the Court held that it had lapsed at the end of the transitional period.

tions. In the exercise of this power, the Community has established various common organizations of the market, created a structural policy for European agriculture, promoted the harmonization of the legislation of the Member States on such matters as animal health, and implemented the financial aspects of the CAP. Article 37 thus forms the main legal basis for all Community legislation implementing the CAP. The Court has rejected arguments by one Member State that harmonizing legislation prohibiting the use of certain hormones in livestock farming should have been based on Article 94, the harmonization provision.[39] In a subsequent case, the Court confirmed the priority of Article 37 over other provisions of the Treaty including Articles 95, 100, 133 and 175, provided the measures are concerned with Annex II products and are intended to achieve one or more of the objectives listed in Article 33.[40] Logically, therefore, if the scope of a measure extends beyond these two conditions, another legal base, such as Article 95, will be needed for the particular measure. Lastly, it must be noted that the scope of Article 37 also extends to measures dealing with international trade in agricultural products.[41]

This article also provides for the consultation of the European Parliament. Disregard of this requirement was held by the Court to be breach of an essential procedural requirement rendering the resulting act void in the case of *Roquette*.[42] This obligation of consultation does not apply to implementing legislation as the Court upheld the validity of such legislation even though the European Parliament had not been consulted.[43]

In other cases dealing with the scope of the Community's legislative power to implement the CAP, the Court has characterized this power as

---

[39] Case 69/86 *UK v Council (Hormones)* [1988] ECR 855. See also Case 131/86 *UK v Council (Battery Hens)* (above n. 6).

[40] Case 131/87 *Commission v Council (Glands)* [1989] ECR 3743. See also Case 11/88 *Commission v Council (Pesticides)* [1989] ECR 3799.

[41] See Cases 51–54/71 *International Fruit* [1971] ECR 1107, Cases 3, 4, and 7/76 *Kramer* [1976] ECR 1279; but also see more recently, Opinion 1/94 [1994] ECR I-5276 discussed in 1.2.4.

[42] Case 138/79 [1980] ECR 3333. See also Case 139/79 *Maizena* [1980] ECR 3393. This obligation does not apply in the event of amendments to a proposal which correspond with those suggested by Parliament itself, see Case C-65/90 *Parliament v Council* [1992] ECR I-4593, Joined Cases C-13/92 to C-16/92 *Driessen* [1993] ECR I-4751 and Case C-280/93 *Germany v Council* (above n. 8).

[43] Case 203/86 *Spain v Council* (above n.12). See also Case 46/86 *Romkes* (above n. 4), Case C-156/93 *Parliament v Commission* [1995] ECR I-2019 and C-417/93 *Parliament v Council* [1995] ECR I-1185. However, see Case C-303/94 *Parliament v Council* [1996] ECR I-2943, where the Court annulled an implementing directive on the basis that it had modified the scope of the basic directive on which Parliament had been consulted.

one in which the institutions enjoy a very wide discretion.[44] In the case of *Westzücker* the Court stated:[45]

> It is consonant to the very idea of the Community that, within the framework of the mechanism of collective discussion set up with a view to the implementation of the CAP, the Member States should emphasise their interests, whilst it falls to the Commission to arbitrate, through the measures taken by it, between possible conflicts of interest from the point of view of the general interest.

By necessary implication, this 'arbitration' of the Commission allows it to take into account all the considerations highlighted in Articles 33 to 38 which would impact on the implementation of the CAP. So, the discretion allowed by the Court permits the Community institutions to balance the political, economic, social and monetary considerations addressed in this part of the Treaty, thus recognizing their political responsibilities. This implication was subsequently confirmed by the Court, who said that 'in matters concerning the common agricultural policy, the Community legislator has a discretionary power which corresponds to the political responsibilities imposed by Articles 40 and 43 [now Articles 34 and 37]'.[46] As a result the role of the Court in reviewing agricultural legislation is limited to 'examining whether it contains a manifest error or constitutes a misuse of power or whether the authority in question did not clearly exceed the bounds of its discretion'.[47]

In its examination of such legislation, the Court can avail itself of the general principles laid down in Articles 33 to 38, which include, for example, an anti-discrimination principle in Article 34(3). With reference to this paragraph, the Court has stated:[48]

> Whilst this wording undoubtedly prohibits any discrimination between producers of the same product it does not refer in such clear terms to the

---

[44] Cases 83 and 94/76 *HNL* [1978] ECR 1209. This wide discretion also extends to the conditions justifying Community financial assistance under various rural development initiatives. See generally, Cases C-258/90 and C-259/90 *Pesquerías de Bermeo* [1992] ECR 2901 and Case T-465/93 *Murgia Messapica* [1994] ECR II-361.

[45] Case 57/72 [1973] ECR 321, p. 341.

[46] For example, in Case 265/87 *Schräder* [1989] ECR 2237, p. 2270.

[47] Above n. 42, p. 3358–59. See also Joined Cases C-267/88 to C-285/88 *Wuidart* [1990] ECR I-435, where the Court stated that the Community institutions were obliged 'in connection with the adoption of rules, to assess their future effects, which cannot be accurately foreseen, its assessment is open to criticism only if it appears manifestly incorrect on the light of the information available at the time of adoption of the rules in question' (p. 481).

[48] Cases 117/76 and 16/77 *Rückdeschel* [1977] ECR 1753, p. 1769. See also Case 165/84 *Krohn* [1985] ECR 3977, where the Court extended the scope of the principle to cover discrimination between importers. The principle does not extend to discrimination between third countries, see Case 52/81 *Faust* [1982] ECR 3745.

relationship between different industrial or trade sectors in the sphere of processed agricultural products. This does not alter the fact that the prohibition of discrimination laid down in the aforesaid provision is merely a specific enunciation of the general principle of equality which is one of the fundamental principles of Community law.

In this particular case, the Court concluded that the Regulation which introduced a difference between producers of quellmehl and of starch was a breach of one of the fundamental principles of Community law and so incompatible with that law. However, not all cases of differences in treatment will amount to discrimination contrary to Article 34(3), and the Court has also declared that where differences can be objectively justified there will be no discrimination.[49] The principle of equality in Article 34(3) has been extended beyond Community legislation to the implementation of that legislation by the Member States.[50]

The constitutional traditions of the Member States are also an additional source of principles for the Court to call on in its review of Community legislation.[51] For example, despite an initial reluctance, the Court has used the principle of proportionality to invalidate agricultural legislation.[52] It has stated:[53]

The principle of proportionality, which is one of the general principles of Community law, requires that measures adopted by Community institutions do not exceed the limits of what is appropriate and necessary in order to attain the objectives legitimately pursued by the legislation in question; when there is a choice between several appropriate measures recourse must be had to the least onerous, and the disadvantages caused must not be disproportionate to the aims pursued.

---

[49] See Case 106/83 *Sermide* [1984] ECR 4209, Case C-309/89 *Codornui* [1994] ECR I-1853 and Joined Cases C-296/93 and C-307/93 *France and Ireland v Commission* [1996] ECR I-795.

[50] See Cases 201 and 202/85 *Klensch* [1986] ECR 3477.

[51] See for example, Case 44/79 *Hauer* [1979] ECR 3727, where the Court held that the relevant legislation did not infringe fundamental human rights, in this Case the right to property. See also Case 265/87 *Schräder* (above n. 46), where the Court held that 'the right to property and the freedom to pursue a trade or profession may be restricted, particularly in the context of a common organization of the market, provided that those restrictions in fact correspond to objectives of general interest pursued by the Community and that they do not constitute an intolerable interference which infringes upon the very substance of the rights guaranteed' (p. 2269).

[52] See Cases 114, 116 and 119–120/76 *Bela-Mühle* (above n.14) and Case 181/84 *E.D. and F. Man* [1985] ECR 2889 and Case 265/87 *Schräder* (above n. 46).

[53] Joined Cases C-133/93, C-300/93 and C-362/93 *Crispoltoni* (above n.16), p. 4905. See also Case C-331/88 *Fedesa* [1990] ECR I-4023 and, more recently, Case C-157/96 *R v Ministry of Agriculture ex parte National Farmers' Union* [1998] ECR I-2211 and Case C-180/96 *United Kingdom v Commission* [1998] ECR I-2265.

The Court has based its decisions on distinctions between primary and secondary obligations; so where failure to comply with a secondary obligation results in a penalty as severe as for failure to comply with a primary obligation, the legislation will be disproportionate.[54] The principle of proportionality has been used to review not just Community measures but also measures taken by the Member States. In *Commission v United Kingdom* it was held that the UK's requirements for an import licence for UHT milk to be obtained before import and for imported UHT milk to be re-treated were not proportionate responses to the perceived public health concerns over UHT milk.[55] Lastly, should a breach of any of the principles developed by the Court, such as equality and legal certainty, constitute a sufficiently serious violation of a superior rule of law for the protection of the individual, the Community could incur non-contractual liability under Article 288(2).[56]

It is the principle of proportionality, discussed above, and the principle of the protection of legitimate expectations which are likely to be most relevant for the individual under the CAP. With respect to the principle of legitimate expectations, the Court has recently stated that although the principle is one of the fundamental principles of the Community:[57]

> ... traders cannot have a legitimate expectation that an existing situation which is capable of being altered by the Community institutions in the exercise of their discretionary powers will be maintained; this is particularly true in an area such as common organization of markets which involves constant adjustments to meet changes in the economic situation.

In the absence of specific assurances by the institutions, it appears unlikely that individuals can claim a breach of the principle of legitimate expectations.[58]

One final matter for discussion in this area is the process of legislating under Article 37. In common with other provisions of the Treaty, the

---

[54] See for example, Case 122/78 *Buitoni* [1979] ECR 667, Case 21/85 *Maas* [1986] ECR 3537, Case C-87/92 *Hoche* [1993] ECR 4623 and Case C-104/94 *Cereol Italia* [1995] ECR I-2983. Contrast with Case 9/85 *Nordbutter* [1986] ECR 2831.

[55] Case 124/81 [1983] ECR 203. See also Case 40/82 *Commission v United Kingdom* [1982] ECR 2793.

[56] See for examples Case 74/74 *CNTA* [1975] ECR 533, Case 238/78 *Ireks-Arkady* [1979] ECR 2985, Cases 326/86 and 66/88 *Francesoni* [1989] ECR 2087, Cases C-258/90 and C-259/90 *Pesquerías de Bermeo* (above n. 44) and Case C-146/91 *KYDEP* (above n. 6).

[57] See for example, Joined Cases C-296/93 and C-307/93 (above n. 49), pp. 849–50. See also Case 120/86 *Mulder* [1986] ECR 2231, Case 170/86 *Von Deetzen* [1988] ECR 2355 and Cases C-133/93, C-300/93 and C-362/93 *Crispoltoni* (above n. 16).

[58] Case T-571/93 *Lefebvre* [1995] ECR II-2379, Case T-521/93 *Atlanta* [1996] ECR II-1707 and Case T-267/94 *Oleifici Italiani* [1997] ECR II-1239.

right of legislative initiative is given to the Commission with the European Parliament being required to give its advice before the Council legislates. Although at the end of the second stage of the transitional period, the Council was supposed to act by qualified majority, the empty chair policy adopted by France, which was resolved by the Luxembourg compromise, led to the continuing use of unanimity after 1966.[59] This particular practice has declined since then.[60] In contrast with other areas of Community legislation, the Council in agricultural matters is assisted not by the Committee of Permanent Representatives (COREPER) but by a Special Committee for Agriculture, which is made up of senior agricultural officials from the Member States.[61] Most agricultural legislation made by the Council is of a general nature, the vast majority being in fact made by the Commission using various Committee procedures.

These various procedures involved in the implementation of CAP measures have now been codified in Council Decision 87/373.[62] This provides for three basic procedures. The first requires the Commission to obtain the opinion of the relevant committee before it acts. The second procedure obliges the Commission to consult the Management Committee, which is chaired by the Commission and is made up of representatives of the Member States, before it can adopt the measure in question. The voting strength of each Member State is weighted in accordance with the qualified majority voting system. If the opinion of the Management Committee is unfavourable, the Commission may still implement the measure but it must inform the Council, who within one month can take a different decision by qualified majority. If no such decision is made, the Commission measure remains in force. A challenge to the legality of this procedure, claiming that it was incompatible with Article 211, in the case of *Köster*, was rejected by the Court. After examining Article 211 and the scope of the Management Committee's powers, it concluded:[63]

---

[59] For a discussion see Olmi, G., 'Common Organization of Agricultural Markets at the Stage of the Single Market' (1967–68) 5 CMLRev 354 and Vasey, M., 'Decision-making in the Agricultural Council and the "Luxembourg' compromise"' (1988) 25 CMLRev 725.

[60] As an example see Vasey, M., 'The 1985 Farm Price Negotiations and the Reform of the Common Agricultural Policy' (1985) 22 CMLRev 649, pp. 664–66.

[61] The Committee was established in 1960, JO 1960 1217. Only if the matter concerns other policy areas in addition to agriculture will COREPER be involved.

[62] OJ 1987 L 197/33. This decision is the result of an amendment to the then Article 145 of the Treaty effected by the Single European Act, requiring the Council to lay down a framework of rules and principles for the procedures for delegating the power of implementation. For discussion of the decision see, as an example, Case C-64/95 *Lubella* [1996] ECR I-5105.

[63] Case 25/70 [1970] ECR 1161, p. 1171. The Court also noted in this Case that it could not 'be a requirement that all the details of the regulations concerning the CAP be drawn up by the Council according to the procedure in Article [37]'.

The Management Committee does not therefore have the power to take a decision in place of the Commission or the Council. Consequently, without distorting the Community structure and institutional balance, the Management Committee machinery enables the Council to delegate to the Commission an implementing power of appreciable scope, subject to its power to take the decision itself if necessary.

Consistent with the Court's interpretation of Article 37, the Court has held that the concept of implementation in Article 211 has to be given a wide interpretation.[64] The scope of that power depends on the relevant legislation. It is clear that the Court will intervene only if either the measures adopted by the Commission are contrary to the legislation adopted by the Council, or if the Commission uses its powers under regulations adopted under Article 37(2) to implement regulations based on other articles of the Treaty.[65] Equally, the Commission may not sub-delegate its powers of implementation, although the vesting of a discretion with the Member States is acceptable.[66]

The final procedure outlined in Decision 87/373 requires the Commission to obtain the consent of the relevant committee before it can act. The Decision was intended to put an end to the proliferation of committees, but Article 4 of the Decision allows for the continuation of existing procedures even when the various acts establishing these committees are amended. So the Decision may not achieve its objective. In addition to the various committees noted above, for structural policy the Commission is assisted by a Committee on Agricultural Structures, known as the STAR Committee, which is made up of the relevant experts from the governments of the Member States. Lastly, through Agricultural Advisory Committees, the Commission consults with the non-governmental sector, including such bodies as the Comité des Organizations Professionelles Agricole (COPA) which represents the major agricultural organizations in the Member States, the Comité Général de la Coopération Agricole (COGECA) which represents agricultural cooperatives, and consumer organizations such as the Bureau Européen des Unions des Consommateurs (BEUC).[67]

---

[64] Case 23/75 Rey Soda [1975] ECR 1300 and Case C-478/93 Netherlands v Commission [1995] ECR I-3081.

[65] See Case 121/83 Franken [1984] ECR 2039, Case 22/88 Vreugdenhil [1989] ECR 2049 and Case C-357/88 Hopermann [1990] ECR 1669.

[66] Compare Rey Soda (above n. 64), where the Court held a provision of an implementing regulation to be invalid because of sub-delegation to Italy, with Cases 103–109/78 Société des Usines de Beauport [1979] ECR 17 where the implementing legislation vesting a discretion with France was held to be acceptable.

[67] See in this respect Commission Decision 98/235 which consolidates all the provisions dealing with agricultural advisory committees and reduces their number to ten: OJ 1998 L 88/59.

2.5 The evolution of the common policy

By virtue of Article 37(1), on the entry into force of the Treaty, the Commission was to convene a conference to evolve the broad lines of a CAP through a comparison of the Member States' agricultural policies. The Conference was duly convened at Stresa in July 1958; but rather than clearing up the ambiguities of the Spaak Report and concretizing the generality of the Treaty provisions on agriculture, it merely added to the confusion by prescribing a further series of objectives which the common policy should seek to achieve. It did, however, reach a number of important conclusions. It was agreed that the structure of European agriculture needed to be reformed; such reform would have to respect the family character of agricultural holdings. It was also agreed that Community-wide prices would be set at a level slightly above world prices; this would lead to the adequate remuneration of farmers without encouraging surplus production. Lastly, the Community would not aim to achieve total self-sufficiency in agricultural production and thus would remain open to international trade, although measures were anticipated which would prevent distortions of competition of external origin.[68]

Taking account of the conclusions of the Stresa Conference, the Commission continued its preparation of proposals to implement the common policy. The slow rate of progress led to disputes between Member States over the speed of industrial tariff cuts. To resolve this dispute it was agreed that the implementation of the CAP would be speeded up. The original Commission proposals of November 1959 were revised and resubmitted to the Council, who in December 1960 made its first substantive decision on the common policy, thus paving the way for the introduction of that policy. The significance of this first decision rests with its establishment of the three basic principles of the CAP.[69] Firstly, common prices, to be achieved through the elimination of barriers to trade and distortions of competition between Member States. Secondly, common financing, through which all Member States would be called on to contribute to the financing of the common organizations of the market to be established over the transitional period. Thirdly, Community preference, to ensure that the Member States enjoyed the advantages of integration foreshadowed by the Treaty.

The threat by France and The Netherlands of vetoing the progress of the Community to the second stage of the transitional period was

---

[68] For the resolution of the Stresa Conference, see JO 1958 291.
[69] Bull. CE 1/61, p. 83.

enough to lead to sufficient progress in the implementation of the common policy in 1961. The original decisions taken on the policy, in the midst of crisis, were to have a profound effect on the future development of that policy. Indeed, it has been noted that the resulting policy was more protectionist than all the previous national policies had been because:[70]

(a) the high price countries fought for comparatively high prices in order to avoid farm income problems;

(b) the range of products covered by protectionist measures was widened in some countries because special protectionist interests in individual countries were extended to Community wide protection; and,

(c) the supply control policies, previously practised in exporting countries were abandoned in the face of the opportunities provided by the Community's market and were replaced, in effect, by a policy of export push by developing the dormant potential of their agriculture.

In the years that followed, common organizations were gradually introduced so that by the end of the transitional period common organizations existed for the bulk of the products listed in Annex II. A single Guidance and Guarantee Fund (known by its French acronym, FEOGA) was introduced in 1962 and split into two separate sections in 1964 – a Guarantee Section to finance the prices and markets policy and a Guidance Section to finance structural operations.[71] Only in the early 1970s did the Community institutions seriously address the need to reform the structure of European agriculture through a reappraisal of the structural policy.[72] The success of this reappraisal would be seriously affected by the difficulties encountered as a result of the collapse of the system of fixed exchange rates. The consequential monetary instability would be dealt with through the introduction of monetary compensatory amounts.[73]

The original principles were designed to meet the situation where Europe was still a net importer of agricultural products. The support of farm incomes through internal price arrangements and the partial or total exclusion of imports for certain products as a result of increased protection at the frontiers of the Community, ensured that the policy met the problems it was initially designed to deal with. However, once this situation had been reached, the instruments of the policy were not changed. As a result surpluses appeared in a number of areas, with a

---

[70] Heidhues, T. et al. *Common Prices and Europe's Farm Policy* (TPRC, London, 1978), p. 7.
[71] For further discussion see 4.2.   [72] For further discussion see Chapter 6.
[73] These are discussed in detail in 4.3.

consequent negative impact on prices, and trade relations with third countries deteriorated with increases in the level of Community subsidized exports and continuing restrictions on imports. To counter these problems the nature of the CAP has undergone a fundamental evolutionary change with the range of measures available under the policy increasing significantly. The core of the policy, however, remains the three principles of common prices, common financing and Community preference. Further principles added over the years, such as producer responsibility, have not yet assumed an overall level of importance equivalent to the three core principles.

Reform of the policy was inevitable, but such reform has been, as noted, evolutionary rather than revolutionary. Gradual reforms were introduced throughout the 1980s. For example, in 1984, to counter major problems in the dairy sector, milk quotas were introduced, thereby confirming the emergence of a fourth principle – producer responsibility – which had made its first appearance in this common organization in 1977.[74] In 1986 and 1987 further limits were imposed on market support for cereals and milk products. In 1988 further stabilization measures were introduced in all market organizations, so confirming the significance of the principle of producer responsibility. Also in 1988, the European Council agreed to place an overall ceiling on agricultural expenditure, linking it to trends in the Community's GDP; a process which was repeated in 1993 and again at the recent Berlin European Council. These reforms represented the beginning of a process of continuing reform of the CAP.

The most significant set of reforms to date emerged in 1992 with the so-called 'MacSharry reforms'. In essence these reforms were two-fold. Firstly, there was a three-year reduction in the level of prices in the arable crops and beef sectors to bring the level of Community prices closer to those on the world market, so improving the competitiveness of Community production. The negative impact of such price reductions on the income of farmers was mitigated by the introduction of compensatory payments, which in the case of certain arable crops was based on the withdrawal of land from production – referred to as the set-aside premium. The impact of these reforms on the common organization of the market in beef would be affected by the outbreak of bovine spongiform encephalopathy (BSE) which necessitated the introduction of a range of additional measures and premiums. The second set of reforms

---

[74] This was the year the co-responsibility levy was introduced. Producer responsibility had always been a feature of the common organization of the market in sugar: see Chapter 3 on this point.

introduced in 1992 built on the compensatory payments by introducing a range of accompanying measures, such as the granting of aid to farmers to encourage the protection of the environment, the landscape and natural resources.

Coupled with this reform, agreement was reached in 1994 in the Uruguay Round of multilateral trade negotiations, including for the first time an Agreement on Agriculture which would establish commitments in several important areas of agricultural policy.[75] Parties to the Agreement would be expected to increase market access, through tariff reductions and the adoption of the process of tariffication for existing non-tariff barriers. Moreover, the level of support offered by domestic agricultural policies would be calculated and reductions would have to be made in certain areas. Finally, budgetary restraints and quantitative limitations would be placed on export subsidies. This Agreement also provided for the introduction of a further Agreement on Sanitary and Phytosanitary Measures, and there would also be stronger and more operationally effective GATT rules. The Uruguay Round Agreement and the new GATT rules would be policed by the newly created World Trade Organization (WTO) which would enforce the rules through the newly effective dispute settlement process. The Agreement on Agriculture and the overall activities of the WTO and its Dispute Settlement Body would accentuate the impact of the 1992 reforms, and emphasize the need for further reform of the policy.

As for an assessment of the 1992 reforms, it must be pointed out that they were not a wholesale reform of the CAP but rather a response to both internal and external problems. In its assessment of the MacSharry reforms the Agenda 2000 document noted a considerable improvement of market balances and continuing improvements in average agricultural incomes, but they have had mixed effects on the environment and had led to increased budgetary expenditure in the sectors affected by the reforms. The reforms were characterized as insufficient to meet the new demands confronting the CAP in the years to come. As the Commission indicated:[76]

> In order to help European agriculture take advantage of the expected positive world market developments, further reform of the CAP must improve the competitiveness of Union agriculture on both domestic and external markets. Greater market orientation will facilitate the progressive integration of new Member States and will help prepare the Union for the next

---

[75] The Agreement is discussed in Chapters 5 and 7.
[76] Agenda 2000 (Brussels, 1997), Chapter 3.3.

44

WTO Round. It will also help the Union to reinforce its position as a major world exporter.

This will involve a 'deepening and extending' of reform through a further package of reforms aimed at converting the primary support mechanism of the CAP from price support to direct payments. The fundamental nature of the CAP will have to continue to change to reflect internal concerns, such as the protection of the environment, animal and consumer welfare, external concerns such as the next round of WTO negotiations and the eastern enlargement of the Community, while at the same time it will have to continue to meet the objectives set for it, within the established budgetary restraints.

In the aftermath of the publication of the Commission proposals considerable discussion occurred between the Member States on the scope of the reform of the CAP. In preparation for the European Council in Berlin in March 1999, the Council eventually reached a political agreement on a compromise package of reforms.[77] Although the political agreement of the Council was endorsed by the European Council in Berlin, various changes were made to the political agreement on reform.The overall agreement on the Agenda 2000 package reached at the Berlin European Council undoubtedly represents an important milestone for the Community. The question to be asked is: Whether or not the reforms agreed will allow the Community to meet the problems identified in the Agenda 2000 document?

[77] See 8.4 for further discussion of this package and the results of the Berlin European Council.

CHAPTER THREE

Common organizations and common prices

3.1 Introduction

According to Article 34(2), in order to achieve the objectives set for the CAP in Article 33, common organizations of agricultural markets were to be established. Although the Community institutions were given three options – common rules on competition, compulsory coordination of the various national market organizations or a European market organization – the choice has almost invariably been to establish a European market organization.[1] There are currently over 20 common organizations of the market for various agricultural products, established by virtue of a Regulation based on Articles 36 and 37 and covering a large percentage of Community agricultural production. The only significant exclusions from the list of common organizations are potatoes and alcohol. All the regulations establishing common organizations share a similar structure. After outlining the scope of the common organization, the market regime is established before the external regime is dealt with, and the concluding provisions deal with such matters as state aids and financing. This chapter will examine the nature of the common organizations before a discussion of the legal aspects of the pricing structure.

3.2 Common organizations

Each of the regulations establishing the common organizations has undergone considerable transformation since the common organization for that particular product was first introduced. This is a reflection not

[1] There are a number of measures applicable to other products which do not bear the name 'common organization of the market'. Special measures apply, for example, to silkworms (Regulation 845/72, OJ 1972 L 100/1). Trading arrangements exist for non-Annex II products (Regulation 3448/93, OJ 1993 L 318/31) and albumens (Regulation 2738/75, OJ 282/104).

only of changes to market and prices policy within the Community as a result of reforms, such as the 1992 MacSharry reforms and the reforms agreed at the recent Berlin European Council, but also of changes brought about by the WTO Agreement on Agriculture.[2] In the discussion which follows the original structure of the common organization is usually discussed before reference is made to the new rules governing that organization.

3.2.1 Cereals

The common organization of the market in cereals extends beyond cereals to include the products of the first processing of cereals, oilseeds, various protein crops and the seed of non-fibre flax. This common organization is of central importance for the Community, not only because of history but also because of its connection with other common organizations, such as pigmeat and eggs, where the prices are set on the basis of the cereal input. As for its history, it was one of the first common organizations to be agreed, and thus acted as a model for other common organizations.

The first common organization of the market in cereals was established under Regulation 19, which set up a system of levies in trade between Member States pending the creation of a single market.[3] When this stage was reached, Regulation 120/67 established a common organization of the market in cereals based on the setting of various prices.[4] The current common organization of the market in cereals is to be found in Regulation 1766/92, as amended, most recently by Regulation 1253/99.[5]

The 'old' pricing structure for this common organization involved setting a target price (a price it was hoped producers would be able to obtain) and an intervention price (the price at which intervention agencies in the Member States would buy cereals). The intervention price thus acted as a minimum price.[6] A third price, the threshold price, calcu-

---

[2] As for the changes adopted at the Berlin European Council, see 8.4. The Agreement on Agriculture was adopted by Decision 1800/94 (OJ 1994 L 336/1) and the text of the Agreement is reproduced in OJ 1994 L 336/22.

[3] Regulation 19, JO 1962 933.

[4] JO 1967 2269. The numerous amendments to the Regulation were consolidated in Regulation 2727/75 (OJ 1975 L 281/1) which itself was subject to numerous amendments, most notably by Regulation 1143/76 (OJ 1976 L 130/1).

[5] OJ 1992 L 181/21 and OJ 1999 L 160/18. See also Regulation 1251/99 (OJ 1999 L 160/1).

[6] Regulation 1900/87 (OJ 1987 L 182/40) introduced the concept of a 'buying-in' price. Under this, when the market price for certain cereals at certain export ports fell below the intervention price, buying-in was to take place at 94% of the intervention price.

lated by reference to the target price, was used as the basis of the external trade regime. It ensured that imports did not arrive on the Community market at such a price as to threaten the intervention price. If such a situation was threatened, an import levy would be applied to imports which would 'reflect the difference between the prices on the world market and those on the Community market. Given a situation where a Community producer wanted to export, the difference between the Community price and the world market price could be made up by granting an export refund. As Usher noted:[7]

> This price structure rests to a very large degree on the premise that the product is one in which the Community is largely self-sufficient and of which Community production is to be encouraged, and that imports will be the exception and must not be allowed to disturb Community prices. It also assumes, in the system of import levies and export refunds, that world prices will be lower than Community prices.

This premise and assumption seemed to run through the price structure not only of the common organization of the market in cereals, but also of all other common organizations. The impact of the price structure and the open-ended commitment to intervention ensured that structural surpluses arose, and although attempts were made to deal with these surpluses, a more thorough reform of the common organization of the market in cereals was needed.[8]

As a result of these reforms, the 'new' pricing structure rests on the setting of an intervention price which will act as a form of safety net for prices. To stop prices within the Community falling below this price, intervention agencies are required to purchase cereals offered to them. However, in contrast to the previous pricing arrangements, there are certain quantity and quality requirements attached to this obligation. For example, the intervention price may be reduced dependent on the quality of the cereals offered. Intervention prices were also gradually increased throughout the year to reflect the increasing costs of storage; these seasonal price corrections have been abolished as a consequence of the reforms agreed at the Berlin European Council. In addition to storage through intervention, private storage is provided for in an attempt to avoid large-scale purchasing by intervention agencies when prices either

[7] *Legal Aspects of Agriculture in the European Community* (OUP, Oxford, 1988), p. 56. See also Usher, J.A., 'Agricultural Markets: Their Price Systems and Financial Mechanisms' (1979) 4 ELRev 147.
[8] See for example, Regulation 1451/82 (OJ 1982 L 164/1), which established a system of guarantee thresholds, and its replacement Regulation 1579/86 (OJ 1986 L 139/29), which established a co-responsibility levy.

fall or are likely to fall as against the intervention price. As for other products covered by this common organization, a minimum price, aligned to official cereal prices, is granted to growers to support potato production for the starch industry and a compensatory payment may be offered as a result of reductions in cereal prices. For oilseeds and protein crops, prices attained by farmers are freely set by the Community market.

As for the import and export arrangements, market access for imports has been modified through the abolition of the import levies as a consequence of the Uruguay Round Agreement on Agriculture.[9] For cereals which can be subject to intervention, the import duty is calculated by increasing the intervention price by 55% and reducing the result by the world price for the particular cereal. The resulting duty may not, however, exceed the rate of duty specified for that product in the Common Customs Tariff.[10] Specific import arrangements, negotiated under the GATT, establish import quotas at either reduced or nil duty. As a further result of the Agreement on Agriculture, export refunds, which may still be offered, are limited in terms of budgetary expenditure and quantities. However, export refunds granted as part of the food aid policy of the Community – for example, as part of the Community's commitments under the Food Aid Convention – are not subject to these financial and quantitative limitations.

The major change introduced by the 1992 reforms has been the increase in the number of other measures which can be taken under the common organization of the market. The 'old' common organization allowed for the grant of subsidies to producers of durum wheat; a much more extensive range of aid measures now forms part of the common organization.[11] The reason for this rests with the changes to the pricing structure of the common organization, in particular the objective of reducing Community prices for cereals towards the level prevailing on the world market, a process which has been continued by the agreement reached at the Berlin European Council. Some form of compensatory aid was required and this is granted under the aid per hectare scheme. Aid is

---

[9] Regulation 3290/94 (OJ 1994 L 349/105) on the adjustment and transitional measures required in the agricultural sector in order to implement the agreements concluded during the Uruguay Round of multilateral trade negotiations, Annex 1. (See also Regulation 1340/98, OJ 1998 L 184/1.)

[10] The new import arrangements do provide for special safeguard measures to be taken. These will be discussed further in Chapter 5.

[11] See Regulation 1765/92 (OJ 1992 L 181/12) for details of these reforms. This regulation will expire at the end of the 2000/01 marketing year and it will be replaced by Regulation 1251/99 (above n. 5). For durum wheat, see for example Regulation 2309/97, OJ 1997 L 321/3.

granted under the scheme after calculation of the average cereal yield for a particular region of a Member State and a calculation of the average number of hectares within a region sown with cereals in the base period of 1989–91. Compensatory payments to individual farmers are granted only for an area not exceeding the regional base area, subject to the total aid granted under the scheme and an obligation to set aside land. This obligation, which forms an integral part of the reform in this area, represents an attempt to curb production and budgetary expenditure within the common organization.

In addition to the link with aid per hectare, there are also temporary (both compulsory and voluntary) and five-year set-aside programmes. The latter scheme applies beyond the cereals sector, and under it the Member States were required to set in place arrangements allowing for farmers to reduce by 20% the arable land available for production.[12] Farmers received compensation, in part financed from the Community, for the loss of income, subject to a maximum amount per hectare. Land set aside under this scheme cannot be counted under the other two schemes. Once the five years have expired, the land which has been set aside can be counted as the voluntary aspect of the temporary set-aside scheme, as part of a renewal of set aside. Under the compulsory aspect of this scheme, every producer claiming compensation for an area greater than that needed to grow 92 tonnes of cereals, must set aside a percentage of his or her land. Various rates have been set over the years, such as a single rate, a rate for rotational set aside and a rate for non-rotational set aside.[13] Land set aside under this scheme may be used to manufacture products not directly intended for either animal or human consumption.[14]

3.2.2 Pigmeat, poultry and eggs

The common organization of the market in pigmeat covers live animals, with the exception of those used for breeding, meat, offal, bacon and fats, and certain processed products, such as sausages.[15] The common organization of the market in poultry covers live poultry, poultry meat,

[12] Regulation 2328/91, OJ 1991 L 218/1. See now Regulation 1257/99 OJ 1999 L 160/80.

[13] By virtue of Regulation 1469/97 (OJ 1997 L 200/2) the compulsory set-aside rate for 1998/99 was set at 5% and extraordinary set-aside was suspended for a further marketing year. For an interpretation of Regulation 1765/92, see Case C-356/95 *Witt* [1997] ECR I-6589.

[14] Regulations 2078/92 (OJ 1992 L 215/85) and 2080/92 (OJ 1992 L 215/96) provided that land set aside for environmental purposes or for afforestation can be counted as compulsory set-aside land; however, no compensation is offered for such land. See also Regulation 1257/99, above n. 12.

[15] Regulation 2759/75, OJ 1975 L 282/1.

offal and liver, fresh, chilled or frozen, and various poultry fat and other preparations.[16] Poultry eggs and other birds' eggs are covered by the common organization of the market in eggs.[17] The reason for joining discussion of these common organizations is not only their connection with the common organization of the market in cereals, but also the fact that the mechanisms of the organizations are broadly comparable.

The common organization of the market in pigmeat continues to rest on the establishment of a basic price, the purpose of which is to ensure market equilibrium by acting as a trigger for private storage aid. By virtue of Article 4 of the Regulation establishing the common organization, the setting of the basic price shall not lead to the formation of structural surpluses in the Community. Intervention is possible under the common organization whenever the Community market price for pig carcasses is below 103% of the basic price and likely to remain at that level. For both poultry and eggs, the common organization of the market has never involved guaranteed prices or intervention arrangements. Instead, both Regulations contain a set of measures designed to improve the organization and quality of production and processing.

As a result of the Agreement on Agriculture, the variable import levy system used in these common organizations has been replaced by fixed customs duties, which under the Agreement are subject to an agreed timetable of reductions over the period of implementation of the Agreement. A similar timetable of reductions is applicable to both budgetary expenditure and quantities benefiting from export subsidies. In addition to these measures a minimum market access quota, with a set customs duty, has been established for pigmeat.[18] Amendments to all three common organizations as a result of the Agreement on Agriculture allow for the imposition of selective safeguard measures provided for in Article 5 of that Agreement.[19]

3.2.3 Beef and veal

Established in 1968, the basic regulation governing this common organization is now Regulation 1254/99.[20] Applicable to live animals, meat (fresh, chilled or frozen), processed products and offal, this common

---

[16] Regulation 2777/75, OJ 1975 L 282/77.   [17] Regulation 2771/75, OJ 1975 L 282/49.

[18] See Regulations 1486/95 (OJ 1995 L 145/58), 1176/96 (OJ 1996 L 155/26) and 2068/96 (OJ 1996 L 277/12). For poultry, see Regulation 1251/96 (OJ 1996 L 161/136).

[19] See above n. 9, Regulation 3290/94, Annex X–XII, Pigmeat, Poultry and Eggs respectively. See also for poultry and eggs, Regulation 1484/95 (OJ 1995 L 145/47).

[20] OJ 1999 L 160/21. The original regulation, Regulation 805/68 (JO 1968 L 148/74) had been subject to numerous amendments, and the consolidation of these amendments formed part of the Agenda 2000 proposals. See also Regulation 1259/99 (OJ 1999 L 160/113).

organization used to rest on the establishment every year of a guide price for calves and a guide price for adult bovine animals. Calculated as a percentage of the guide price, there was also an intervention price at which point intervention was triggered. However, with the emergence of structural surpluses, the nature of the common organization has been transformed. The common organization of the market in beef and veal no longer involves the establishment of guide prices.

One of the more important measures under this common organization is now the intervention system under which beef and veal can be bought into intervention. This may occur in two situations. Firstly, where the average market price in the Community for a particular grade of beef is below 84% of the relevant intervention price and the average national market price for that grade is below 80% of the intervention price. If this situation occurs, buying in to intervention will occur within set quantitative limits for the entire Community. Under the second situation, a further safety net is introduced if, for two consecutive weeks, the average Community market price for certain cattle falls below 78% of the intervention price and the average national market price falls below 60% of that price. Products bought in under this latter scheme do not count towards the maximum quantities set for intervention. Private storage aid may also be granted in order to avoid or reduce the impact of a fall in prices. However, as in the common organization of the market in cereals, the major reform of this sector has been the widespread introduction of a system of premiums which are designed to alleviate the consequences of the gradual reduction in intervention prices.

The most important of these premiums is the suckler cow premium which is granted to two categories of producers. Firstly, those producers who deliver no milk or dairy produce from their farms for a period of one year from the date of application for the premium and who keep for six months following that date a number of suckler cows at least equal to that specified in the application. Secondly, small dairy farmers, provided they keep for a period of six months after the application for the premium a number of suckler cows at least equal to that specified in the application. The amount of the premium is laid down under the Regulation and may be restricted by an individual ceiling which is set according to the number of animals for which a premium is granted in a reference year selected by the Member State. An additional premium for suckler cows may be awarded by the Member States, which is partly funded by the Community for those regions of a Member State which specialize in suckler herds or which are not as developed as other regions. Another premium, known as the special premium, is payable to producers keeping male cattle on their farms, subject to a ceiling set at regional level, and which are kept for fattening for at least two months. Payment of the suckler cow premium and the special premium is limited according to the application of a 'density factor' established on the basis of the number of 'livestock units' per hectare of forage for the animals for which the application for a premium has been made.

There are a number of other premiums for which producers may be eligible. These include a deseasonalization premium (payable as a result of postponing the date of slaughter under certain conditions), an extensification premium (payable in addition to the special and/or suckler cow premium where the density factor is less than one livestock unit per hectare), a premium for the fattening of young male calves and a premium for the early slaughter of calves. Further measures of direct support were introduced as a result of the problems emerging in this common organization as a result of the spread of BSE in the United Kingdom. The measures introduced include a Community contribution to the cost of slaughter of cows and calves, not only in the United Kingdom but also in Belgium, France, The Netherlands and Portugal.[21]

BSE first emerged in the United Kingdom in 1986, and the response of the Community was to adopt a series of measures designed to stop the spread of the disease to other cattle and to protect consumers. For example, the inclusion in ruminant feed of mammalian meat and bone meal was prohibited and minimum criteria were established for the rendering of cattle and other ruminant material.[22] The situation would change significantly as a result of declaration by the United Kingdom's Spongiform Encephalopathy Advisory Committee (SEAC) of a potential link between BSE and a number of cases of new-variant Creutzfeldt-Jakob Disease. The immediate response of the Community was to adopt Decision 96/239, which prohibited the export from the United Kingdom of live cattle, their semen and embryos, the meat of cattle slaughtered in the UK, products obtained from cattle slaughtered in the UK destined for use in medicinal products, cosmetics or pharmaceutical products or mammalian-derived meat and bone meal.[23]

---

[21] See for example, Decision 96/381 (OJ 1996 L 149/25) and Decision 98/653 (OJ 1998 L 311/23) on a plan for eradicating BSE in Portugal. See also Decision 97/18 (OJ 1997 L 6/43) on a plan for eradicating BSE in France.

[22] Decision 94/381 (OJ 1994 L 172/23) as amended by Decision 95/160 (OJ 1995 L 55/43). See also Decision 96/449 (OJ 1996 L 184/43) requiring all animal waste from mammalian animals in the Community to be processed, demonstrated to deactivate the agents of scrapie and BSE. See also Decision 90/200 (OJ 1990 L 105/24), which was replaced by Decision 94/474 (OJ 1994 L 194/96) as amended by Decision 95/287 (OJ 1995 L 181/40).

[23] OJ 1996 L 78/47. See also Decision 92/290 (OJ 1992 L 152/37) which had imposed strict conditions on the export of embryos. Decision 96/362 (OJ 1996 L 139/17) lifted the ban on semen.

The validity of this total export ban, based on Article 37 and Directives 89/662 and 90/425 dealing with veterinary checks in intra-Community trade and which were designed to complete the internal market,[24] was brought before the Court in two cases – *R v Ministry of Agriculture, ex parte National Farmers' Union and others* and *United Kingdom v Commission*.[25] The question asked by the High Court in the first of these cases was:

> Is Article 1 of Commission Decision 96/239 ... invalid in whole or in part, in particular because the Commission lacked the power or else misused the power to adopt the Commission decision, or because it infringes the principle of proportionality?

The claim of the parties was that the exercise of the Commission's competence was not based on affording protection against any serious hazard to human health as required by the Directives. Moreover, these Directives did not contain any provision allowing for the Commission to ban exports from the United Kingdom to third countries. Such a ban, it was also argued, should not have been adopted under measures aimed at the internal market, but rather under more specific measures governing trade with third countries. It was further asserted that the complete export ban went beyond what was necessary in the circumstances of the case.

With respect to the plea of lack of competence, the Court found that Article 37 was an appropriate and sufficient legal basis with regard to trade in agricultural products. Moreover, there was nothing in the secondary legislation used to suggest that the powers of Commission were limited to the protection of public health within the Community, thus confirming the broad discretion enjoyed by the Community institutions in matters concerning the CAP.[26] In its analysis of this secondary legislation, the Court considered that the new information offered by SEAC altered the perception of the risk involved and thus authorized the Commission to adopt the necessary safeguard measures under this legislation. Having dismissed the plea of lack of competence, the Court also dismissed the plea of misuse of power. As for the claim of a breach of the principle of proportionality, given the great uncertainty as to the risks posed by BSE the Court considered that protective measures might be taken without having to

---

[24] OJ 1989 L 395/13 and OJ 1990 L 224/29. The latter directive was amended by Directive 92/118 (OJ 1993 L 62/49) and action taken under it was upheld in Joined Cases T-481/93 and T-484/93 *VELV* [1995] ECR II-2941.

[25] Case C-157/96 [1998] ECR I-2211 and Case C-180/96 [1998] ECR I-2265. See also Case C-263/97 *Fair City Trading* (unreported, judgment of 29 September 1998).

[26] See also discussion of Article 37 in 2.4 above.

wait until the existence or extent of the risk became fully apparent. The measures taken were not inappropriate and not therefore a breach of the principle of proportionality.

In the second of these cases, the United Kingdom government also sought the annulment of the Decision and, in the alternative, the annulment of Article 1 in so far as it applied, for example, to live exports permitted under Decision 94/474, and to meat from animals certified to come from BSE-free herds. Numerous pleas in law were advanced in support of the application, in addition to those outlined above. They included a breach of the principles of non-discrimination and legal certainty and an infringement of Article 38(1). Those claims which were also made, and dismissed, in the first case suffered a similar fate in this case, as did the additional claims made here.

The restrictions applicable under Decision 96/239 were partially alleviated in March 1998 in a decision which provided for the lifting of the export ban on beef and beef products derived from animals born and reared in Northern Ireland.[27] One reason for the decision to lift the ban only for Northern Ireland related to the system used there for the identification and registration of bovine animals. A similar system has been formally adopted for the rest of the Community as a result of Regulation 820/97, which also sets various rules for the labelling of beef and beef products.[28] The Regulation requires identification by means of eartags and identification papers for all animals born after 1 January 1998. The identity of all animals and their movement will be stored in a computer database to be created by each Member State. The database will operate alongside a register to be kept by all producers for all cattle in their holdings. A compulsory labelling system, to replace the existing optional scheme, will be introduced from 1 January 2000.[29] Regulation 820/97 is part of the strategy to eradicate the problems arising from BSE and to restore consumer confidence in beef. This strategy includes a plan for the eradication of BSE in the United Kingdom[30] and the introduction of a system to ensure the eradication of the agents causing BSE, so-called

---

[27] Decision 98/256 OJ 1998 L 113/32 implemented by Decision 98/351 OJ 1998 L 157/110.

[28] OJ 1997 L 117/1.

[29] The original Commission proposal (COM (97) 103) proposed two measures to be adopted under Article 95. The resulting regulation which combined the two proposals was based on Article 37, and in March 1997 the Commission decided to institute proceedings challenging the use of Article 43 (Bull. EU 3-1997, point 1.3.132).

[30] Decision 96/385, OJ 1996 L 151/39. See also conclusions of the Florence European Council, Bull. EU 6-1996, point I.8.

specified risk materials, in the processing of animal waste.[31] On 25 November 1998, the Commission formally endorsed the UK's date-based export scheme, combined with the decision of the Agriculture Council on 23 November that the beef export ban should be lifted.[32] After the completion of the necessary inspections, beef exports from the United Kingdom resumed in August 1999.

To complete the analysis of the common organization of the market in beef and veal, various changes have been made to the trading regime as a result of the Agreement on Agriculture. Export refunds will continue to be granted on the basis of the difference between world prices and prices within the Community.[33] In relation to imports, a fixed customs duty will replace the system of customs duties and variable import levies which had been applied before the implementation of the Agreement on Agriculture. Various other market access opportunities will also exist as a result of a series of quotas.[34]

3.2.4 Sheepmeat and goatmeat

In contrast to the other common organizations of the market, that covering sheepmeat was not established until 1980, ten years after the end of the transitional period.[35] Regulation 1837/80 originally limited the scope of the organization to sheepmeat[36] and it allowed for a further four-year transitional period during which reference prices would gradually converge on the basic price.[37] The aid provisions of the common organi-

---

[31] Decision 96/449, OJ 1996 L 184/43. See also Decision 97/734 (OJ 1997 L 294/7) concerning certain protection measures with regard to trade in certain types of mammalian waste. The prohibition on the use of specified risk materials introduced by Decision 97/534 (OJ 1997 L 216/95) was suspended until 1 January 1999. See also Decision 98/248 (OJ 1998 L 102/26) which suspended this decision.

[32] See Commission Decision 98/692, OJ 1998 L 328/28. The arrangements will apply only to boned beef and beef products from animals born after 1 August 1996 and aged between six and 30 months.

[33] By virtue of Regulation 2634/97 (OJ 1997 L 356/13) the payment of export refunds on consignments of live animals is conditional on compliance with the Community's animal welfare rules.

[34] See Regulation 1203/95, OJ 1995 L 119/3, and Regulation 500/96 (OJ 1996 L 75/13).

[35] In this period there had been a number of disputes between the two main producers in the Community: see for example, Case 232/78 *Commission v France* [1979] ECR 2729.

[36] OJ 1980 L 183/1.

[37] The validity of this additional period was upheld by the Court in Case 106/81 *Kind* [1982] ECR 2885. In essence, during this period a series of regional markets existed. To ensure that the variable slaughter premium used at this time by the United Kingdom did not disrupt trade, a premium, known as the clawback premium, was payable on exports from the UK. See Joined Cases C-38/90 and C-151/90 *Lomas* [1992] ECR I-1781, where aspects of the regulation laying down detailed rules for the premium were declared invalid. See also Regulation 1922/92 (OJ 1992 L 195/10), Case C-212/94 *FMC* [1996] ECR I-389 and Case T-455/93 *Hedley Lomas* [1997] ECR II-1095.

zation were extended to cover goatmeat as a result of Greek accession to the Community.[38] The common organization of the market in sheepmeat and goatmeat is currently governed by Regulation 2467/98.[39]

Under this Regulation every year a basic price, which is adjusted throughout the year to take account of seasonal variations, is fixed for fresh or chilled sheep carcasses. Since 1988 the basic price has been subject to a 'stabilizer' which sets a guaranteed maximum number of ewes for the Community; whenever that maximum is exceeded the basic price is reduced by 7% irrespective of the percentage by which the maximum is exceeded. The basic price is used as a reference point for intervention measures, which usually take the form of private storage aid, when, for example, the market price in a particular region and the Community market price are less than a fixed percentage of the seasonally adjusted basic price and are likely to remain so.[40] The basic price is also used to calculate aid under the common organization where a distinction is made between producers. Aid is granted, in the form of a ewe premium, where it is necessary to compensate for losses of income suffered by producers during a marketing year, and it is calculated by determining the difference between the basic price and the mean of market prices in the Community during the marketing year. For light lamb producers, that is those who market ewe's milk or any product based on this milk, the loss of income suffered is multiplied by 80% of the figure emerging from this calculation.[41] For heavy lamb producers, that is all other producers, the ewe premium is calculated by multiplying the loss of income by a figure representing the annual average production of lamb per ewe throughout the Community. A goat premium, equivalent to 80% of the ewe premium, is payable for goats in certain mountain and less favoured areas, provided that they are mainly intended for production.[42]

In an effort to limit expenditure on aid under this common organization, since 1992 each producer has been able to receive premiums only within the limits received for the 1991 marketing year. From 1992 to 1994, a difference was made in the application of this measure between producers in less favoured areas and producers in other areas, whereby the former would receive the full premium up to a limit of 1,000 animals as compared to 500 animals for other producers. Since 1995 these ceil-

[38] See Regulation 3523/85, OJ 1985 L 336/2.
[39] OJ 1998 L 312/1. This repealed Regulation 3013/89 (OJ 1989 L 289/1).
[40] The percentages are set at 90% and 70%; the difference gives rise to different procedures for initiating private storage aid.
[41] Light lamb producers may also receive the heavy producer's premium if it can be shown that at least 40% of the lambs born on their farms are fattened into heavy carcasses for slaughter.
[42] A fixed premium is also payable for ewes and goats in mountain and less favoured areas, see Regulation 193/98 (OJ 1998 L 20/18).

ings have been abolished, although the Member States are required to recalculate the individual limits in such a way as to maintain the principle that payments over the limits are to be reduced by 50%. As in other common organizations, major changes were made as a result of the Agreement in Agriculture. In this common organization, where external protection had usually been effected by means of voluntary restraint agreements, these were transformed into more generous market access quotas. Import levies were replaced by duties which were reduced on meat and live animals. Finally, export refunds are no longer payable.

3.2.5 Milk

The common organization of the market in milk, which covers milk and cream (fresh, preserved, concentrated or sweetened), butter, cheese and curd, lactose and lactose syrup, and milk-based compound feeds for animals, was established by virtue of Regulation 804/68 and is now governed by Regulation 1255/99. [43] Under this common organization a target price is set for milk and an intervention price for butter and skimmed milk powder. A threshold price for 'pilot products' used to be set as part of the calculation of the variable import levy. The price is no longer set as, under the Agreement on Agriculture, the variable levy has been replaced by fixed customs duties. To protect the Community market a special safeguard mechanism allowing for quotas has been provided for in accordance with the provisions of the Agreement on Agriculture. Lastly, export refunds may be granted, but under the Agreement these refunds must respect budgetary and quantitative limitations agreed by the Community and these limitations are to be reduced over the period of implementation of the Agreement.

The common organization of the market in milk is of legal interest because it is in this organization that the greatest (and longest) efforts have been made to curb surplus production and increased budgetary expenditure. The first such attempt was the co-responsibility levy imposed by virtue of Regulation 1079/77 as a measure to reduce the costs of milk support under the common organization of the market.[44] In 1982, the levy was replaced by a system of guarantee thresholds for milk and milk products based on production figures for 1981 plus a margin of 0.5%.[45] It was agreed that appropriate measures would be

---

[43] JO 1968 L 148/13 and OJ 1999 L 160/48.
[44] OJ 1977 L 131/6. The validity of the measure as a measure to stabilize markets was upheld by the Court in Case 138/78 *Stölting* [1979] ECR 713. This is discussed further in 4.5.
[45] Regulation 1183/82, OJ 1982 L 140/1.

taken to offset the additional expenditure if the threshold was exceeded. Measures were taken but they failed to stem the tide of increased production, and in 1984 a quota and additional levy system were introduced.[46] Originally the quotas were set on the basis of the guarantee threshold plus 0.5%, but as this led to a situation of continuing over-production, they were subsequently reduced.[47] The system operated through the division of the global Community figure into figures for each of the Member States. This quota was then further divided, into reference quantities for both deliveries and sales for direct consumption, and if these quantities were exceeded a levy was payable either by milk producers (Formula A), or purchasers of milk or other milk products (for example, dairies) who recovered the amount from the producers (Formula B). The individual reference quantities might be increased, but only within the confines of the figure for the total quantities set for each Member State. The reference quantity is transferred whenever an undertaking is sold, leased or transferred by inheritance. As originally set up, a Community reserve was created to meet the needs of a Member State(s) which had difficulty implementing schemes for controlling milk production. The reserve has now been abolished and the quantities incorporated into the global Community figure.

Amendments to the 1984 Regulation establishing the additional levy were simplified and consolidated in Regulation 3950/92.[48] This Regulation confirms that if the national quota is exceeded, an additional levy is imposed on those producers or dairies who have exceeded their quotas. The levy, which is payable for a period of seven years beginning in April 1993, is set at 115% of the target price. The levy is shared between those producers who have exceeded their quota, after a decision of the Member State on whether or not to reallocate unused reference quantities, thus pointing to the existence of national reserves. Such reserves, and the power to allocate reference quantities, are an important element in the restructuring of milk production at national or regional level.[49] In the

---

[46] Regulation 856/84, OJ 1984 L 90/10. For a discussion of the original scheme, see Freidberg, A., 'Milk Surpluses Till the Cows Come Home?' (1984) 7 *World Economy* 421.

[47] See for example, Regulations 1355/86 (OJ 1986 L 119/19) and 775/87 (OJ 1987 L 78/5).

[48] OJ 1992 L 405/1 as amended by Regulation 1256/99 (OJ 1999 L 160/73) which extends the scheme for a period of eight years starting on 1 April 2000. See also the rules for application in Regulation 536/93 (OJ 1993 L 51/12) and Regulation 551/98 (OJ 1998 L 73/1) which extends the special arrangements under the Regulation applicable to the new German *Länder*.

[49] Under Article 3 of Regulation 857/84, special reference quantities could be granted to producers adopting milk production development plans under the Community's structural policy for agriculture, for example Directive 72/159 (this Directive is discussed further in Chapter 6).

event that the amount collected exceeds the levy, the Member State may use the proceeds to give a refund to producers who are in an exceptional position resulting from a national provision unconnected with the quota system. The Member State may also use the proceeds to fund restructuring programmes, through giving compensation to producers who undertake to abandon milk production.[50]

Beyond the quota system there is intervention for butter and for skimmed milk powder, although the latter intervention is open for a defined period and is subject to a maximum quantity. If intervention is suspended for skimmed milk powder there is the possibility that private storage aid may be granted. There is also a vast range of measures designed to promote the use of products subject to this common organization. For example, for skimmed milk powder aid is granted when it is used for calf feed or feed for other animals and for the processing of skimmed milk powder into casein. For milk, aid is granted for the use of denatured liquid skimmed milk for calf feed or feed for other animals. There are also a number of measures promoting the consumption of milk and milk products, such as the school milk programme.[51]

3.2.6 Sugar

Whereas surplus production measures were introduced into many common organizations in the 1970s and 1980s, surplus production measures have always been part of the common organization of the market in sugar as established by Regulation 1009/67.[52] By virtue of the original Regulation, the system was to expire in 1975, but it is now a permanent feature of this common organization.[53] The common organization applies to cane sugar and beet sugar, molasses and various other processed products. The scope of the common organization was extended in 1977 to include isoglucose, and in 1994 to include inulin syrup.[54] Under the current Regulation, Regulation 1785/81, various prices are set each year which include an intervention price for white

---

[50] See for example, Regulation 1183/90 (OJ 1990 L 195/23) which established a Community programme financing the discontinuation of milk production. The reference quantities so released were to be used to implement a programme for the restructuring of small holdings' production.

[51] See Regulation 1842/83 (OJ 1983 L 183/1). For other promotion measures, see as an example Regulations 2073/92 (OJ 1992 L 215/67) and 3582/93 (OJ 1993 L 326/23).

[52] JO 1967 L 308/1.

[53] The production arrangements were extended to 2000/01 by Regulation 1101/95 (OJ 1995 L 11/1).

[54] The common organization was extended to isoglucose by Regulation 1111/77 (OJ 1977 L 134/4) and to inulin syrup by Regulation 133/94 (OJ 1994 L 22/11).

sugar and a target price for white sugar to which the intervention price applies.[55]

The price guarantees and the intervention arrangements are offered for only limited quantities of the main products covered by the common organization, known as A and B quotas. The basic Regulation establishes overall production quotas for each Member State and it is up to the Member State to allocate a quota to each sugar refinery in its territory. The difference between A and B quota sugar rests on the price guarantee offered to producers. The A quota established the quantities of sugar for which full price support is offered. Since 1986 an elimination levy, set at 2%, has been imposed on all sugar producers to ensure that the cost of disposing of production surplus to internal consumption requirements was met by producers.[56] (At the same time a special elimination levy was introduced to help in the elimination of the surpluses which had arisen.[57]) The elimination levy applies to all producers of sugar under both A and B quota arrangements. As for the B quota, the price guarantee is limited to 68% of the intervention price, with the possibility of a reduction to 60.5% if the revenue arising from the levy is not sufficient to meet the cost of disposing of surplus sugar production. Production above the quantities set by the sum of the A and B quotas, known as C sugar, may not be marketed in the Community and must be exported without the aid of an export refund.

As a consequence of the Agreement on Agriculture, as in other common organizations, import levies have been replaced by import duties. To offer protection equivalent to that provided by import levies, a special safeguard mechanism was introduced. Export refunds are similarly subject to the budgetary and quantitative restrictions established by the Agreement. One further factor must be taken into account in the trading regime established by this common organization and it is a reflection of the fact that sugar constitutes an important product for some developing countries associated with the Community. A feature of Protocol 3 of the 1975 Lomé Convention, establishing an association between the Community and various African, Caribbean and Pacific Countries, was the offer by the Community to import 1.3 million tonnes per annum from these countries.[58] Protocol 3 has been re-enacted with each new

---

[55] OJ 1981 L 177/4. A basic price is also fixed for beet sugar and a minimum price for beet processed into sugar.

[56] Regulation 934/86, OJ 1986 L 87/1. See also Regulation 1107/88, OJ 1988 L 110/20.

[57] Regulation 1914/87, OJ 1987 L 183/5. See also Regulation 1108/88, OJ 1988 L 110/25.

[58] Protocol 3 is discussed in 5.4 as part of the assessment of the external impact of the CAP.

Lomé Convention since 1975 and will continue to apply until 2000/01 by virtue of Regulation 1101/95.[59]

3.2.7 Other products

Given the range of common organizations of the market it is not possible to discuss all of them within the confines of this work. The most important products covered by the CAP are either listed above, or have market organizations similar to those outlined above. One common organization which does not fall into either of these categories is the common organization of the market in fruit and vegetables. This was one of the first common organizations, and the basic regulation is now Regulation 2200/96 which entered into force on 1 January 1997.[60] The instruments of the common organization involve the establishment of common standards, applicable to all stages of marketing, for the products subject to the Regulation.

One of the interesting features of the common organization is the system for the recognition of producer associations, who may receive Community assistance to help finance withdrawal of products from the market. The Community will also give financial assistance to such associations to help with the establishment of operational funds. Such funds will help finance the functions of producer associations, which are to include the planning of production, the promotion of marketing, the reduction of production costs and the stabilization of producer prices. The Regulation also allows for the creation of interbranch organizations, that is organizations representing a significant share of the production of and/or trade in, and/or processing of, products covered by the common organization in one or more specific regions. Such organizations, to be set up on the initiative of their members, must carry out the operations which are exhaustively listed in the Regulation. The agreement, decisions or concerted practices of these organizations are to be notified to the Commission.[61]

Beyond the encouragement given to producer associations and interbranch organizations, the common organization establishes intervention arrangements for certain products. Producers receive compensation in the event of intervention. The level of this compensation, according to Annex V of the Regulation, is to be progressively reduced over a five-year period, as are the quantities which will be received into

---

[59] Above n. 53. See also Regulation 1915/95 (OJ 1995 L 184/16) on arrangements covering the import of special preferential sugar from the ACP States and India into Portugal.
[60] OJ 1996 L 297/1.
[61] See discussion in 1.2.3, 'The agricultural provisions and the rules on competition'.

intervention. As for processed fruit and vegetables, these are governed by Regulation 2201/96 which established a series of production aids for various processed products.[62] There is very limited intervention under this common organization, but the Regulation does provide for specific measures to be adopted to improve the competitiveness of products which are of major local or regional importance in economic or ecological terms and which face strong international competition.

3.3 Legal aspects of the pricing structure

The above analysis of the various pricing mechanisms of a number of common organizations reveals the extent to which the nature of those mechanisms has changed over the years. Initially characterized by the setting of just three prices – the target, intervention and threshold prices – most common organizations rely now only on the setting of an intervention price. As part of the compensation package for the reduction in the level of common prices, the range of premiums or additional payments available to producers has increased significantly and has become more important. Production restraints also became more important as the Community struggled (and continues to struggle) with the problem of surplus production. As a result the legal aspects of the pricing structure have grown beyond the setting of common prices to encompass the new elements introduced in the 1980s and 1990s.

3.3.1 Prices and producers

An examination of the 'old' pricing structure reveals that it was never the intention for the target price to replace the market price. The aim of that price, according to the Court, was to help in the realization of the objectives of the CAP, for example, to guarantee a fair income for agricultural producers in accordance with Article 33(1)(b).[63] In *Pool* the Court made it clear that:[64] 'Those prices are to determine on the one hand the implementation of the various measures of intervention in the market and on the other to adjust the level of levies and refunds applicable in trade with non-Member States.' After pointing out the advantages of Community prices being higher than world prices, the Court continued:

[62] OJ 1996 L 297/29.
[63] See as examples, Case 5/71 *Schöppenstedt* [1971] ECR 975 and Case 60/75 *Russo* [1976] ECR 45.
[64] Case 49/79 [1980] ECR 569, p. 581.

It is true that the prices obtained by individual producers are indirectly determined by the combination of intervention in the market and the arrangements for the Community's external trade, but in spite of that it is not possible to take the view that the price system guarantees to individual traders that their produce will be disposed of at the precise level determined by the Community rules.

Thus there was no guarantee to the individual producer that the market price would be around the level of the common price.

So in the setting of common prices the Community institutions were not promoting individual interests but the wider Community interest. For example, it has been noted that:[65]

The essential aim of the machinery of the common organization of the market is to achieve price levels at the production and wholesale stages which take into account both the interests of Community production as a whole in the relevant sector and those of consumers, and which guarantee market supplies without encouraging over-production.

Such an intention can also be gleaned from the regulations establishing the various common organizations. For example, Article 4 of the Regulation establishing the common organization of the market in pigmeat provides that the setting of the basic price shall not lead to the formation of structural surpluses in the Community. However, the decline of the target price evident in the above discussion of the various common organizations is a reflection of the fact that it was set at a level which generated surplus production and thus was an inappropriate instrument to achieve the overall goals of the CAP. This may be seen as the inevitable consequence of giving the power to make decisions on the level of prices to a political body, such as the Council, rather than allowing it to remain with the Commission. Moreover, the decision was vested in the Ministers of Agriculture rather than in Finance Ministers, hence the impact of prices on agricultural producers was a more important consideration than the budgetary consequences of such decisions. The result was that the high-price countries fought for comparatively high prices in order to avoid farm income problems.[66] The resulting impetus to production was not seen as a problem given the fact that for most of the 1960s the Community was not self-sufficient in products covered by the common organizations of the market.

The negative consequences of the Council of Agricultural Ministers fixing the level of common prices could have been avoided had the

---

[65] Case 297/82 *De Samvirkende Danske Landboforeninger* [1983] ECR 3299, p. 3318.
[66] Heidhues, T. et al., *Common Prices and Europe's Farm Policy* (TPRC, London, 1978), p. 7.

wording of the Treaty been followed, but it was not. Instead of moving to a system of qualified majority voting at the end of the second stage of the transitional period, the Luxembourg compromise ensured that unanimity would remain the standard voting procedure for a considerable period. Such a system encouraged the continuation of the process of setting high common prices.[67] Political agreement at the 1988 Brussels European Council to tackle the budgetary consequences of high common prices, and the resulting Institutional Agreement on Budgetary Discipline, signalled the beginning of the end of such prices. As a result of the compensation package for the reduction in the level of common prices, there has been a significant increase in the number of additional measures or premiums, designed to secure the objectives of the CAP and, in particular, the objective of guaranteeing a fair standard of living for producers.[68] It also helps to explain the return to the original goal of intervention as a safety net, so as to prevent market prices falling too far below a level, for example, at which farmers would receive a fair income.

3.3.2 Intervention

The intervention price represents a form of guarantee to the producer which is met if the producer satisfies the criteria for intervention.[69] In the period of high common prices intervention had merely acted as an additional outlet for Community agricultural production, thus increasing stocks and expenditure. During this time the producer could sell any amount of a product for which intervention arrangements existed and would receive the intervention price.[70]

> As regards the legal effect of an offer, it must be pointed out that the Community rules on market intervention derogate from ordinary law in so far as the national intervention agency is obliged to accept an offer of sale from an economic agent if the conditions for intervention are fulfilled.

The Court continued by noting that the fact that the intervention agency may not turn down the offer is sufficient to justify a prohibition imposed on the producer from withdrawing the offer of the products to intervention where this would run counter to the aims of the intervention system. The possibility of withdrawing an offer could, the Court argued,

---

[67] For a discussion see Vasey, M., 'Decision-making in the Agricultural Council and the "Luxembourg" compromise' (1988) 22 CMLRev 725.

[68] See for example, Case C-132/95 *Jensen* [1998] ECR I-2975 and Joined Cases C-36/97 and C-37/97 *Kellinghusen* [1998] ECR (unreported, judgment of 22 October 1998).

[69] Case 2/75 *Mackprang* [1975] ECR 607, p. 616.

[70] Case C-28/89 *Germany v Commission* [1991] ECR I-581, p. 615.

lead to results not in accordance with goals pursued by Community rules.

As a result of the reform process, intervention is, as noted above, returning to its original goal of acting as a safety net or, as the Court noted in *Kaas*, a mechanism 'to restore the balance between supply and demand'.[71] Although the obligation to buy in products which qualify for intervention which are offered to them is a Community obligation, the Community does not acquire ownership of the products as the intervention agencies are established under national law. However, the Commission is responsible for the management of the products bought into intervention and the Community is responsible for the cost of storage and processing.[72] Products bought into intervention must be disposed of in a way which does not undermine the intervention price.[73]

In addition to intervention, which is a form of public storage, various common organizations provide for private storage aid, either in addition to intervention or as the sole means of withdrawing a product from the market. Such aid is conditional on the conclusion of a storage contract between the intervention agencies and satisfaction of the conditions laid down by Community law for such storage.[74]

3.3.3 Production controls

Just as common prices have declined in significance and intervention has returned to acting as a safety net for producers, the range of production controls in various common organizations has increased significantly. Two particular types of production controls have given rise to significant legal problems: the use of quotas in the common organization of the market in sugar, and the use of the additional levy scheme in the common organization of the market in milk.[75] The jurisprudence of the Court in both these areas has confirmed various general principles of Community law, notably the prohibition on discrimination and the respect for various other human rights principles.

The common organization of the market in sugar was considered by the Court in *Eridania* in the context of a claim that the quantity allocated to Italy did not fully reflect Italian consumption of sugar.[76] In contrast to other Member States, Italy had been allocated an A quota

---

[71] Case 237/82 [1984] ECR 483, p. 502.
[72] Case C-174/89 *Hoche* [1990] ECR I-2702, p. 2712.
[73] Case 79/87 *OBEA* [1988] ECR 937.
[74] See for example, Case 215/88 *Casa Fleischhandels* [1989] ECR 2789.
[75] The financial aspects of Producer Levies are discussed below in 4.5.
[76] Case 250/84 [1986] ECR 117. See also Case 151/78 *Nykøbing* [1979] ECR 1 and Case C-1/94 *Cavarzere Produzioni Industriali* [1995] ECR I-2363.

which was lower than its internal consumption, with the result that Italian sugar producers could only export B sugar which involved the payment of levies. As for the legality of the quota system, the Court noted:[77] 'It must be borne in mind in this regard that the aim of the quota system is not to support the least profitable undertakings but to provide a degree of control over production, whilst re-orientating it towards the needs of the market.' For the Court this constituted a justification for not taking into account differences in production costs between Member States in the allocation of quotas. As a result it considered that the higher levy on B sugar than on A sugar did not infringe the principle of non-discrimination.

The Court has also upheld the use of the quota system in the milk sector. Two years after the introduction of the milk quota scheme, further regulations provided for a reduction in the total quantities guaranteed to each Member State.[78] In the case of *Spain v Council*, the Court rejected a challenge to the validity of these latter regulations, characterizing the measures as intending 'to stabilize the market in milk products, in which structural surpluses resulting from an imbalance between supply and demand are endemic'.[79] In reaching this decision the Court rejected the argument that the regulations infringed Article 33(1)(b) of the Treaty. In *Erpedling*, the Court confirmed that the primary purpose of the milk quota scheme was to re-establish the balance between supply and demand in the milk market, and it went on to reject the argument that the failure to allocate a reference quantity to a producer, as a result of the fact that the plaintiff's herd was repeatedly struck by disease during the period within which reference quantities were to be set, constituted a breach of the right to enjoy property.[80] Affirming the decision in *Erpedling*, the Court has held that the primary purpose of the quota scheme does not allow for the aggregation of the reference quantities for direct sales and for deliveries, which are independent of each other, in order to determine whether or not there has been over-production at national level.[81] However, after reaffirming the goal of market balance,

---

[77] *Ibid.*, p. 143.

[78] Regulations 1335/86 and 1343/86, OJ 1986 L 119/19 and 34. The reduction was to be made through the Community purchase of milk quotas, Regulation 1336/86, OJ 1986 L 119/21.

[79] Case 203/86 [1988] ECR 4563, pp. 4599–4600. See also Joined Cases T-466/93, T-469/93, T-473/93, T-474/93 and T-477/93 *O'Dwyer* [1995] ECR II-2071, where the Court of First Instance rejected a challenge to reduction in the level of guaranteed quantities. A similar decision was reached by the Court in Case C-22/94 *Irish Farmers Association* [1997] ECR I-1809.

[80] Case 84/87 [1988] ECR 2647. See also Case 113/88 *Leukhardt* [1989] ECR 1991, Case C-177/90 *Kühn* [1992] ECR I-35 and Case C-122/92 *Schultz* [1993] ECR I-6885.

[81] Case C-196/94 *Schiltz-Thilmann* [1995] ECR I-3991.

the Court has concluded that there is nothing to preclude national legislation empowering national authorities to waive the levy in exceptional
circumstances on the grounds of personal equity.[82]

It was only to be expected that the milk quota system would give rise
to considerable litigation. In *Klensch*, the Court considered that the prohibition on discrimination contained in Article 34(3) required an
interpretation of Regulation 857/84 precluding Member States who had
opted for Formula B, under which the additional levy was payable by
purchasers of milk and milk products, from adding the reference quantity from a producer who had ceased production to a purchaser who had
been supplied by this producer.[83] Such a quantity should have gone to
the national reserve. So the relevant provision of the Regulation, Article
7, covered not only the complete or partial replacement of one purchaser
by another but also a change of purchaser freely made by the producer.
In *Neu*, Luxembourg legislation, adopting Formula B, which provided
that in the event of a change of purchaser during a year, a reference
quantity equal to that allocated to the supplier had to be deducted from
the first purchaser's reference quantity and added to the new purchaser's
quantity, was contrary to Community law.[84] The effect of the legislation
was to disadvantage the producer, and so the Court ruled that it was
contrary to the general principles of Community law, in particular the
freedom to choose with whom to do business which was a specific
expression of the freedom to pursue a trade or profession.[85]

The ruling in *Klensch* was confirmed in *Cornée*, where the Court also
considered the discretion vested in the Member States by Article 3 of
Regulation 857/84, which allowed for the allocation of special reference
quantities for those producers who had adopted a milk production
development plan under Directive 72/159 on farm modernization.[86] It
held that Article 3 precluded national authorities implementing that provision in such a way that all producers covered by it would receive a
single fixed quantity. However, national rules giving a special reference
quantity to producers whose milk deliveries did not exceed a specified
ceiling were permissible. The Court concluded by noting that the principle of legitimate expectations did not prevent a reduction in the
reference quantities from those allocated in the previous year, even for

---

[82] See Case C-290/91 *Peter* [1993] ECR I-2981. See also Case C-285/93
Dominikanerinnen-Kloster Altenhohenau [1995] ECR I-4069.
[83] Cases 201 and 202/85 [1986] ECR 3503. See also Case C-67/89 *Berkenheide* [1990]
ECR I-2615; and with respect to Formula A see Case C-351/92 *Graff* [1994] ECR I-
3361.
[84] Cases C-90/90 & C-91/90 [1991] ECR I-3617.
[85] This decision was confirmed in Case C-307/91 *Hendel* [1993] ECR I-6835.
[86] Joined Cases 196–198/88 [1989] ECR 2309. See also Case C-16/89 *Spronk* [1990]
ECR I-3185 and Case C-63/93 *Duff* [1996] ECR I-569.

those producers who had a milk production development plan approved before the entry into force of the levy system.

In the case of *Wachauf*, a tenant applied for compensation for discontinuing milk production even though he was not engaged in such production.[87] Such compensation would have been granted under Regulation 857/84 if the landlord of the property consented, but in this case the landlord had withdrawn consent. The Court, in response to the doubts of the referring court, held that a holding under the legislation covers all land which is subject to a lease, even if that land had neither dairy cows nor the technical facilities for milk production. This established the principle that the reference quantity is transferred with the land that gives rise to the allocation.[88] Furthermore, it did not matter that the lease did not impose an obligation on the tenant to engage in milk production. To deprive the lessee of his rights without compensation would, in the opinion of the Court, be incompatible with the requirement of the protection of fundamental rights in the Community legal order. Compensation would therefore have to be offered to the departing lessee to reflect the contribution made to building up milk production on the land; however, the reference quantity freed up as a result could not be put at the disposal of the lessor.[89]

In contrast to Wachauf, who had never produced milk, the applicant in *Mulder* had entered into an agreement not to deliver milk for a period of five years which ended on 30 September 1984; such an agreement had been introduced under a previous scheme to control milk production.[90] His application for a reference quantity was rejected by the Dutch authorities on the ground that he had not provided proof of milk production during 1983, the year chosen for applying the system of additional levies, and the applicant did not seem to fall within any of the exceptions allowed by Regulation 857/84. According to the Court, the applicant could be awarded a reference quantity only in so far as the guaranteed quantity for the particular Member State was not exceeded. However, the Court went on to hold Regulation 857/84 to be invalid to the extent that it did not provide for the allocation of a reference quantity to producers like Mulder, as it was a breach of the legitimate

---

[87] Case 5/88 [1989] ECR 2609.

[88] See Case 177/90 *Kühn* above n. 80, Case C-189/92 *Le Nan* [1994] ECR I-26, Case C-463/93 *St Martinus Elten* [1997] ECR I-255 and Case C-15/95 *EARL de Kerlast* [1997] I-1961.

[89] See also Case C-2/92 *Bostock* [1994] ECR I-955, where the Court noted that: '... the protection of the right to property guaranteed by the Community legal order does not require a Member State to introduce a scheme for payment of compensation by a landlord to an outgoing tenant and does not confer a right to such compensation directly on the tenant' (p. 985).

[90] Case 120/86 [1988] ECR 2321.

expectations of producers who had participated in the previous scheme to control production.

As a result of the judgment in *Mulder* and a similar ruling in *Von Deetzen*,[91] Regulation 764/89 amended Regulation 857/84 by adding a new Article 3a, which allowed a special reference quantity to be granted to producers who had not delivered milk during the reference year as a result of undertakings made under previous schemes to control production.[92] This addition to Regulation 857/84 was in turn declared invalid by the Court on the grounds of breach of the principle of protection of legitimate expectations.[93] As a result of these rulings, Regulation 1639/91 introduced a new method of calculating special reference quantities to ensure that producers resuming production would not be subject to restrictions affecting them specifically because of their previous non-marketing premiums, and that they should not be given an advantage over other producers.[94] The validity of this Regulation was upheld by the Court in *Kamp*.[95] In May 1992 the Court in *Mulder II* upheld a claim for compensation from a producer who had not been allocated a reference quantity under the original regulation because he had entered into a non-marketing or conversion undertaking.[96]

Given the large number of producers affected by this ruling, and the situation where individual compensation packages would have to be negotiated, the Council and the Commission issued a communication.[97] This promised legislation to deal with the matter, and this was duly provided by Regulation 2187/93 which offered flat-rate compensation to those producers who had been denied a reference quantity under the original regulation but who had received reference quantities under Regulations 764/89 and 1639/91.[98] The validity of Regulation 2187/93

---

[91] Case 170/86 [1989] ECR 2355.

[92] OJ 1989 L 84/2. As for the effect of these changes, see Case C-98/91 *Herbrink* [1994] ECR I-223.

[93] Case C-189/90 *Spagl* [1990] ECR I-4539, Case C-217/89 *Pastätter* [1990] ECR I-4585 and Case C-314/89 *Rauh* [1991] ECR I-1647.

[94] OJ 1991 L 150/35.

[95] Case C-21/92 [1994] ECR I-1619. However, the anti-accumulation rule which had been a feature of Regulation 764/89 was declared invalid in Case C-264/90 *Wehrs* [1992] ECR I-6285. See also Case C-81/91 *Twijnstra* [1993] ECR I-2455. The rule was abolished by Regulation 2055/93 (OJ 1993 L 187/8). See Case C-127/94 *R v MAFF ex parte Ecroyd* [1996] ECR I-2731 and Case C-165/95 *R v MAFF ex parte Lay, Gage and Gage* [1997] ECR I-5543.

[96] Cases C-104/89 and C-37/90 [1992] ECR I-3061.

[97] Communication 92/C 198/04, OJ 1992 C 198/4.

[98] OJ 1993 L 196/6. For details of the previous compensation package see Regulation 1637/91 (OJ 1991 L 150/30) and Case C-152/95 *Macon* [1997] ECR I-5429. See also Regulation 2055/93 (OJ 1993 L 187/8) introducing rules for calculating special reference quantities where part of a holding is transferred, and Case C-165/95 *R v MAFF ex parte Lay, Gage and Gage* (above n. 95).

has been upheld by the Court of First Instance which has tried to bring this particular saga to a conclusion through, for example, an interpretation of the Regulation providing a definitive period for compensation.[99] However, as a result of the decision of the Court of First Instance in the case of *Quiller and Heusmann*, it has been necessary to offer another scheme of compensation for those producers denied compensation under the previous schemes.[100] Regulation 2330/98 deals with what are referred to as 'SLOM III' producers and follows the model provided by Regulation 2187/93.[101]

The legislative and judicial saga instituted by Regulation 857/84 appropriately illustrates the extent to which the control of production has been particularly problematic for the CAP. The problem lies not only with the Community's attempt to achieve the objectives set by Article 33(1), but also with the implementation of Community measures by Member States.[102]

---

[99] On validity see, for example, Case T-541/93 *Connaughton* [1997] ECR II-549. On interpretation of the Regulation see Case T-544/93 *Saint and Murray* [1997] ECR II-563 and Case T-20/94 *Hartmann* [1997] ECR II-595.

[100] Cases T-159/94 and 202/94 [1997] ECR II-2247. See also Case T-222/97 *Steffens* (unreported, judgment of 25 November 1998).

[101] OJ 1998 L 291/4.

[102] For example, although the additional levy scheme was introduced in 1984, in Italy mechanisms to control production were not introduced until 1989; see Special Report 4/93 of the Court of Auditors on the implementation of the quota system intended to control milk production (OJ 1994 C 12/1). See also Case 394/85 *Commission v Italy* [1987] ECR 2741 and Case C-69/95 *Italy v Commission* [1996] ECR 6233.

CHAPTER FOUR

Common organizations and common financing

4.1 Introduction

According to Article 34(3), the price policy pursued by the Community under the CAP was to be based on common criteria and uniform methods of calculation. Originally expressed in units of account and then in European Currency Units (ECUs), such prices as from 1 January 1999 are expressed in euros. The establishment of a common currency will have a profound effect on the operation of the CAP, as over time it should lead to the elimination of monetary compensatory amounts. These were introduced in the 1970s as a mechanism to reduce the impact of monetary fluctuations on the operation of the CAP and represented a considerable challenge to the nature of the policy. Their operation forms a major part of the discussion in this chapter, which begins with an examination of the Community budget before an analysis of the operation of the European Agricultural Guidance and Guarantee Fund, which includes a brief discussion of the fight against fraud in the Community.

4.2 The Community budget

According to Strasser, there were six categories of expenditure on agriculture from the Community budget: export refunds, public or private storage aid, compensatory aid, guidance premiums, expenditure on obligations under other policies and monetary compensatory amounts.[1] As for income, the import levies and production levies under the common organization of the market in sugar constitute part of the

---

[1] See Strasser, D., *The Finances of Europe* (OOPEC, Luxembourg, 1981), Chapter XI, pp. 172–3.

Community's own resources.[2] Given the original open-ended nature of the principle of common financing, expenditure on agriculture constituted a substantial proportion of the Community's budget. Action to remedy this situation had been advocated for a considerable period of time. For example, at the Hague Summit of December 1969, the Heads of State and of Government of the then six Member States asked:[3]

> ... governments to continue without delay, within the Council, the efforts already made to ensure a better control of the market by a policy of agricultural production, making it possible to limit the burden on budgets.

Despite this encouragement, and numerous proposals for reform of the CAP, agricultural expenditure continued to remain a very significant element of the Community's budget.[4] Eventually, in 1988, the European Council meeting in Brussels set a maximum annual amount of expenditure, a budgetary guideline, for the market and price policy aspect of the CAP for the years 1988–1992. The basis for the guideline was the actual expenditure incurred in 1987, with expenditure not being allowed to rise by more than 74% of the rate of increase of the Community's gross national product (GNP) over this period.[5] The discipline was incorporated by Decision 88/739.[6]

The discipline provided by the Interinstitutional Agreement on Budgetary Discipline and Improvement of the Budgetary Procedure was confirmed and extended at the 1993 Edinburgh Summit until 1999, at which stage the share of the Community budget devoted to the market and price policy was to have decreased to 45% from 50% in 1993.[7] Under the Agreement, which could not be changed without the consent of the parties to it, Community expenditure, by broad category, was to develop in an orderly manner and within the limits of the Community's

---

[2] Revenue from the various levies, such as the milk co-responsibility levy, are not considered part of the Community's own resources. These will be discussed in 4.5.

[3] EC Bull. 1–1970, Ch. 1, paragraph 6 of the Communiqué.

[4] In their 1980 document *Reflections on the CAP* (COM (80) 800), the Commission noted that there were four budgetary difficulties encountered by the CAP. The overall burden which agriculture imposes on public funds is too high in absolute terms; the agricultural share of the budget is too large, retarding the development of other Community policies; some Member States are net contributors while others are net beneficiaries; and agricultural appropriations are spent on ever larger structural surpluses without reducing the income disparities in the agricultural sector. This last criticism was the only one which was accepted by the Commission.

[5] The per annum growth rate from 1988–92 would be 1.9% per annum in real terms over this period in contrast to a figure of 7.5% in the period 1975–88.

[6] OJ 1988 L 185/29. See also the Interinstitutional Agreement on Budgetary Discipline and Improvement of the Budgetary Procedure, OJ 1985 L 185/33.

[7] Interinstitutional Agreement of 29 October 1993 (OJ 1993 C 331/1), enshrined in Decision 94/729, OJ 1994 L 293/14.

own resources. Annual adjustments to the budgetary discipline, to be proposed by the Commission, were to be limited to technical adjustments in line with the movement in GNP and prices. When the Commission presented these adjustments to the Council and the Parliament, it could also present proposals for further adjustments necessitated by changes in the conditions of implementation, or if unforeseen measures had to be initiated. The Commission could also present proposals for the use of the reserves created as a result of the Edinburgh European Council. One of these three monetary reserves was intended to cover the impact of significant and unforeseen developments in the dollar/ecu parity on agricultural budget expenditure. This particular reserve could also have been used to absorb the budgetary costs incurred arising from monetary realignments within the European Monetary System whenever these costs could not be absorbed within the agricultural guideline.

Under the 1993 Interinstitutional Agreement, the Commission was to present proposals by 1 July 1998 for a new medium-term financial perspective. An early indication of the nature of these proposals arose from the Agenda 2000 document.[8] As for the medium-term outlook for agricultural expenditure, the Commission considered that maintaining the current method of calculating the agricultural guideline would not cause any difficulties in meeting anticipated expenditure needs. As a result of the reform process, initiated in 1992 and which would be continued under other proposals made in the Agenda 2000 document,[9] the costs of market intervention measures and export refunds would fall whereas direct compensation for producers would rise, and new measures, such as pre-accession aid for the countries of Central and Eastern Europe, would have to be financed. Only the existing accompanying measures, that is those of a structural nature arising, in part, from the 1992 reforms, would require a proposal for appropriate adjustments to the existing financial regulations. A large margin of error was, however, recommended to cover market uncertainties and further reform of the CAP. That reform, it was recognized, should allow for the phasing out of the agricultural monetary reserve by 2003.

An overall assessment of the functioning of the existing system led the Commission to conclude that it was possible 'to face the challenges posed by the necessary reforms of some of the most important Community policies and those deriving from a first wave of accessions' without the need for an increase in the existing own resources ceiling of

[8] COM (97) 2000. Part 3, The New Financial Framework.
[9] These are discussed further in Chapter 8.

1.27% of Community GNP.[10] This conclusion was predicated on the further reform of the CAP, which, it is admitted, will initially lead to additional expenditure, and the fact that during the period of the new budgetary guideline, transitional arrangements would apply to any new Member State. If reform were not to be as extensive as that proposed by the Commission, the margin for error might be exceeded. Even assuming that it was not, the anticipated development of the guideline showed an increase in expenditure over the period to 48 billion ECU.[11]

Discussion of the Agenda 2000 document ended with Agreement on a New Financial Perspective at the Berlin European Council in March 1999.[12] Even though the reforms agreed were not as extensive as those advocated by the Commission, the new financial perspective envisages that agricultural expenditure (price support, rural development and accompanying measures) will rise from 45,220 million euros in 2000 to 46,030 million euros in 2006. In an attempt to control expenditure on the CAP, the European Council instructed the Commission and the Council to pursue additional savings to ensure that average annual agricultural expenditure, excluding rural development and veterinary measures, did not exceed 40.5 billion euros. So it appears that the anticipated increase in expenditure is not as great as first thought; and to ensure that it does not rise above the guideline adopted by the European Council, the Commission will in 2002 submit a report on the development of agricultural expenditure. Appropriate proposals may at that stage be advanced by the Commission, and the European Council has instructed the Council to take the decisions necessary to maintain the process of reform.

4.3 The European Agricultural Guidance and Guarantee Fund

By virtue of Article 34(4), one or more Agricultural Guidance and Guarantee Funds could be established in order to enable the common organizations of the market to realize their objectives. Regulation 25/62 established a single fund forming part of the Community budget from

---

[10] Above n. 8, Part 3, III, The Financing Arrangements.
[11] *Ibid.*, Table 2. The table confirms that at current prices and under the current policy, expenditure will rise to nearly 55 billion ECU.
[12] *Presidency Conclusions Berlin European Council*, Part I.I (The New Financial Perspective) available on the europa website. See also European Commission Directorate General of Agriculture Newsletter, *Berlin European Council: Agenda 2000, Conclusions of the Presidency* (Brussels, 1999).

which export refunds and intervention purchases would be financed and into which the revenue from import levies would be paid.[13] In 1964, the fund was split into two sections: a Guarantee Section, which would relate to the various aspects of the market and price policy followed by the Community; and a Guidance Section, which would relate primarily to the measures needed to implement the structural policy of the Community.[14] After the end of the transitional period, the existence of the European Agricultural Guidance and Guarantee Fund (EAGGF) as part of the Community budget was confirmed by Regulation 729/70, which also laid down the mechanisms for the management of the fund. As a result of numerous amendments, this Regulation has now been replaced by Regulation 1258/99 with effect from 1 January 2000.[15]

By virtue of Article 1(3) of the Regulation, the Guidance Section is to finance various rural development measures.[16] Articles 1 and 2 of this Regulation confirm that the fund is to finance export refunds and intervention activities, the latter comprising all internal market measures under the various common organizations of the market.[17] Revenue from the operation of the market and price policy is to form part of the system of the Community's own resources.[18] As the administration of the Community's agricultural legislation is the responsibility of the Member States, they become liable for the payment of any amounts due to individuals under the market and price policy.[19] Thus no rights accrue to individuals benefiting from the market and price policy of the Community as a result of the Regulation. Individual rights arise against the Member State and the liability of the Member State, to make payments under a common organization of the market exists even in those cases where the Community refuses to reimburse such payments or where resources are insufficient to meet them.[20] This requires that the

---

[13] JO 1962 991.   [14] Regulation 17/64, JO 1964 586.

[15] JO 1970 L94/13 (Article 1) and OJ 1999 L 160/103.

[16] This can be contrasted with Article 11 of Regulation 17/64 which listed the action taken by the Guidance Section as being related to (a) the adaptation and improvement of conditions of production in agriculture; (b) the adaptation and guidance of agricultural production; (c) the adaptation and improvement of the marketing of agricultural products; (d) the development of outlets for agricultural products.

[17] See Regulation 1883/78 (OJ 1978 L 216/1) for a declaratory list of these activities.

[18] See Decision 70/243 (JO 1970 L 94/19) replaced by Decision 85/257 (OJ 1985 L 128/15).

[19] Case 93/71 *Leonesio* [1972] ECR 287 and Case C-48/91 *Netherlands v Commission* [1993] ECR I-5611.

[20] Case 99/74 *Grand Moulins* [1975] ECR 1531 and Joined Cases 89/86 and 91/86 *Étoile Commerciale and CNTA* [1987] ECR 3005. In the event of disputes between the Commission and the Member States as to who is to bear the costs of a particular item of expenditure, a conciliation body may be established (Decision 94/442, OJ 1994 L 182/45). The conclusions of this body are not, however, binding on the Commission.

Member States (and traders) know exactly the scope of the obligations imposed on them, and it does not allow the Commission to choose to interpret those obligations in a manner inconsistent with their normal meaning.[21] Regulation 3183/87 confirms these obligations imposed on the Member States.[22]

The general obligations arising from this Regulation are confirmatory of the jurisprudence of the Court, where it has repeatedly stated that, in the absence of detailed Community law, Article 10 of the Treaty requires the Member States to take all measures which are necessary to ensure the effective supervision and enforcement of provisions which give rise to budgetary expenditure by the Community.[23] This requires the Member States to ensure:[24]

> ... that infringements of Community law are penalized under conditions, both procedural and substantive, which are analogous to those applicable to infringements of national law of a similar nature and importance and which in any event, make the penalty effective, proportionate and dissuasive.

By virtue of Regulation 3508/92, the Member States are required to set up an integrated administration and control system, applying to the support systems introduced in the arable crops sector under Regulation 1765/92 and various premiums awarded under the common organizations of the market in beef and veal and sheepmeat and goatmeat.[25] The Community would make a contribution to the expenditure on the establishment of this integrated system.

Previously various aid schemes, administered and controlled by the Member States, had operated under separate rules, thus giving rise to the possibility of incorrect application and irregularities. The new integrated system is to include a computerized database, an alphanumeric identification system for agricultural parcels, an alphanumeric identification and registration system for animals and an integrated control system. The last would constitute an important element covering all aid applica-

---

[21] See in particular Case 348/85 *Denmark v Commission* [1987] ECR 5225.
[22] OJ 1987 L 304/1.
[23] See Case 39/72 *Commission v Italy* [1973] ECR 101, Joined Cases 205–215/82 *Deutsche Milchkontor* [1983] ECR 2633 and Case C-348/93 *Commission v Italy* [1995] ECR I-673. See also Joined Cases 212–217/80 *Salumi* [1981] ECR 2735 and Cases C-31/91–C-44/91 *Lageder* [1993] ECR I-1761, where the Court recognized that in the absence of relevant Community provisions, it was for the national legal systems of the Member States to lay down rules and conditions for the collection of Community financial charges and agricultural levies.
[24] Case 68/88 *Commission v Greece* [1989] ECR 2965, p. 2985.
[25] OJ 1992 L 355/1. This regulation will cease to apply at the end of the marketing year 1999/2000; the measures will then be replaced by those in Regulation 1251/99 (OJ 1999 L 160/1).

tions, on which Member States are to carry out, in addition to administrative checks, various on-the-spot checks or checks by remote sensing. Detailed rules for the implementation of the Regulation, in particular the administrative and other checks, were laid down in Regulation 3887/92.[26] The new system was seen as necessary given the 1992 reform of the CAP which had reorientated the focus of the policy away from common prices towards direct income support. It was also seen as necessary to assist in the implementation of Article 8 of Regulation 729/70, which required the Member States to take all the necessary measures to satisfy themselves that transactions financed by EAGGF were actually carried out and executed correctly.

Expenditure will be financed by the fund only if undertaken 'in accordance with the Community rules within the framework of the common organization of the agricultural markets'. It is for the Commission to prove an infringement of the rules governing the common organization of the markets, and once the Commission has satisfied this burden of proof, a Member State can demonstrate that the Commission committed an error as to the financial consequences to be drawn from such an infringement.[27] So, expenditure which can be classified as 'unlawful' – for example, through the misapplication of Community rules – will not be met by the fund. If such expenditure were to be met, the Court has asserted that it would lead to a distortion of competition between the Member States and lead to inequality between producers and/or traders within the Community.[28] As examples of misapplications of Community rules, if a regulation lays down specific measures of supervision, the Member States must apply them, even if they consider that another system would be more efficient. Equally, if there are difficulties in the implementation of a Community measure, that does not justify a Member State in unilaterally absolving itself from observing its obligations.[29]

The only exception emerges from a series of cases brought by The Netherlands, France and Germany, seeking annulment of the

---

[26] OJ 1992 L 391/96.
[27] See for example, Case C-281/89 *Commission v Italy* [1991] ECR I-347 and Case C-55/91 *Italy v Commission* [1993] ECR I-4813. The Court in Case 349/85 *Denmark v Commission* [1988] ECR 169 noted that until accounts have been cleared, the Commission is required by Article 2 of Regulation 729/70 to refuse to charge to the EAGGF refunds which have not been granted in accordance with Community rules. See also Case C-50/94 *Greece v Commission* [1996] ECR I-3331.
[28] Case 347/85 *United Kingdom v Commission* [1988] ECR 1749 and Case C-48/91 *Netherlands v Commission* (above n. 19).
[29] See Case 819/79 *Commission v Germany* [1981] ECR 21, Case C-39/88 *Commission v Ireland* [1990] ECR I-4271 and Case C-54/91 *Germany v Commission* [1993] ECR I-3399.

Commission's decision relating to the discharge of Guarantee Section expenditure for 1971 and 1972.[30] The provision at issue was Article 8(2) of Regulation 729/70, which provided that in the absence of total recovery, the financial consequences of irregularities or negligence were to be borne by the Community, save where the irregularities or negligence were attributable to the Member States. The Court concluded that Article 8 contained 'too many contradictory and ambiguous elements' to provide a clear answer in the case, so it decided to use Articles 2 and 3 of the Regulation. Using these provisions, the liability of the Community was to be limited to 'sums paid in accordance with the rules laid down' by the various common organizations of the market. All other sums would have to be borne by the Member State.[31] The legal basis of the fund's liability was thus clearly established as being limited to those cases where there has been an erroneous application of Community law which is attributable to a Community institution.

A definition of 'irregularity' emerges from Article 1(2) of Regulation 2988/95 on the protection of the Communities' financial interests.[32] This provides that irregularity shall mean:

> ... any infringement of a provision of Community law resulting from an act or omission by an economic operator, which has, or would have, the effect of prejudicing the general budget of the Communities or budgets managed by them, whether by reducing or losing revenue accruing from own resources collected directly on behalf of the Communities, or by an unjustified item of expenditure.

With respect to an unjustified item of expenditure, further detail is added by the Convention on the protection of the Communities' financial interests which deals with fraud affecting those interests.[33] These definitions will assist the Member States in taking those measures which are necessary, in the words of Article 8 of Regulation 729/70 (and

---

[30] Case 11/76 *Netherlands v Commission* [1979] ECR 245, Cases 15 and 16/76 *France v Commission* [1979] ECR 321 and Case 18/76 *Germany v Commission* [1979] ECR 343. See also Case 327/85 *Netherlands v Commission* [1988] ECR 1065, Case C-197/90 *Italy v Commission* [1992] ECR I-1 and Case C-49/94 *Ireland v Commission* [1995] ECR I-2683.

[31] In Case C-28/89 *Germany v Commission* [1991] ECR I-581, the Court noted that 'National authorities cannot justify a failure to rectify irregularities by relying on the length of administrative or judicial proceedings commenced by an economic agent.'

[32] OJ 1995 L 312/1.

[33] OJ 1995 C 316/48. Article 1(1) defines fraud in respect of expenditure as: 'any intentional act or omission relating to (a) the use or presentation of false, incorrect or incomplete statements or documents, which has as its effect the disappropriation or wrongful retention of funds from the general budget ...; (b) non-disclosure of information in violation of a specific obligation, with the same effect; (c) the misapplication of such funds for purposes other than those for which they are originally intended.'

Regulation 1258/99), 'to satisfy themselves that transactions financed by the EAGGF are actually carried out and are executed correctly'.[34]

To help in the realization of the other aspect of Article 8 – that is, to prevent and deal with irregularities and to recover sums lost as a result – a number of legislative initiatives have been taken. For example, Regulation 4045/89 reinforced the scrutiny by Member States of transactions forming part of the Guarantee Section of the EAGGF, in this particular case export refunds.[35] The Regulation provides for the scrutiny of commercial documents of undertakings receiving or making payments relating directly or indirectly to the EAGGF Guarantee Section,[36] the preparation of annual scrutiny programmes and reports by the Member States,[37] and for mutual assistance between the Member States. The effectiveness of the Regulation was assessed in a Special Report by the Court of Auditors which considered that the general lack of effective risk analysis constituted a serious weakness in the scrutiny procedure.[38] In addition to this and a number of other problems with the Regulation, the report pointed to various failures by the Member States in cooperating in the scrutiny of supranational undertakings, where the Court of Auditors considered that a more dynamic approach was needed to promote the full effectiveness of the Regulation. The overall conclusion was one challenging the effectiveness of the Regulation as a means of controlling EAGGF income and expenditure, the effectiveness of the Commission in this area and the extent to which the Member States had fulfilled their obligations under the Regulation.

With respect to the other instrument examined in the Special Report, Regulation 595/91, the Court was more positive but still critical.[39] This Regulation sets up an information system to deal with irregularities and

---

[34] Case 8/88 *Germany v Commission* [1990] ECR I-2321. See also Joined Cases 146/81, 192/81 and 193/81 *BayWa* [1982] ECR 1503 and Case 2–93 *Exportslachterijen van Oordegem* [1994] ECR I-2283. A series of cases decided on 1 October 1998 also confirm this point: Case C-209/96 *United Kingdom v Commission*; Case C-232/96 *France v Commission*; Case C-233/96 *Denmark v Commission* and Case C-238/96 *Ireland v Commission*.

[35] OJ 1989 L 388/18, which replaced Directive 77/435 (OJ 1977 L 172/17). The Regulation has since been amended – see for example, Regulation 3094/94 (OJ 1994 L 328/1) and Regulation 3235/94 (OJ 1994 l 338/16). See also the implementing regulation, Regulation 1863/90 (OJ 1990 L 170/23) which has also been amended (Regulation 2992/95 (OJ 1995 L 312/11) and Regulation 2278/96 (OJ 1996 L 308/30)).

[36] Article 2(2) set various figures for the entities; for those receiving more than 200,000 ECU scrutiny was to occur once every two years.

[37] Article 3. The annual programmes were to be scrutinized by the Commission to ensure that the terms of the Regulation were being complied with.

[38] Special Report 7/93 OJ 1993 C 53/1. See also Special Reports 2/90 (OJ 1990 C 133/1) and 2/92 (OJ 1993 C 101/1) on export refunds.

[39] *Ibid.*, Chapter 4 of the Report.

the recovery of sums wrongly paid under the CAP.[40] Under Article 2 of the Regulation, the Member States are to communicate to the Commission the provisions laid down in national law for the application of Article 8 of Regulation 729/70 (and Regulation 1258/99) and the list of authorities and bodies responsible for the application of these measures. Every quarter, each Member State is to communicate to the Commission detailed information on irregularities which have been the subject of primary administrative or judicial findings of fact. Such information, plus any suspicions of irregularities, must also be reported to other Member States. Subsequent action taken by the Member States must also be notified to the Commission. Investigations of the irregularity are usually carried out by the Member State, but may also be conducted by the Commission in association with the Member State(s). Various failings in the notification system were highlighted in the Special Report of the Court of Auditors.[41] The Report also noted that in the period 1972–91, 5,775 cases of fraud and irregularity had been reported by the Member States, giving a total, which the Report recognized as an underestimate, of some 725.5 million ECU.[42] Of this amount only 10.7% had been recovered; and of the 109 cases (1.1%) that were considered unrecoverable, the Community had accepted responsibility for 67 cases. It was recommended that greater efforts should be made to recover all sums paid as a result of irregularities or fraud.

The Report commented unfavourably on the fact that at the time no Community definition of 'irregularity' or 'fraud' existed.[43] This problem has, as noted above, now been remedied. In addition, the fight against fraud has gained added impetus as in 1993 the anti-fraud unit, known as Unité de Coordination de la Lutte Anti-Fraude (UCLAF), recommended greater coordination of existing anti-fraud activities within the Commission, such as those of the Agriculture Directorate and the Customs Directorate.[44] Further legislative support has been offered to protect the Communities' financial interest against fraud and other irregularities through, for example, Regulation 2185/96 concerning on-

---

[40] OJ 1991 L 67/11. This replaced the original Regulation, Regulation 283/72 (OJ 1972 L 36/1). See also Regulations 4253/88 (OJ 1988 L 374/1) and 1681/94 (OJ 1994 L 178/) which establish similar mechanisms for Structural Funds, and Regulation 2988/95 (OJ 1995 L 312/1) which deals with penalties. As for the relationship with Regulation 729/70, see Case C-476/93P *Nutral* [1995] ECR I-4125. As for the situation before the Regulation, see for example Case C-41/94 *Germany v Commission* [1996] ECR I-4733.

[41] Above n. 38, paras 4.13–4.20.   [42] *Ibid.*, paras 4.26–4.27.   [43] *Ibid.*, para. 4.9.

[44] See COM (93) 141. The unit was created by the Commission in 1988 in response to demands by the Council, Parliament and Court of Auditors and is located within the Secretariat General of the Commission. See Court of Auditors Special Report 8/98 concerning the Commission departments responsible for fighting fraud, notably UCLAF (OJ 1998 C 230).

the-spot checks and inspections,[45] and Regulation 515/97 establishing cooperation between the administrative authorities in the Member States and the Commission to ensure the correct application of agricultural law.[46] Details of irregularities so detected are kept on a database, which complements the advanced warning system for agricultural transactions introduced by Regulation 1469/95.[47]

As for the impact of these measures, the 1997 report on the *Fight Against Fraud* reveals that that year witnessed a decline in both detected fraud and irregularities to 317 million ECU, although there was a slight increase in the number of cases detected.[48] Progress in the recovery of sums paid remains disappointing with over 75% of sums still to be recovered. As a result of Regulation 1663/95, four years seems to be considered the period within which there is a realistic chance that sums paid can be recovered.[49] The analysis offered in the Annex to the Report notes that irregularities formally notified to the Commission under Regulation 595/91 for the four-year period 1994–97 totalled 7,414 cases involving 1018 million ECU.[50] As for the recovery situation regarding irregularities communicated before 1994, 22% of cases involving nearly 7 million ECU involved sums which still had to be recovered.[51] As for the global impact of these irregularities and those detected by the Commission, the Report concludes by noting that they amounted to 0.79% of agricultural expenditure concerning EAGGF Guarantee measures in 1997 as against 0.85% in 1996.[52]

One final point to be made in this area relates to the Amsterdam Treaty, which provides for a continuation of the fight against fraud affecting the financial interests of the Community. According to Article 280 of the Treaty, 'Member States shall take the same measures to counter fraud affecting the financial interest of the Community as they take to counter fraud affecting their own financial interests.' In addition there will be coordinated action to afford effective and equivalent protection in the Member States of the Community's financial interests, and close and regular cooperation between the Commission and the relevant

---

[45] OJ 1996 L 292/2. This instrument was used to detect the illegal trade in UK beef.

[46] OJ 1997 L 82/1. The Regulation also promotes mutual assistance between the administrative authorities of the Member States. Under the previous Regulation, Regulation 386/90 (OJ 1990 L 42/6), customs authorities held details of irregularities arising from these physical controls. The new system also allows checks to be carried out by UCLAF officials.

[47] OJ 1995 L 145/1. See also Regulation 745/96 (OJ 1996 L 102/15). The system is designed to identify traders considered to be 'unreliable'!

[48] COM (98) 276. *Fight Against Fraud*, Annual Report 1997, pp. 6 and 11.

[49] OJ 1995 L 158/6. This argument rests on the fact that the Regulation sets a four-year period for the clearance of the accounts of the EAGGF Guarantee Section.

[50] Above n. 48, Graph 2.   [51] *Ibid.*, Table 4.   [52] *Ibid.*, Table 5.

national authorities. Whether or not this, and the proposed creation of an independent fraud unit, will lead to greater success in the fight against fraud remains an open question.

4.4 Monetary compensatory amounts

The system of price support established through the common organizations of the market required the setting of a Community-wide price level and, in the absence of a common currency, a common denominator for the currencies involved. This common denominator was the agricultural unit of account, as defined by Regulation 129/62, Article 1 of which adopted the 1934 value of gold in terms of the United States dollar as the value of the unit of account.[53] The adoption of this gold/dollar standard and the principle of fixed exchange rates through the Bretton Woods Agreement was to act as the foundation stone for the establishment of the principle of common financing.[54] Under Article 2(1) of the Regulation, each amount the value of which had been fixed in units of account would be expressed in national currencies according to the exchange rate communicated to and recognized by the International Monetary Fund (IMF).

Regulation 129/62 demonstrated the confidence of the Member States in the Bretton Woods system of fixed exchange rates by making it impossible for any alteration of an exchange rate which exceeded the limits set down by the IMF. This situation was remedied by Regulation 653/68, which set down the conditions for alteration to the value of the agricultural unit of account.[55] The principle of automatic adjustment in the event of one or more Member States changing their rate of exchange was applied only once in the manner envisaged by the amended Regulation 129. This was to occur in the cases of the French franc devaluation and German mark revaluation of 1969. The application of these rules to these events entailed an increase and a decrease, respectively, in agricultural prices. Unwilling to countenance such a drastic change in the common prices, France was allowed a transitional period during which there would be a progressive realignment with the common prices. Germany was allowed a similar period. To avoid problems arising with agricultural trade, the Council provided for a system of import refunds and export levies in the case of France, and import levies and

---

[53] JO 1962 2553.
[54] See Braakman, G., 'Monetary Evolutions and the Common Agricultural Policy' (1978) 15 CMLRev 157, p. 162.
[55] JO 1968 L 123/4.

export refunds for Germany.[56] To all intents, this marked the end of the phenomenon of common prices.

In May 1971, the German and Dutch governments decided to float their respective currencies, a decision which led to the introduction of Regulation 974/71 and monetary compensatory amounts.[57] The floating of the US dollar later that year, and the decision of Belgium, Luxembourg and Italy to float their currencies, plus that of France to adopt a system of multiple exchange rates, led to the extension of the monetary compensatory amounts system to all the Member States.[58] The incorporation of the system of monetary compensatory amounts into the CAP occurred through Regulation 2746/72, which rendered their application obligatory in cases where deviations from the par value of a currency of a Member State, as communicated to and recognized by the IMF, occurred.[59] The Regulation also confirmed that expenditure and revenue arising from monetary compensatory amounts should be met by, and accrue to, the Community budget. The legal basis of the measure was changed from Article 99 to Articles 26, 37 and 308.

Following the enlargement of the Community in 1973, Regulation 222/73 created representative rates for the currencies of the United Kingdom and Ireland, in an effort to ensure that the applicable conversion rate reflected economic reality rather than the official parity for the currency involved.[60] The concept of green currency or rates thus became a feature of the system. Subsequently, Regulation 509/73 extended the monetary compensatory amounts system to currencies which had depreciated as well as to those which had appreciated.[61] The decision of the United States government to float the dollar in April 1973 led to the end of its use as a reference point for the agricultural unit of account. In its place was substituted an agreement by some of the Member States, known as the 'snake', by which they agreed to limit their currency fluctuations within fixed margins of 2.25%.[62] For those Member States participating in the 'snake', monetary compensatory amounts were granted on the difference between the representative rate of the currency in question and the conversion rate deriving from the central rate of that

---

[56] See Regulation 1586/69, JO 1969 L 202/1 (France); Decision 69/336 (JO 1969 L 250/69) and Decision 69/348 (OJ 1969 L 253/23). The difference in the nature of the measures was a result of the fact that the French measures were based on Article 99, whereas the German measures were based on Article 226 of the original Treaty. When the latter measures expired, they were continued through Regulation 2464/70 (OJ 1970 L 312/4) which was based on Article 99.

[57] JO 1971 L 106/1. This measure was based on Article 99, not Article 37.

[58] Regulations 2887/71 and 2888/71, OJ 1971 L 288/57.

[59] JO 1972 L 291/148.   [60] OJ 1973 L 27/4.   [61] OJ 1973 L 50/1.

[62] Regulation 112/73, OJ 1973 L 114/4.

currency which was held to reflect the true value of the currency. Given the requirement of the 'snake', the monetary compensatory amounts had a fixed character and were granted only when their official or green rates were changed. For those Member States not participating in this exchange rate arrangement – that is, Ireland, Italy, the United Kingdom, and later, France – monetary compensatory amounts were in principle the difference between the representative rate for their currency measured against the central rate for the 'snake' currencies and the spot market rate for the currency as against each currency in the 'snake'. As these rates changed constantly, monetary compensatory amounts were fixed on a weekly basis.

In 1975 green currencies were introduced for all Member States as a result of Regulation 475/75.[63] When the unit of account was replaced by the European Currency Unit (ECU) in 1979, no substantive changes were made to the monetary compensatory amounts system as the ECU continued to be converted, like the unit of account had been, at the agricultural conversion rate.[64] Monetary compensatory amounts were thus calculated on the basis of the difference between the central rate of the currency expressed in ECU and the green rate. To avoid the situation where the difference in the measurement mechanism for the unit of account and the ECU created positive monetary compensatory amounts, common prices and amounts were multiplied by a coefficient. The system as a whole was consolidated in Regulation 1676/85, which established the general rules on the value of the unit of account and conversion rates.[65]

As part of the gradual process of dismantling the system, Regulation 1677/85 introduced the green ECU, which was calculated by taking the strongest currency within the European Monetary System and multiplying it by a corrective factor.[66] The purpose of this switchover mechanism was to avoid the creation of positive monetary compensatory amounts, as the elimination of these amounts would lead to the reduction of common prices as expressed in national currencies. The result was that as all other green rates were below this green ECU, negative monetary compensatory amounts were created which were easier to eliminate.[67] Regulation 1889/87 established a gradual programme for the elimination of monetary compensatory amounts through an increase in the corrective factor. In the event of exchange rate modification there was to

---

[63] OJ 1975 L 52/28. [64] Regulation 652/79 OJ 1979 L 84/1.

[65] OJ 1985 L 164/1. See also Regulation 1678/85, OJ 1985 L 164/11.

[66] OJ 1985 L 164/6. See also Regulation 855/84, OJ 1984 L 90/1.

[67] See Strauss, R., 'The Economic Effects of Monetary Compensatory Amounts' (1983) JCMS 261.

be an automatic realignment of currencies modified as against the ECU currency against which the revaluation was the highest. The Regulation also made provision for the reduction of common prices as the elimination of negative monetary compensatory amounts increases prices in national currency.

Given the complexity of the monetary compensatory amounts system, it is not surprising that it has been the subject of extensive jurisprudence by the Court.[68] For example, in an early case disputing the validity of Regulation 974/71, the Court recognized that monetary compensatory amounts represented a breach of the principle of market unity:[69]

> Although the compensatory amounts do constitute a partitioning of the market, here, they have a corrective influence on the variations in fluctuating exchange rates which in a system of market organizations for agricultural products based on uniform prices, might cause disturbance in trade in those products.

However, the Court recognized that such unity would result not only from the operation of the CAP, but also from the coordination of the economic and monetary policies of the Member States.[70] Given the lack of such coordination, monetary compensatory amounts were considered necessary to preserve some semblance of market unity. As the Court noted:[71]

> Diversion of trade caused solely by the monetary situation can be considered more damaging to the common interest bearing in mind the aims of the Common Agricultural Policy, than the disadvantages of the measures in dispute.

The Court in a subsequent case would suggest that the failure to coordinate the economic and monetary policies of the Member States was contrary to Article 105 of the Treaty.[72]

Having accepted the need for such measures, the Court turned its

---

[68] See Usher, J., 'Agricultural Markets: Their Price Systems and Financial Mechanisms' (1979) 4 ELRev 147 and Gilsdorf, P., 'The System of Monetary Compensatory Amounts from a Legal Standpoint' (1980) 5 ELRev 341 and 433.

[69] Case 9/73 *Schlüter* [1973] ECR 1135, p. 1158. See also Case 10/73 *Rewe* [1973] ECR 1175 and the 1980 Resolution of the European Parliament on Monetary Compensatory Amounts, OJ 1980 C 97/33.

[70] In Case 5/73 *Balkan* [1973] ECR 1091 the Court noted that: 'These measures, intended to compensate temporarily for the harmful effects of national monetary measures, so that the process of economic integration may meanwhile continue its progress, are of an essentially transitory nature ...' (p. 1108).

[71] Above n. 69, p. 1159. See also Case 43/72 *Merkur* [1973] ECR 1055.

[72] Cases 80 & 81/77 *Ramel* [1978] ECR 927.

mind to operation of the monetary compensatory amounts system, stating that:[73]

> ... the introduction of monetary compensatory amounts is intended to correct the effects of unstable variations in the rates of exchange which, within a system of organization of the markets in agricultural products based on common prices, are capable of causing disturbances in trade and in particular of jeopardizing the system of intervention laid down in respect of such products.

The system was designed to protect the common price system rather than national markets[74] or the individual interests of traders. In this latter area, a contrast can be drawn between the case of *CNTA*, where the Community was held liable for the abolition of monetary compensatory amounts even though transitional measures had been adopted,[75] and subsequent cases where liability has not been found. For example, in *Merkur* the Court held that the Community could be held liable for damage to the legitimate expectations of traders only if it were to abolish or modify the monetary compensatory system applicable immediately without adopting transitional measures and a prudent trader could not reasonably foresee such abolition or modification.[76]

The Court has also confirmed that the system was not designed to offer protection against imports from third countries.[77] Indeed the Court stated in *Providence Agricole* that the system of monetary compensatory amounts differed fundamentally from the system of levies and refunds applicable to trade in agricultural products with third countries.[78] To remedy the situation where an importer could be subject to a form of double taxation (that is an import levy and a monetary compensatory amount), the Commission introduced a regulation which provided for the calculation of monetary compensatory amounts through the use of a corrective coefficient.[79] This approach to the problem was upheld by the Court in *Kühlhaus Zentrum*, where the applicant claimed that the mon-

---

[73] Case 4/79 *Providence Agricole* [1980] ECR 2823, p. 2845. See also Case 67–85/75 *Lesieur Cotelle* [1976] ECR 391, p. 408, Case 152/80 *Debayser* [1981] ECR 1291 and Case C-153/95 *André* [1997] ECR I-311.

[74] See Case 46/84 *Nordgetreide* [1985] ECR 3127.

[75] Case 74/74 [1975] ECR 533.

[76] Case 97/76 [1977] ECR 1063. See also Case 146/77 *British Beef* [1978] ECR 1347.

[77] See Case 236/84 *Malt* [1986] ECR 1923. This case also contains an excellent summary of the Court's jurisprudence on the legality of monetary compensatory amounts under Community law.

[78] Above n. 73, pp. 2845–46. However, accession compensatory amounts, which fulfil a different function from monetary compensatory amounts, are equivalent to import levies and export refunds, see Case 6/78 *Union Française de Céréals* [1978] ECR 1675.

[79] Regulation 1463/75 (OJ 1973 L 146/1). See also consolidating Regulation 1380/75 (OJ 1975 L 139/37) and Regulation 3153/85 (OJ 1985 L 310/4).

etary compensatory amount should have been reduced by a corrective coefficient.[80] The problem in the case related to the fact that the imports in question, frozen beef from Argentina, were granted an exemption from import levies through a GATT arrangement. In the next case, *Wagner*, which concerned an export refund granted for exports from Germany to Bulgaria, the application of the corrective coefficient was declared invalid.[81] The reason for this was that the system of invitation to tenders used national currencies, so by applying the corrective coefficient which was applicable to units of account, and which reduced the size of the export refund, the Commission had acted contrary to the Regulation.[82] In both cases the Court stressed the neutrality of the system of monetary compensatory amounts.

One further aspect of the neutrality of the monetary compensatory amounts system was discussed in *Milac*, in which the Court assessed the validity of a Commission regulation imposing monetary compensatory amounts on powdered whey.[83] Under Article 1(2)(b) of Regulation 974/71, the charging or granting of monetary compensatory amounts on products was authorized if two conditions were met: if the price of the product depended on the price of products covered by intervention arrangements under the common organization of agricultural markets; and if the product in question was governed by a common organization of the market. Powdered whey did not fulfil the first of these conditions, so monetary compensatory amounts could not be applied to it as there was no correlation between its price and the price of the relevant intervention product, skimmed milk powder. The problem of derived products would arise again in *Providence Agricole*, where it was alleged that the monetary compensatory amount on the derived product was, contrary to the Regulation, greater than that on the original product. After emphasizing the neutrality of monetary compensatory amounts, the Court continued:[84]

> If the result of the method of calculation employed is persistently to apply to processed products monetary compensatory amounts the burden or, as the case may be, the benefit of which continually exceeds the amount necessary to take account of the incidence of the monetary compensatory amount applicable to the basic product, the objective of the provisions

---

[80] Case 79/77 [1978] ECR 611.   [81] Case 108/77 [1978] ECR 1187.

[82] Shortly afterwards, and to avoid a repeat of the situation, the Commission enacted Regulation 1392/78 (OJ 1978 L 167/53) allowing for the corrective coefficient to be applied to refunds and levies set in national currencies. See also Case 162/78 *Wagner* [1979] ECR 3467.

[83] Case 131/77 [1978] ECR 1041.   [84] Above n. 73, p. 2848.

establishing these amounts may no longer be deemed to neutralize the effects of the currency fluctuations between the Member States.

As the Commission had exceeded the limits of its discretion the measure was declared invalid.[85] Given the nature of the complex monetary difficulties faced by the Community during the monetary compensatory amount saga, it was rare for the Court to overrule the discretionary power of the institutions.[86]

As for other aspects of the agri-monetary situation, such as green rates, the Court has upheld their legality. In *Stölting* the applicant claimed that the conversion of the milk co-responsibility levy, which had been established in units of account, not national currencies, led to discrimination given the differences in green rates between the Member States.[87] After pointing to the reasons for the adoption of the systems and its advantages and disadvantages, which included the impression of discrimination, the Court concluded:[88] 'Although it is not without serious drawbacks, the adoption of the system of so-called green exchange rates is therefore justified by the prohibition on discrimination and the requirements of the Common Agricultural Policy.' A similar conclusion was reached in *Pool* with respect to the validity of the green pound, where the applicant alleged discrimination as a result of the maintenance of inadequate green rates.[89]

Commentators on the CAP have been divided on the effect of the monetary compensatory amounts system on the CAP. For some the system allowed 'Member States considerable freedom in determining the level of their domestic farm-product prices and in general ... intercountry transfers which are politically acceptable and economically reasonable'.[90] Yet other commentators have stated:[91]

> Ever since their introduction, monetary compensatory amounts have represented the non-attainment of the objectives set by the Community of gradual harmonization in economic and monetary policies, in that they

---

[85] See also Case 109/79 *Maïseries de Beauce* [1980] ECR 2883, Case 145/79 *Roquette* [1980] ECR 2917 and Case 33/84 *Fragd* [1985] ECR 1605, where the applicants were also successful. Compare with Case 39/84 *Maizena* [1985] ECR 2115 and Case 46/84 *Nordgetreide* (above n. 74), where the applicants were unsuccessful.

[86] See for examples, Case 154/73 *Becher* [1974] ECR 19 and Case 29/77 *Roquette* [1977] ECR 1835.

[87] Case 138/78 [1979] ECR 713.   [88] *Ibid.*, p. 723.

[89] Case 49/79 [1980] ECR 569. See Grant, W., 'The Politics of the Green Pound 1974–79' (1981) 19 JCMS 313.

[90] Heidhues, T. et al., *Common Prices and Europe's Farm Policy* (TPRC, London, 1978), p. 33.

[91] Buckwell A. et al., *The Costs of the Common Agricultural Policy* (Croom Helm, London, 1982), p. 91.

have enabled countries to enjoy somewhat different price levels for agricultural products despite the declaration of 'common' prices in Brussels each year.

As such they represented a partial 'renationalization' of the common price element of the CAP, as even if the declaration of common prices involved a price freeze or a reduction in prices, prices received by agricultural producers could still be increased as a result of changes to the green rates. The differentiation in green rates for various products further increased the variations in common prices throughout the Community. Such a situation was clearly unacceptable from the point of view of a policy of common prices, a point recognized by the Court of Auditors in their 1989 Special Report on the Agri-monetary System, which also noted the objective of the Council and Commission to abolish the system in the context of meeting the aim of creating a single market within the Community.[92]

With the establishment of the single market, and thus the need to eliminate controls on the free movement of goods, Regulations 1676/85 and 1677/85 were repealed but the agri-monetary system continued. Regulation 3813/92 provided for the immediate adjustment of agricultural conversion rates in the event of a currency realignment.[93] Under this Regulation, agricultural conversion rates could be adjusted in one of three situations: on the adoption of protective measures covering the application of CAP legislation; on the adoption of specific measures to prevent the risk of market distortions occurring as a result of monetary problems; and where monetary gaps exceeded the established thresholds at the end of a reference period. All changes in the agricultural conversion rates would involve reductions in monetary gaps. In the event of revaluations or devaluations, the new conversion rate would be calculated on the basis of the new representative market rate and the desired monetary gap, the latter being defined as half the gap actually recorded. Agricultural conversion rates would also be adjusted when the difference between that rate and the representative market rate exceeded a certain threshold.

This agri-monetary system also provided for compensation for loss of income through temporary and digressive aid, partly financed by the

---

[92] OJ 1989 C 128/1, see Chapter 3, 'The Impact of Green Rates on the System of Common Prices'.

[93] OJ 1992 L 387/1 as amended by Regulation 150/95 (OJ 1995 L 22/1). See also Regulation 1068/93 (OJ 1993 L 108/106) on detailed rules for determining and applying the agricultural conversion rate, and Case C-244/95 *Moskof* [1997] ECR I-6441 for a discussion of the Regulation and its implementation.

Community, in the event of appreciable currency revaluations.[94] Such revaluations occur when the thresholds set for the adjustment of the difference between the agricultural conversion rate and the representative market rate exceed the threshold for a second reference period. They were deemed 'appreciable' after an assessment of the impact of changes of the agricultural conversion rates over a period of three years. Compensation was payable in a number of circumstances – for example, if there was a loss of income for farmers over the previous year despite the measures taken by the Council to realign the agricultural conversion rate with the representative market rate.

Two other features of this agri-monetary system need to be noted. Firstly, as a result of increased budgetary pressure and the impact which it had on increasing agricultural production, the switchover mechanism, introduced in 1984 and which created the green ECU, was abolished on 31 January 1995.[95] As in the changeover from the unit of account to the ECU in 1979, to ensure that the effect of the abolition of the green ECU was neutral in terms of national currencies, common prices and amounts were multiplied by a coefficient. Secondly, as a result of further changes introduced in 1995, the agricultural conversion rate for certain currencies for the purposes of certain forms of aid would remain unchanged until 1 January 1999.[96]

As for the future of the agri-monetary system, this date was significant. The agri-monetary system was introduced because the system of price support and other measures established through the common organizations of the market, setting Community-wide price and aid levels, required a common denominator for the currencies involved. As from 1 January 1999, there is a common denominator, the euro,[97] so there is no longer any need to convert common prices and amounts of aid payments. Thus the distortions which gave rise to the agri-monetary system in the 1970s will cease. However, for at least the first period of the euro, the common currency will apply to only 11 of the existing 15 Member States, so it will still be necessary to continue the system of converting

[94] See Regulation 724/97 (OJ 1997 L 108/9) as amended by Regulation 942/98 (OJ 1998 L 132/1). See also Regulation 805/97 (OJ 1997 L 115/13).

[95] Regulation 150/95, above n. 93. The switchover mechanism was severely criticized in the Special Report of the Court of Auditors (above n. 92) as undermining the Community's efforts to impose stricter budgetary discipline on agricultural expenditure (see Chapter 4 of the Report).

[96] Regulation 1527/95 (OJ 1995 L 148/1) and Regulation 2990/95 (OJ 1995 L 268/3). The affected currencies were those of Austria, Belgium, Denmark, Germany, Luxembourg, The Netherlands and Sweden. The affected programmes were aid per hectare, aid per livestock unit and aid under certain structural and environmental schemes.

[97] Regulation 974/98, OJ 1998 L 139/1.

common prices and amounts of aid payments from euros into national currencies. Pending the completion of the general transitional stage on 1 January 2002, transitional measures will have to be applied under the CAP, and arrangements are also needed to establish the agri-monetary arrangements for the euro. These measures were adopted by Regulations 2799/98 and 2800/98.[98]

Under Regulation 2799/98 establishing the agri-monetary arrangement for the euro, for the first time since 1969 there will be no specific agricultural conversion rate. The rate to be applied for Member States participating in the euro will be the fixed and irrevocable parity established on 1 January 1999. For those Member States not participating in the euro it will be the currency market exchange rate between the euro and the national currency at the time of the operative event. The concept of 'operative event' relates to the event whereby the economic aim of a particular operation is attained; for example, in the case of export refunds, at the time of acceptance of the customs declaration. The concept of appreciable revaluation is also retained but is re-defined to reflect the abolition of the agricultural conversion rate, and will now cover a situation where the annual average exchange rate is below a threshold defined as the lowest average annual exchange rate of the preceding three years and the exchange rate on 1 January 1999. Aid, partly financed by the Community, will still be granted in the event of an appreciable valuation.[99] In the case of compensatory aid arising from an appreciable revaluation, such aid will not apply after 31 December 2001. A similar date is set under Regulation 2800/98 for digressive compensatory aid, which may also be granted where an appreciable revaluation occurs as a result of the disappearance of the agricultural conversion rate for all Member States.

Only when all Member States are members of the common currency, and the Community truly has a common currency, will the agri-monetary system cease to be an integral part of the CAP. According to the Court of Auditors, three factors will determine whether or not the abolition of the system will be acceptable to the Member States:[100]

(a) progress towards economic and monetary convergence would reduce the frequency and intensity of currency movements: if movements are few and relatively small, Member States may be able to absorb their impact more easily;

---

[98] OJ 1998 L 349/1 and 8. See also implementing Regulations 2808/98, 2810/98 and 2813/98 (OJ 1998 L 349/36, 44 and 48)
[99] In essence this continues the system established by Regulation 724/97, above n. 94.
[100] Above n. 92, point 7.17.

(b) agreement on a genuine common price level for Community agriculture that reconciles the requirements of efficient agricultural markets and of producer incomes;

(c) a reduction in the role of agricultural support prices in determining agricultural market prices. If this link is weakened, as it has been to some extent in several markets under the pressure of budgetary discipline, then the adjustment of agricultural prices in the market following a currency realignment will be more gradual.

The future of the agri-monetary system depends therefore not only on the success of economic and monetary union but also on the continuing reform of the CAP.

4.5 Producer levies

Under the original decision on the system of the Communities' own resources, a distinction was made between 'contributions and other duties provided for within the framework of a common organization of the markets in sugar' and 'revenue accruing from other charges introduced within the framework of a common policy'. Whereas the levy imposed in the common organization of the sugar market constituted part of the Communities' own resources, other levies would constitute own resources only in so far as the procedures provided for in Article 269 of the Treaty had been complied with. In this respect, producer levies, introduced as part of the efforts to stem the tide of increasing structural surpluses and budgetary expenditure, which have been adopted using the procedure in Article 37, have been challenged before the Court.

The first such levy was the co-responsibility levy imposed by virtue of Regulation 1079/77 as a measure to reduce the costs of milk support under the common organization of the market in milk.[101] By virtue of Article 5 of the Regulation, the levy was to be considered as forming part of a number of measures to stabilize agricultural markets and was to be allocated to promote this stability. Article 5 made it clear that the revenue emerging from the levy was not to be considered as a source of general revenue constituting a part of the Communities' own resources.[102] The validity of the measure was upheld by the Court in

---

[101] OJ 1977 L 131/6.

[102] See also the Commission's response to a question from the European Parliament on the nature of co-responsibility levy, where they characterized it as 'a financial contribution by producers to help reduce the cost to the Community of disposing of surpluses' (OJ 1981 C 67/11).

Stölting, where it commented: 'As it is directed towards restraining production in the face of the surpluses observed, the co-responsibility levy contributed to the attainment of the objective of stabilizing markets.'[103] The validity of the co-responsibility levy was also upheld in the case of *Bozzetti,* where the Court confirmed that it served an essentially economic purpose similar to that performed by other types of intervention within the common organization of the milk market.[104]

The common organization of the market in sugar, which has always had production constraints, has also introduced various levies. The levy on the production of isoglucose was upheld by the Court in two separate cases which confirmed that Article 37 was the proper legal basis for the adoption of these measures.[105] In response to the argument that the legal basis for the levy should have been Article 269 rather than Article 37 because the levy did not come within the decision on the Communities' own resources, the Court noted that the purpose of that decision was:[106]

> ... to define own resources allocated to the Community budget and not to stipulate the Community institutions which are competent to impose duties, taxes, charges, levies or other forms of revenue. As a measure adopted under budgetary law, that decision does not prevent the Council from creating a levy such as the one imposed on the production of isoglucose where the power of the Council has its basis, as has been said, in the provisions of the Treaty relating to the Common Agricultural Policy.

The Court also noted that it was not conceivable that the scope of that decision could be limited to those levies which existed at that time, as this would not allow for the need to adapt the common organization of the market in sugar to reflect developments in production and marketing.

A further opportunity for the Court to rule on the levy system in the common organization of the market would arise as a result of the introduction in 1986 of an elimination levy, set at 2%, imposed on all sugar producers to ensure that the cost of disposing of production surplus to internal consumption requirements was met by producers.[107] At the

---

[103] Case 138/78 [1979] ECR 713, p. 722.
[104] Case 179/84 [1985] ECR 2301.
[105] Case 108/81 *Amylum* [1982] ECR 3107 and Case 110/81 *Roquette Frères* [1982] ECR 3159.
[106] *Ibid.,* paras 32 and 38 respectively of the judgments.
[107] Regulation 934/86, OJ 1986 L 87/1. See also Regulation 1107/88, OJ 1988 L 110/20. As for when liability to pay the elimination levy arises, see Case C-172/95 *Société Sucrière Agricole de Maizy* [1996] ECR I-5581. The case also discusses when liability to pay the storage, production and special elimination levies arises. See also Case C-19/94 *SAFBA* [1995] ECR I-1051.

same time a special elimination levy was introduced to help in the elimination of the surpluses which had arisen.[108] The validity of this special elimination levy was challenged in *Suderdithmarschen* where it was alleged, *inter alia*, that the levy breached the principle of non-retroactivity.[109] The Court dismissed this argument, pointing to previous jurisprudence which had upheld the validity of retroactive legislation as an exceptional measure if demanded by the situation and if the legitimate expectations of those concerned have been duly respected.[110] It also dismissed the argument on the proper legal basis of the measure for the same reasons as it had identified in *Amylum* and *Roquette Frères*.

Confirmation that Article 269 was not the appropriate legal basis for measures introducing levies merely because they entailed the collection of revenue was also given by the Court in *Schräder*, in which a challenge was made to the co-responsibility levy in the cereals sector.[111] The Court concluded:[112]

> The fact that the co-responsibility levy has a financial aspect, inasmuch as it contributes to limiting the costs of operating the market mechanisms in the cereals sector, is not a reason to base the regulation at issue also on Article 201 of the Treaty [now Article 269]. As the Council and the Commission rightly point out, Article 201 concerns only revenue which is intended to finance the Community's general budget, to the exclusion of agricultural charges which apply in a specific agricultural sector and are allocated to the financing of costs in that sector alone.

Reflecting the political responsibilities conferred on the Community institutions by Articles 34 and 37, under which these institutions enjoy a wide discretion, the Court has generally endorsed their use of levies as a mechanism for controlling production.[113]

---

[108] Regulation 1914/87, OJ 1987 L 183/5. See also Regulation 1108/88, OJ 1988 L 110/25.

[109] Cases 143/88 and C-92/89 [1991] ECR 415.

[110] See for example, Case 98/78 *Racke* [1979] ECR 69 and Case 99/78 *Decker* [1979] ECR 101.

[111] Case 265/87 [1989] ECR 2237. The levy had been introduced by Regulation 1579/86 (OJ 1986 L 139/29).

[112] *Ibid.*, pp. 2266–67.

[113] With respect to the validity of the cereals co-responsibility levy, see also Case C-8/89 *Zardi* [1990] ECR I-2515, Case 203/89 *Van Landschoot* [1990] ECR I-3525 and Case C-411/92 *Commission v France* [1994] ECR I-3069.

CHAPTER FIVE

Common organizations and Community preference

5.1 Introduction

The concept of Community preference is derived from the original Article 44 of the Treaty. Paragraph 1 of that provision allowed the Member States to introduce a non-discriminatory system of minimum prices during the transitional period in the event that the progressive establishment of a single market could result in prices likely to jeopardize the attainment of the objectives of Article 33. By virtue of paragraph 2, these minimum prices 'shall not be applied so as to form an obstacle to the development of a natural preference between Member States'. In a case challenging the validity of a regulation imposing a levy on the import of grapes into the Community, the Court noted the conflicting nature of the objectives in Article 33, especially in relation to the interests of producers and consumers. It continued:[1]

> In balancing these interests the Council must take account in the present case of the Community preference principle, which tends to favour the agricultural producer and which is one of the Treaty's principles, which finds expression, so far as agriculture is concerned, in Article 44(2).

Advocate General Jacobs has commented that the principle could not be regarded as a legal principle, and indeed questioned whether the original Article 44 could provide a foundation for a general principle of Community preference.[2] The impression that Community preference is a matter of policy rather than a legal principle seems to be confirmed by the introduction of an element of Community preference within the structure of common organizations of the market, as part of the gradual integration of new Member States within the CAP, and by the repeal of

---

[1] Case 5/67 *Beus* [1968] ECR 83, p. 95.
[2] Case C-353/92 *Greece v Council* [1994] ECR I-3411, pp. 3432–3434.

Article 44 by the Treaty of Amsterdam.[3] Breach of the principle has not been used by the Court as a ground for invalidating Community legislation.[4]

As for converting this principle/policy, which the original Article 44 seemed to limit to the transitional period, into a general principle of the CAP, the Community institutions would express it, in part, through the introduction of import levies. Such levies would not be the only means of protecting the common organizations of the market, as most regulations establishing such organizations would contain a safeguard clause. Just as a fundamental reform of the pricing structure occurred in the early 1990s as a result of the internal reform of the CAP, a fundamental reform of the import arrangements of most common organizations was necessary as a result of the Agreement on Agriculture concluded as part of the Uruguay Round of multilateral trade negotiations.[5] One of the three elements of the reform package introduced by the Agreement was new rules governing market access which, in addition to the usual concessions on import duties, would involve the conversion of then existing non-tariff barriers, such as import levies, into import duties. Furthermore, restrictions would be placed on the use of safeguard mechanisms by the parties to the Agreement. Another aspect of the Agreement on Agriculture's reform package was agreement on the use of export subsidies or refunds. In contrast to non-tariff barriers, such subsidies or refunds were not to be abolished but would be subject to both budgetary and quantitative limitations. The goal of the reform package is to achieve a fairer and more market-orientated agricultural trading system in the years to come. Such a system will, it is hoped, result in fewer complaints about the CAP by third countries in the future, as the old system of import levies, safeguard clauses and export refunds had led to complaints about the protectionist nature of the CAP. This chapter will end with a discussion of this aspect of the CAP, which will focus on developing countries, after discussing the other aspects outlined above.

---

[3] See for example, Case 6/78 *Union Française* [1978] ECR 1675 and Case 119/86 *Spain v Council and Commission* [1987] ECR 4121.

[4] See for example, Case 58/86 *Coopérative Agricole d'Approvisement des Avirons* [1987] ECR 1525. See also Case C-353/92 (above n. 2), p. 3451, where the Court stated: 'Community preference is not in any case a legal requirement the violation of which would result in the invalidity of the measure concerned.'

[5] The text of the Agreement is reproduced in OJ 1994 L 336/22.

5.2 Import levies and duties

In the case of *Neumann*, the Court had made it clear that although import levies imposed under the common organization of the market bore a resemblance to customs duties, the levy did not constitute a customs duty; rather it was a charge regulating external trade connected with the common price policy.[6] As such, external protection for agricultural products would be guaranteed through this system, in contrast to other products where protection would be offered through the Common Customs Tariff. In *Frecassetti*, the Court declared that the purpose of the import levy was, through preventing fluctuations on the world market from affecting the Community market, to protect and stabilize the Community market.[7] Given that prices on the world market were variable, the resulting import levies were also variable. In these, and further, cases on the purpose of the import levy, the Court would confirm that the levy was designed to help to achieve the objectives of the CAP through the implementation of the principle of Community preference.[8]

A further aspect of the principle of Community preference was the possibility of imposing safeguard measures in the event that the normal mechanisms used within the common organization were not sufficient.[9] Each of the regulations establishing a common organization of the market allowed for the imposition of safeguard measures in the event that the Community market experienced, or was threatened with, serious disturbances endangering the objectives of Article 33. If such an event occurred, the Community institutions were allowed to take appropriate measures until the disturbance, or threat thereof, had ceased.[10] By their nature, the safeguard mechanisms vested a wide discretionary power with the Community institutions, and, in accordance with the Court's case law on such powers, the scope for judicial review of these measures was limited. For example, the threat of disturbance involved an assessment of a complex economic situation, and so long as the institutions acted objectively their assessment could not be challenged. This was made clear in *Schröder*, where the Court also confirmed that although

---

[6] Case 17/67 [1967] ECR 441. See also Case 26/69 *Commission v France* [1970] ECR 565.
[7] Case 113/75 [1976] ECR 983.
[8] Case 6/77 *Schouten* [1977] ECR 1291 and Case 58/86 *Coopérative Agricole d'Approvisement des Avirons* (above n. 4).
[9] See Case 112/80 *Dürbeck* [1981] ECR 1095 and Case 345/82 *Wünsche* [1984] ECR 1995.
[10] See for example, Case 265/87 *Schräder* [1989] ECR 2237, Case C-24/90 *Faust* [1990] ECR I-4905 and Case C-81/92 *Dinter* [1993] ECR I-4601. See also Sack, J., 'The Commission's powers under the safeguard clauses of the common organizations of agricultural markets' (1983) 20 CMLRev 157.

the affected 'market' had to be delimited, it was to be interpreted in a broad sense as meaning the Community market.[11] Furthermore, the Community institutions enjoyed a wide discretion as to the scope and duration of the measures adopted, with the result that the Community could discriminate between third countries.[12] Despite the breadth of the discretion enjoyed, legislation has been declared invalid on occasion – for example, when in particular it constitutes a breach of the principle of proportionality.[13]

As a consequence of the Uruguay Round Agreement on Agriculture, not only were import levies to be replaced by import duties but strict controls were to be imposed on the use of safeguard mechanisms. The results of the market access negotiations were recorded in the national schedule of concessions annexed to the Uruguay Round Protocol that forms an integral part of the Final Act.[14] In addition to the usual reductions in the levels of tariffs reflected in Appendix IA of the Uruguay Round Protocol, there were also to be concessions on non-tariff measures. These latter concessions are the result of the adoption of the process of tariffication that applies to nearly all types of non-tariff barriers. According to a note to Article 4(2) of the Agreement on Agriculture, the measures to be converted include:[15]

> ... quantitative import restrictions, variable import levies, minimum import prices, discretionary import licensing, non-tariff measures maintained through state trading enterprises, voluntary export restraints and similar border measures other than ordinary customs duties, whether or not the measures are maintained under country-specific derogations from the GATT 1947.

The starting point for this process is the conversion of existing non-tariff barriers into tariff barriers to provide for an equivalent level of protection. For the Community, this involved the replacement of variable

---

[11] Case 40/72 [1973] ECR 125.

[12] See for example, Case 52/81 *Faust* [1982] ECR 3745 and Case 245/81 *Edeka* [1982] ECR 2745. See also Case T-489/93 *Unifruit Hellas* [1994] ECR II-1201 and Case C-51/95 *Unifruit Hellas* [1997] ECR I-727.

[13] See, for example, the saga in relation to protective measures against imports of cultivated mushrooms, Case 345/82 *Wünsche* (above n. 9), Case 69/85 *Wünsche* [1986] ECR 947, Case C-24/90 *Faust* [1991] ECR I-4905, Case C-25/90 *Wünsche* [1991] ECR I-4939, Case C-26/90 *Wünsche* [1991] ECR I-4961, Case C-295/94 *Hüpeden* [1996] ECR I-3375 and Case C-296/94 *Pietsch* [1996] ECR I-3409.

[14] Article 4(1) of the Agreement on Agriculture notes that 'market access concessions contained in Schedules relate to bindings and reductions of tariffs and to other market access commitments as specified therein.' Above n. 5.

[15] Measures which will not be converted are limited to measures maintained under balance-of-payments provisions or under other general, non-agriculture-specific provisions of the GATT 1994 or of the other Multilateral Trade Agreements in Annex 1A of the WTO.'

import levies by import duties and a commitment to effect an average reduction of 36% of these duties over the implementation period, which for developed countries is to be six years, expiring in 2000.

The process of tariffication also requires that existing access opportunities be maintained; and in those cases where current access falls below 3% of domestic consumption, minimum access tariff quotas are to be established. These quotas are to be expanded over the implementation period. According to Article 4(2) of the Agreement on Agriculture, 'members shall not maintain, resort to, or revert to any measures of the kind which have been required to be converted into ordinary customs duties' except as authorized under Article 5 and Annex 5. Annex 5 represents an attempt to counter concerns raised during the negotiations relating to the tariffication of non-tariff barriers on particularly sensitive products. There are strict limits on the use of this special treatment:[16]

(a) imports of the designated products comprised less than 3 per cent of corresponding domestic consumption in 'the base period';

(b) no export subsidies have been provided since the beginning of the base period for the designated products;

(c) effective production restricting measures are applied to the primary agricultural product;

(d) such products are designated with the symbol 'ST-Annex 5', in Section IB of Part I of a Member's Schedule annexed to the Uruguay Round (1994) Protocol as being subject to special treatment reflecting factors of non-trade concerns, such as food security and environmental protection; and

(e) minimum access opportunities in respect of the designated products correspond, to 4 per cent of base period domestic consumption of the designated products from the beginning of the first year of the implementation period and, thereafter, are increased by 0.8 per cent of corresponding domestic consumption in the base period per year for the remainder of the implementation period.

The cumulative effect of these conditions indicates that there will be few exemptions from the full scope of the tariffication process. Even in the situation where the provisions of the Annex can be used, minimum access opportunities will rise from 4% at the beginning of the implementation period to 8% at the end of the period. Annex 5 states that if a member ceases to apply special treatment:[17]

... the Member concerned shall maintain the minimum access opportunities already in effect at such time and increase the minimum access

---

[16] Above n. 5, Annex 5, A.1(A).   [17] *Ibid.*, Annex 5, A.2.

opportunities by 0.4 per cent of corresponding domestic consumption in the base period per year for the remainder of the implementation period.

Should the member wish to continue affording special treatment to the designated product, the percentage shall be the subject of negotiations. These negotiations may allow for the continuation of the special treatment on the condition that the member provides additional and acceptable concessions. If special treatment is not continued after these negotiations, the minimum access opportunities at the end of the implementation period are to be maintained at 8%. An additional exception is provided for in section B of Annex 5, but it can be invoked only by developing countries.

In addition to the above measures, Article 5(4) of the Agreement allows for a special safeguard measure to be taken with respect to tariffed products if:

(i)   the volume of imports of that product entering the customs territory of the Member granting the concession during any year exceeds a trigger level[18] which relates to the existing market access opportunity...; or, but not concurrently:

(ii) the price at which imports of that product may enter the customs territory of the Member granting the concession, as determined on the basis of the c.i.f. import price of the shipment concerned expressed in terms of its domestic currency, falls below a trigger price equal to the average 1986 to 1988 reference price for the product concerned.

In addition to these conditions, the agricultural product must also be designated in the member's schedule as being the subject of a concession in respect of which Article 5 may be invoked.

The special safeguard measure envisaged by Article 5 is the introduction of an additional duty. A strict schedule is established in Article 5(5) detailing the amount of this additional duty, and it is to be maintained only until the end of the year in which it is imposed. In essence, what Article 5 provides is a specific safeguard measure for agriculture drafted in such a way that its application will be transparent.[19] For example, the additional conditions imposed include the giving of notice, the provision of statistical information and the opportunity for consultations. Moreover, the use of Article XIX, the traditional GATT safeguard provision, and the Agreement on Safeguards will no longer be applicable to

---

[18] *Ibid.*, Article 5(4). The trigger level varies according to the existing level of market opportunities.
[19] *Ibid.*, Article 5(7).

safeguard measures in relation to market access for agricultural products. So, specific safeguard measures, which would frustrate the process of reform, will be adopted only on the satisfaction of very strict criteria. The products that may benefit from these measures must be flagged from a very early stage. The measures adopted will be temporary, and provision is made for consultation with affected Contracting Parties. These criteria and the overall transparency of the process will ensure that the process of liberalization is not derailed by such safeguard measures.

As for the impact of the Agreement on Agriculture on the Community's import arrangements, market access for various products subject to common organizations has been modified through the abolition of the import levies.[20] These products include cereals, pigmeat, eggs and poultry, and milk. In the common organization of the market in sheepmeat and goatmeat, where external protection had usually been effected by means of voluntary restraint agreements, these agreements were transformed into more generous market access quotas. For those cereals which can be subject to intervention, the import duty is now calculated by increasing the intervention price by 55% and reducing the result by the world price for the particular cereal; the resulting duty may not, however, exceed the rate of duty specified for that product in the CCT. Specific import arrangements, negotiated under the GATT, for cereals and beef, establish import quotas at either reduced or nil duty. The Community has also through various amendments to the common organizations of the market in cereals, pigmeat, poultry and eggs, milk and sugar, designated a number of products as being subject to the imposition of special safeguard measures provided for in Article 5.

5.3 Export subsidies

According to the regulations establishing the various common organizations of the market, subsidies or refunds are to be provided to enable the export of the products of the common organizations.[21] The value of the subsidy or refund would depend on the difference between the price prevailing on the Community market and that on the world market; in the

---

[20] See Regulation 3290/94 (OJ 1994 L 394/105) on the adjustment and transitional measures required in the agricultural sector in order to implement the agreements concluded during the Uruguay Round of multilateral trade negotiations. See also Regulation 1340/98 (OJ 1998 L 184/1).

[21] Refunds may also be granted for non-Annex II products, see for example Case 94/86 *Maizena* [1987] ECR 2941.

event that the latter were greater than the former, an export levy or tax could be imposed.[22] However, given that prices on the Community market have usually exceeded those on the world market, it is the export subsidy which is more usual. The purpose of the export subsidy was made clear by the Court in *Westzücker* where it was characterized as a means of ensuring the proper functioning of the market by allowing for the export of agricultural products.[23] As such the subsidy does not represent an income guarantee for the exporter, by, for example, allowing him or her to achieve a price equivalent to the intervention price on the internal market, or assuring the exporter of the most favourable opportunities for export.[24]

As with respect to those cases on the purpose of the import levy, the Court's jurisprudence with respect to export subsidies would confirm that the subsidy was designed to help to achieve the objectives of the CAP by allowing Community products to compete on the market of non-member countries.[25] Indeed, where export subsidies have led to a situation where the exporter had been overcompensated for the difference between the Community and world market price, the Court has declared such subsidies illegal.[26] However, the Court has also confirmed that the calculation of an export subsidy is not just an automatic calculation of the difference between the Community and world market price.[27] The basic regulations governing the common organizations of the market made it clear that other considerations, such as the state of the Community market in, and the proposed destination of, the products to be exported were also to be taken into account.[28] Detailed legislation on the use of export subsidies was established by Regulation 3665/87.[29]

The use of export subsidies by the Community, for example to export agricultural surpluses, has caused great friction between the Community

[22] See, for example, Regulation 865/97 (OJ 1997 L 123/23) imposing an export tax on common wheat and durum wheat as a result of the development of prices on the world markets in these products.

[23] Case 57/72 [1973] ECR 231.

[24] See Case 62/83 *Eximo* [1984] ECR 2295 and Case C-94/91 *Wagner* [1992] ECR I-2765.

[25] See for example, Case 89/83 *Dimex* [1984] ECR 2815. This case confirms that the completion of customs formalities constitutes evidence of importation and so triggers the payment of the subsidy. See also Case C-27/92 *Möllman-Fleisch* [1993] ECR I-1701 and Case C-321/91 *Tara Meat Packers* [1993] ECR I-2811.

[26] Case 167/82 *Nordgetreide* [1983] ECR 1149.

[27] Case 263/87 *Denmark v Commission* [1989] ECR 1081.

[28] See for example, Case 89/83 *Dimex*, above n. 25.

[29] OJ 1987 L 351/1, as amended by Regulation 354/90 (OJ 1990 L 38/34). See also Regulation 3846/87 (OJ 1987 L 366/1) establishing an agricultural product nomenclature for export subsidies. On the interpretation of the Regulation, see, for example, Case C-299/94 *Anglo Irish Beef Processors International* [1996] ECR I-1925 and Case C-263/97 *Fair City Trading* (judgment of 29 September 1998).

and its trading partners.[30] Attempts to deal with the resulting problems eventually resulted in the inclusion of export subsidies within the Uruguay Round Agreement on Agriculture, where it was agreed that in future certain export subsidies would be subject to a commitment to reduce the budgetary outlay and quantities benefiting from such subsidies. The approach of the Agreement on Agriculture is to list those export subsidies subject to the reduction commitments. Six specific examples are listed in Article 9(1). These include:

(a) The provision by governments or their agencies of direct subsidies, including payments-in-kind, to a firm, to an industry, to producers of an agricultural product, to a cooperative or other association of such producers, or to a marketing board, contingent on export performance.

(b) The sale or disposal for export by governments or their agencies of non-commercial stocks of agricultural products at a price lower than the comparable price charged for the like product to buyers in the domestic market.[31]

These and the other examples relate mainly to the provision of direct export subsidies. The export subsidy commitments undertaken by the members of the agreement may relate to budgetary outlay and export quantity.[32] For developed country members, such as the Community, the commitment is to reduce the budgetary outlays of the export subsidies and the quantities benefiting from such subsidies, over the implementation period covered, to a level 36% and 21% below the levels in the 1986–1990 base period.

Provision is made in Article 9(2)(b) for members to grant export subsidies in excess of the corresponding annual commitment levels provided that certain conditions are satisfied.[33] The conditions seek to ensure compliance with the reduction commitments, allowing for an annual excess of up to 3% of the base period budgetary outlays and 1.75% of the base period quantities. The potential effect on the reduction process is limited by Article 9(2)(b)(iii), which states that:

The total cumulative amounts of budgetary outlays for such export subsidies and the quantities benefiting from such export subsidies over the entire implementation period are no greater than the totals that would have resulted from full compliance with the relevant annual commitment levels specified in the Member's Schedule.

[30] For further discussion of this point, see 7.2 'The GATT and agriculture'.
[31] Above n. 5, Article 9(1).   [32] Uruguay Protocol, Appendix V, pt IV, section II.
[33] Above n. 5, Article 9(2)(b).

For those export subsidies that conform to the provisions of the Agreement there will be an exemption from actions based on Article XVI of the GATT, the traditional GATT provision on subsidies, or Articles 3, 5, and 6 of the Subsidies Agreement.

Those export subsidies not covered by Article 9(1) are not to be applied in a manner that results, or may result, in the 'circumvention of the export subsidy commitments'.[34] These non-listed export subsidies will be subject to the Subsidies Agreement, which establishes three categories of subsidies: prohibited,[35] actionable,[36] and non-actionable.[37] In addition, Article 13(3)(a) of the Agreement on Agriculture makes clear that subsidies covered by Article 9(1) can continue to be subject to countervailing duties in limited circumstances.[38] Lastly, the obligation not to circumvent the reduction commitments also applies to non-commercial transactions. Article 10(4) states that members that donate international food aid must ensure:

(a) that the provision of international food aid is not tied directly or indirectly to commercial exports of agricultural products to recipient countries;

(b) that international food aid transactions, including bilateral food aid which is monetized, shall be carried out in accordance with the FAO 'Principles of Surplus Disposal and Consultative Obligations' including, where appropriate, the system of Usual Marketing Requirements; and

(c) that such aid shall be provided to the extent possible in fully grant forms or on terms no less concessional than those provided for in Article IV of the Food Aid Convention 1986.

---

[34] Above n. 5, Article 10(1).

[35] Article 3. These subsidies are subject to a new dispute settlement procedure outlined in Article 4, the main feature of which is an expedited timetable for action by the dispute settlement body. Countermeasures will be authorized if the prohibited subsidy is not withdrawn within a specified period.

[36] Article 5. These provide that such subsidies shall not have adverse impact on the interests of other signatories. An adverse impact is defined as injury to a domestic industry, nullification or impairment of direct or indirect benefits arising under the GATT, or serious prejudice to the interests of another signatory. If the dispute settlement body determines that an adverse impact exists, the subsidy must be either withdrawn or the adverse effects removed.

[37] Article 6. If serious adverse effects to a domestic industry of a member arise from these subsidies, that member may seek a determination and recommendation from the committee.

[38] Above n. 5. Under Article 13(3)(a), Article VI of the GATT, the traditional GATT provision on dumping, and part V of the Subsidies Agreement may be invoked 'upon a determination of injury or threat thereof based on volume, effect on prices, or consequent impact'.

Export subsidies will continue to play a role in international agricultural trade. Total elimination, as demanded during the Uruguay Round negotiations by the United States and the Cairns Group, remains a long-term goal.[39] Export subsidies will be subject to the discipline provided for in the Agreement in Agriculture; subsidies falling outside this discipline will be subject to the discipline provided by the Agreement on Subsidies and Countervailing Duties.

As for the impact of the Agreement on the Community's export arrangements, refunds, which may still be offered, are limited in terms of budgetary expenditure and quantities in the common organizations in cereals, pigmeat, beef and milk.[40] Export refunds are no longer payable in the sheepmeat and goatmeat common organization. Lastly, export refunds granted as part of the food aid policy of the Community – for example, as part of the Community's commitments under the Food Aid Convention – are not subject to these financial and quantitative limitations.

To complete the analysis of the principle of Community preference, a system of import and export licences exists to monitor trade flows, thus providing the Community institutions with advance warning of problems likely to emerge in the operation of the CAP. The validity of such a system has been upheld by the Court. For example, in the case of *Internationale Handelsgesellschaft* the Court noted that the system allowed the Community and the Member States to collect information which would help them to determine the best method of achieving the objectives of the CAP, a goal which was made more important by the heavy financial responsibilities imposed by the policy on both the Community and the Member States. It continued:[41]

> ... import and export licences, which create an obligation on the part of the holders to carry out the contemplated operation since it is secured by the posting of a bond, are a necessary and appropriate means to permit the authorities to choose the most effective interventions on the ... market.

This reveals the basic features of the licensing system as an authorization and an obligation to import/export enforced through a system of deposits/securities.[42] If an importer/exporter meets all the conditions for the grant of a licence, he or she has a right to the licence.[43] The period of

---

[39] See Breen, J., 'Agriculture' in Stewart, T. (ed.), *The GATT Uruguay Round: A Negotiating History (1986–1992)* (Kluwer, 1993), pp. 125–254.
[40] Full details are available in Regulation 3290/94, above n. 20.
[41] Case 11/70 [1970] ECR 1125, p. 1134–35.
[42] See Regulation 3183/80 (OJ 1980 L 338/1). This Regulation has been the subject of frequent amendment. See also Regulation 2220/85 (OJ 1985 L 205/5) which contains detailed rules for the application of the system of securities for agricultural products.
[43] Case 25/70 *Koster* [1970] ECR 71.

validity of the licence will begin as from the date of issue, although it may be suspended pending changes to import/export arrangements by the Commission. The obligation to import/export must be exercised during the period of the licence and will be met by the completion of customs formalities.[44] When such formalities have been completed, the deposit/security is released.[45] In the event that import/export does not take place within the period of validity of the licence, the deposit/security is forfeited except in the case of *force majeure*.[46] The Court has made it clear that this concept is not limited to cases of absolute impossibility:[47] 'It follows that, in principle, an importer who has exercised all reasonable care is released from the obligation to import when external circumstances render it impossible for him to complete the importation within the period of validity.' In this particular case, where the licence was lost in the post, the Court held that it was for the national courts to decide whether the trader had acted with all reasonable care.[48]

5.4 A study of the external impact of the CAP

The problem facing agricultural exports from developing countries to developed countries prior to the Uruguay Round was the high degree of protection which the latter countries accorded to their domestic producers. Through various measures, such as market price support and border protection, developed countries, such as those of the Community, sought to restrict the import of directly competitive products. Insulated from the effects of the impact of the world market, domestic producers in developed countries often produced quantities in excess of domestic demand. Faced with the build up of surpluses, some developed countries resorted to export subsidization as a means of surplus disposal. Developing countries were thus doubly penalized by the agricultural policies pursued by some developed countries; not only were their exports to the latter's markets subject to limitations, but in their efforts

---

[44] Case 122/78 *Buitoni* [1979] ECR 677. See now Article 29 of Regulation 3183/80, noted above in n. 42.

[45] For a discussion of the system of securities, see Barents, R., 'The System of Deposits in Community Agricultural Law: Efficiency v. Proportionality' (1985) 10 ELRev 239.

[46] Regulation 3183/80, Article 32 (above n. 42). See for example, Case C-12/92 *Huygen* [1993] ECR I-6381, Case C-347/93 *Boterlux* [1994] ECR I-3933, Case C-299/94 *Anglo Irish Beef Processors International* (above n. 29) and Case C-263/97 *Fair City Trading* (above n. 29).

[47] Case 158/73 *Kampffmeyer* [1974] ECR 101, p. 110. See also Case C-124/92 *An Bord Bainne* [1993] ECR I-5061 and Case C-136/93 *Transáfrica* [1994] ECR I-5757.

[48] For a thorough discussion of *force majeure*, see Barents, R., *The Agricultural Law of the EC* (Kluwer, Deventer, 1994), Chapter 14.

to place these exports elsewhere, they were faced with competition arising from the export subsidization of surplus production.

Moreover, the presence of domestic agricultural policies tended to restrict the generosity of developed countries in their trade arrangements with developing countries. In the assessment which follows of Community practice in this respect, three particular areas will be examined: the Lomé Conventions, the Mediterranean Agreements and the Generalized System of Preferences (GSP). Thereafter, some consideration is given not only to the impact of the Agreement on Agriculture on developing countries, but also to the future scope of Community policy in this area. The latter is now informed by the introduction of a specific chapter on development cooperation policy by the Treaty on European Union, according to which:

> Community policy in the sphere of development cooperation, which shall be complementary to the policies pursued by the Member States, shall foster:
> – the sustainable economic and social development of the developing countries and more particularly the most disadvantaged among them;
> – the smooth and gradual integration of the developing countries into the world economy;
> – the campaign against poverty in the developing countries.

According to Article 178, the Community is to take account of these objectives in the policies which it implements which are likely to affect developing countries. Some indication of the nature of the task confronting the Community in the implementation of this Article emerges as a result of the assessment below, which concludes with a discussion of the initial attempts of the Community to meet the demands of Article 178.

The Lomé Conventions represent the most generous range of concessions granted by the Community to developing countries. The first Convention in 1975 acted as a replacement of the then existing relationship, established through two Yaoundé Conventions, and as an extension of the scope of cooperation between the Community and developing countries.[49] With respect to agricultural concessions, the trade provisions of the Convention repeated almost *verbatim* the trade treatment provisions of the second Yaoundé Convention of 1969.[50] This had established the principle of free trade in industrial products, but such free trade could not be allowed for those agricultural products falling within the scope of the CAP as these countries would receive a

---

[49] OJ 1975 L 25/2.   [50] JO 1970 L 282.

level of preference as against all other third countries. The range of agricultural concessions granted by the Community to the beneficiaries of the Lomé Convention, collectively known as the African, Caribbean and Pacific (ACP) countries, include duty-free access for various tropical products, various forms of relief from the import measures relating to imports of products subject to the CAP and imports of various products under arrangements made by protocols to the Convention. The concessions on products covered by the CAP range from exemption from customs duties without a marketing timetable to progressive abolition of the customs duties within a marketing timetable.[51] These concessions have been characterized as follows:[52]

> ... although ACP countries may enjoy relative preferences over non-ACP suppliers outside the EU, they still face the barriers of protectionism in the EU erected in the interest of domestic EU producers. The ACP's relative disadvantage vis-à-vis EU suppliers is still substantial.

The scope of the preferential treatment offered by the Convention for agricultural products has been gradually expanded as a result of the renegotiations of the Conventions and as a result of consultations with the ACP States concerning their requests for preferential treatment for products not already covered by such treatment. However, this has been a painstakingly slow process.

To the agricultural preferences received by the ACP must be added the concessions made to them under various protocols to the Conventions which give the ACP special trade treatment for a number of products; this is usually in the form of allowing them to maintain traditional export patterns. One of these arrangements is for sugar, and it involves an undertaking by the Community to 'purchase and import at guaranteed prices' specific quantities of cane sugar which the ACP States undertake to deliver to it.[53] Article 1 of Protocol 8 continues by noting that the implementation of these undertakings is to take place within the common organization of the Community market in sugar, and this common organization should not prejudice the undertaking given by the Community. The quantity of sugar benefiting from the Protocol is set at 1.3 million tonnes, and this is subdivided between those ACP States

---

[51] For full details of the concessions, see Annex XL Lomé IV. The text of the Lomé IV Convention is reproduced in OJ 1991 L 229/3.

[52] Davenport, M., Hewitt, A. and Koning, A., *Europe's Preferred Partners? The Lomé Countries in World Trade* (ODI, 1995), p. 12.

[53] Protocol 8 Lomé IV; reproduces Protocol 3 to Lomé I. The Protocol derives from Protocol 22 of the Act of Accession of the UK, in which the Community undertook to safeguard the interests of those ACP States 'whose economies depend to a considerable extent' on the export of sugar.

listed in the Protocol.[54] Despite the fact that the number of ACP States has increased, no provision exists for the quantity of sugar to be delivered to the Community to be increased. Under Article 5 of the Protocol, the sugar is to be marketed in the Community at prices freely negotiated between buyers and sellers. The Community agreed to intervene only when quantities of sugar could not be marketed within the Community at a price equivalent to or in excess of the guaranteed price. Although the Protocol represents a limited guarantee of free and assured access for one important commodity to the Community, its provisions have been subject to criticism.

Two aspects of the Protocol which have caused the most problems are the provisions on price and those on quantities. Although the Protocol calls for genuine annual negotiations on price, there has been little evidence of negotiation, with the Community usually making an offer on a 'take it or leave it' basis. The problem was that as agricultural price policy within the Community was adapted as part of an effort to deal with the problems of agricultural expenditure and surpluses, the Community found itself hamstrung. The logic of the Community's position was that it could hardly offer a price increase to ACP producers if domestic producers were experiencing price decreases.[55] Similarly, efforts to limit production within the Community have resulted in the adoption of a negative attitude by the latter to ACP requests for additional export quantities to be allocated under the Protocol. As one commentator has noted:[56]

> The idiosyncratic arithmetic of the [CAP] would have it that the cost of stocking and exporting Europe's huge current surplus of beet sugar is directly attributable to ACP sugar. Never mind that when the Protocol was signed, Europe was a net importer of sugar. Never mind the concept enshrined in the Protocol that its implementation would be 'carried out within the framework of the common organization of the sugar market.' The consummation of this train of logic would be that prices paid to ACP sugar producers by *commercial buyers and refiners*, whose viability as a

---

[54] *Ibid.*, Article 3. Although only 13 countries are listed in this Article, 18 countries actually benefit from the Protocol.

[55] Concern about the evolution of prices was the subject of discussions at a Special Ministerial Conference of the ACP in May 1990, where the Secretary-General of the ACP group commented: 'The prolonged freeze of the guaranteed sugar price, which has now turned into a decrease, combined with the reluctance of the Community so far to adopt other measures to counteract the effects of such actions and to alleviate the effects of international developments, pose a serious threat to the ability of the protocol to meet its objectives' (*The Courier* No. 122 (July–August 1990), p. 35).

[56] Jackman, R., 'The Sugar Protocol' *The Courier* No. 75 (September–October 1982), p. 59.

Community industry depends directly on ACP cane sugar, should somehow be seen as a form of aid.

A solution to the problems of the allocation of quantities under the Protocol was possible as a result of the offer by Portugal on accession to the Community to buy 0.3 million tonnes of ACP sugar.[57] Instead, the Commission and the ACP negotiated a five-year agreement providing for an annual quota based on demand within the Community, this additional quota being outside the context of the Sugar Protocol.[58]

A similar pattern of failure to respond adequately to the needs of developing countries emerges with respect to the next most important set of arrangements concluded by the Community with developing countries – the Mediterranean Agreements. The guiding principle of the 1963 Association Agreement with Turkey for industrial or manufactured products was one of free trade (with the exception of textile products), whereas for agricultural products subject to the CAP the guiding principle was one of preferential treatment, a reflection of the fact that the degree of competition between Mediterranean and Community producers can be very acute.[59] Even the adoption of a Global Mediterranean Policy by the Community in 1973 did not alter the fundamental nature of the agricultural trade relations established with the Mediterranean countries. For example, Articles 15 to 23 of the Cooperation Agreement with Algeria merely provided for a percentage reduction in the level of customs duties for certain products, the introduction of certain import calendars, reductions in the protective charges imposed by the CAP and minimum price levels.[60] Agricultural concessions given to the Mediterranean countries reflected the trading interests of these countries, yet the concessions granted were not the same for all countries – for example, the Maghreb countries were granted a 80% reduction in the customs duties applicable to oranges, whereas the concession for the Mashreq countries was only 60%. Even the more advanced agreement concluded at that time with Israel, which was supposed to lead to the creation of a free trade area between the parties, only granted Israel a certain level of preferential treatment through percentage reductions for certain products, tariff quotas and reductions in the protective charges applied under the CAP.[61]

This brief review of the Lomé and Mediterranean relationships highlights the extent to which domestic pressures arising from the CAP have impacted on the most generous trade arrangements of the Community

---

[57] *The Courier* No. 89 (January–February 1985), p. 6.
[58] Regulation 1915/95 (OJ 1995 L 184/16). See also Decision 95/284 (OJ 1995 L 181/22).
[59] JO 1964 217/64.   [60] OJ 1978 L 263/2.   [61] OJ 1975 L 136/3.

with developing countries. For those developing countries trading under the least generous range of concessions, the GSP, the situation is even more adverse. For example, the commercial cooperation agreements concluded between 1974 and 1976 with India, Bangladesh, Pakistan and Sri Lanka offered various concessions in the context of the Community's GSP in an effort to compensate these countries for the loss of trading opportunities resulting from enlargement.[62] An Annex to the agreements relating to the future development of the GSP provided that the Community, when improving the GSP, would take into account the interests of these countries. However, as the Commission noted in its 1980 review of the first ten years of the Community's GSP scheme, when discussing the possibility of wider product coverage, especially for agricultural products:[63]

> Given the constraints of the CAP and the need to safeguard opportunities for access for the ACP countries, or in the case of certain products, opportunities for the Mediterranean countries and the possibility of the accession of new countries, it would be inappropriate to widen the present product coverage.

The European Parliament acknowledged this conclusion by accusing the policy of being protectionist and thus hampering the agricultural development of developing countries, especially through the disposal of surplus production as food aid.[64]

The Commission, in its first memorandum on development policy in 1971, pointed to a very generous GSP as evidence of the Community's consideration of the needs of developing countries.[65] By parity of reasoning, the paucity of the GSP offer on agricultural products at this time was evidence of the failure of the CAP to take into account the interests of developing countries. To allow for the demands of development cooperation policy to be taken into account in the operation of the CAP, the Commission noted:[66]

> [The] necessary integration of development cooperation aims into internal policies will of course have to come about gradually and according to a programme so that abrupt social and economic repercussions within the

---

[62] OJ 1974 L 82/2 (India), OJ 1976 L 319/2 (Bangladesh), OJ 1976 L 168/2 (Pakistan) and OJ 1975 L 247/2 (Sri Lanka).

[63] COM (80) 104, p. 6.

[64] EPWD1-603/83, *Report on the context of the future ACP-EEC Convention to follow Lomé II*, p. 41.

[65] Bull. EC Supp. 5/71, *Commission memorandum on a Community policy for development cooperation*.

[66] *Ibid.*, p. 23.

Community are avoided. But it is indispensable if the effectiveness of cooperation is to be secured and the Community's credibility in the developing countries ensured.

An examination of the various agreements above demonstrated how the generosity of the Community was hampered by the domestic pressures catered for by the CAP. The situation may change as a result of the inclusion of Article 178 and as a consequence of the Uruguay Round Agreement on Agriculture.

What developed countries wanted from the Uruguay Round was a mechanism to restrain the budgetary consequences of their policies, whereas developing countries wanted the reform of those aspects of developed countries' agricultural policies which had frustrated the process of agricultural development. Numerous studies have been conducted to assess the impact of the Uruguay Round agreements. Given the range of these studies and the range of models used in such studies, there is little agreement on the impact of the changes to agricultural trade and policy in temperate agricultural products effected by the Agreement on Agriculture on the developing countries.[67] A note submitted by the GATT Secretariat to the GATT Committee on Trade and Development in 1994 indicated that the average percentage reduction by developed countries for agricultural products would be 37%, and for tropical products 43%.[68] For some products the reductions will be above average (oilseeds, tropical beverages and flowers), and for others below average reductions are to be made (sugar and dairy products). Adding the results on market access to those on the impact of tariffication, domestic support and export subsidies, the GATT Secretariat concluded that new opportunities would exist for developing countries exporting temperate agricultural products.[69] Page and Davenport, in their analysis of the impact of the trade reform on developing countries, estimate that for temperate agricultural products the net price effect is an average rise of 5% with a net trade effect of less than 0.1%.[70] Greater

---

[67] See Francois, J., McDonald, B. and Nordström, H., *A User's Guide to Uruguay Round Assessments* (WTO Staff Working Paper RD-96-003). See also Hertel, T., 'Agricultural Trade Liberalization and the Developing Countries: A Survey of the Models' in Goldin, I., and Knudsen, D. (eds), *Agricultural Trade Liberalization: Implications for Developing Countries* (OECD/World Bank, Paris, 1990), pp. 19–35. See also the other studies in this publication.

[68] *Developing Countries and the Uruguay Round: An Overview* (1994), Table 6: Developed economy imports and tariff reductions on agricultural products.

[69] A similar conclusion is reached in the November 1994 GATT Study: *The Results of the Uruguay Round on Multilateral Trade Negotiations: Market Access for Goods and Services: Overview of the Results*.

[70] *World Trade Reform: Do Developing Countries Gain or Lose?* (ODI, London, 1995), p. 33.

impact would have been achieved had the percentage reductions, especially in the area of market access, been larger and the time period chosen to calculate the reductions different.

If for agricultural products there may not be significant gains for developing countries, the situation is different with respect to tropical products. For these products, the major change will be the reduction in the tariffs of the Community on coffee and cocoa. These existed to give some level of preferential treatment to the ACP countries and the reduction in the levels of tariffs will lead to ACP preference erosion on tropical products; the estimated loss of revenue for these two products is $55 million and $19 million respectively.[71] Although preferential margins will continue for these and other tropical products, the total loss to the ACP as a result of changes to trade in tropical products is estimated at $177 million.[72] This loss may be offset by the continuation of existing tariff exemptions on CAP products as existing quantitative barriers are to be replaced by tariffs, as a consequence of tariffication. This assumes, however, that the ACP will continue to enjoy tariff exemption for these products and does not reflect the impact of changes in prices for temperate agricultural products. For example, Davenport, Hewitt and Koning estimate that the net loss resulting from guaranteed price reductions for temperate agricultural products to be $226 million, with losses being particularly serious for those ACP countries who export products under the various protocols to the Convention.[73]

Overall the loss resulting from the various measures agreed to the ACP as a group is greater than that to the developing countries as a group. Page and Davenport conclude that the loss to the latter from reforms is minimal, whereas the loss to the ACP is minus 1.5% or some $720 million. When other reforms, such as those to the Multifibre Agreement, are included, the ACP suffer a further 0.2% decline in contrast to an overall net gain to developing countries of 1.3%.[74] The parties to the Lomé Convention had recognized that the outcome of the Uruguay Round would affect the trading position of the ACP. The Joint Declaration on trade liberalization attached to the 1990 Lomé IV Convention stated that the Community was conscious of the need to ensure that the competitive position of the ACP States would have to be maintained on the Community market where their advantages were affected by measures relating to general trade liberalization.[75] A further declaration noted that amendments to the trade regime might be neces-

---

[71] *Ibid.*, p. 39.   [72] Above n. 52, p. 44 and Table A9 (pp. 93–94).
[73] *Ibid.*, Table 4.1 (p. 41) and Table A7 (pp. 89–91).   [74] Above n. 70, pp. 61 and 62.
[75] Above n. 51, Annex XXIX.

sary 'for access for agricultural products in order to take account of the outcome' of the Uruguay Round.[76] The mid-term review of the Convention offered the Community the opportunity to realize changes to the trade regime to take account of the effect of the Uruguay Round, but the main focus of the changes to the trade regime related to the provisions on trade development. Limited changes were made to the trade regime by expanding the coverage of preferential treatment and through the relaxation of quantitative restrictions and/or expansion of the import calendars for certain agricultural products.[77]

A second opportunity to compensate the ACP for the impact of all these changes will arise shortly with the renegotiation of the current convention which began in 1998 and which will be concluded, it is hoped, with the signing of a new convention in 2000. As for the future of the ACP–EC trading relationship, the choice is between a continuation of the security and stability of existing arrangements, or an amendment of those arrangements to encompass the new international trade reality arising from the creation of the WTO.[78] The Commission favours the latter as it identifies as one of the guidelines for the future that existing policy should be refocused on the complementary objectives of sustainable economic and social development, the alleviation of poverty and integration into the world economy through the negotiation of new cooperation agreements with the ACP. For the Commission this entails greater support for regional integration efforts within the ACP through the negotiation of differentiated agreements as part of the process of global integration.[79] Such agreements would take the form either of economic cooperation agreements, which would not be totally reciprocal, or of economic partnership agreements, which could include free trade areas. An exception to the WTO rules would be needed not only for the continuation of existing arrangements, pending the negotiation of new agreements, but also for the economic cooperation agreements. A similar exception would be needed for the continuation of the existing product protocols. Given the differentiation envisaged by the Commission in the

---

[76] *Ibid.*, Annex XXVII.

[77] See OJ 1997 L 28/31 (Agreement in the form of an exchange of letters between the Community and the ACP States concerning Annex XL to the fourth ACP–EC Convention relating to the Joint Declaration concerning agricultural products referred to in Article 168(2)(c)(ii)). See also Regulation 1706/98 (OJ 1998 L 215/12) on agricultural imports from the ACP and the amended text of Lomé IV, OJ 1998 L 156/3.

[78] *Green Paper on relations between the European Union and the ACP countries in the eve of the 21st century: Challenges and options for a new partnership* notes that: '... future cooperation between the EU and the ACP countries must be seen against a radically changed international backdrop' (COM (96) 570, p. 35).

[79] COM(97) 537, *Guidelines for the negotiation of new cooperation agreements with the African, Caribbean and Pacific (ACP) countries*, p. 24.

new arrangements and the narrow interpretation adopted by both the Panel and the Appellate Body in the banana dispute of the existing Lomé waiver, it is by no means certain that such an exception will be obtained.[80] Moreover, the free trade areas option, which will involve the complete elimination of obstacles to substantially all the trade between the parties if it is to be WTO-consistent, will come up against the significant obstacle of the CAP.

In relation to the Euro–Mediterranean agreements which are part of the goal of promoting a Euro–Mediterranean Economic Area, Article 16 of the Tunisian agreement lists the aim of the gradual liberalization of reciprocal trade.[81] Protocol 1 deals with the import of Tunisian agricultural products into the Community, and an annex to the Protocol lists the trade treatment applicable to certain products. This includes the complete elimination of customs duties applicable to imports, either within or without a tariff quota and with or without an import calendar, reduction in the levels of *ad valorem* duties and the exemption from customs duties of imports within established reference quantities. These reference quantities may be transformed into tariff quotas as a consequence of the annual review of trade flows. This annual review may also be used as a justification for the imposition of reference quantities or tariff quotas on those goods which are to benefit from the complete elimination of import duties. Under Article 1(5) of the Protocol, some of the products subject to either tariff quotas or reference quantities may be increased from 1997 to 2000 by 3% *per annum*; this covers such products as cut flowers, new potatoes, almonds, apricots, tomato concentrate and fresh oranges. The limited number of products benefiting from this concession can be contrasted with the large number of products which may be subject to the imposition of either reference quantities or tariff quotas under Article 1(6) of the Protocol. As justification for this, the Commission pointed to the fact that the stability of the Community market could be upset if the move to more open trading were to proceed too rapidly.[82] The response of the Council was to stress:[83]

> ... the importance of taking account, when defining the Community position in negotiations with third countries, of the characteristics of the Community agricultural market and of the socio-economic repercussions of the proposed concessions on that market, as well as of the need to develop a consistent overall strategy on the subject.

[80] See discussion of the WTO Panel and Appellate Body in 7.4.5.
[81] OJ 1997 L 97/2.
[82] COM (97) 477, *Mediterranean Concessions Impact Study*.
[83] Conclusions of 16 December 1997, reproduced in Bulletin EU 12–1997, point 1.2.224.

It could be argued that a consistent overall strategy does exist; it is expressed, for example, in Article 177. Yet it seems that that strategy must give way to the need to maintain the principle of Community preference, and that principle requires a restrictive approach to the question of granting agricultural concessions to developing countries.[84]

This conclusion appears to be vindicated by the Community's response to the WTO initiative to adopt a comprehensive Action Plan in favour of the least developed countries, agreed in Singapore in December 1996. Existing opportunities within the Community market for the least developed countries include the Lomé trade provisions (the vast majority of the countries listed as least developed are ACP countries) and the GSP (for the remaining least developed countries). For agricultural products, the Commission has pointed out that around 4% of total Community agricultural imports come from the least developed countries, with very few imports not receiving some sort of preferential treatment.[85] In terms of further moves to increase market access possibilities for the least developed, although results would be difficult to predict, the potential for the least developed to 'flood' the Community market is seen as limited. Despite this acknowledgement, the Commission concluded that any liberalization package would have to include safeguard mechanisms to guard against unforeseen surges in imports. Complete, instantaneous duty-free imports could not be envisaged, not only because it would go further than either the existing Lomé and GSP arrangements but also because of possible difficulties on the Community market.

Possible exceptions to liberalization of agricultural trade were addressed by the Commission against the background of previous liberalization efforts. These included the negotiation during the Kennedy Round of a concession on manioc (cassava flour) which was used as evidence of the unpredictability of liberalization. This unpredictability had led the Community in the 1980s to conclude voluntary export restraint agreements with Thailand and Indonesia.[86] Analysing the consumption, production and export statistics of the least developed countries and comparing them with equivalent statistics for Community consumption, production and imports, the Commission concluded that for eight products liberalization could be contemplated as there was no, or effectively

---

[84] See the new GSP scheme for agricultural products, Regulation 1256/96 (OJ 1996 L 160/1). See also Regulation 1154/98 (OJ 1998 L 160/1) applying the special incentive schemes referred to in Articles 7 and 8 of the GSP regulations. For a discussion of the scheme, see Driessen, B., 'On Very Sensitive Cauliflowers and the (P)Re-cooked EU Agricultural Generalised Scheme of Preferences' (1996) 30 JWT (No. 6) 169.

[85] COM(97) 156, *Improving Market Access for Least Developed Countries*, p. 8.

[86] Decisions 82/495 and 82/496 (OJ 1982 L 219/52 and 56).

no, Community production.[87] For the remaining products, clear export potential existed for bananas and rice and a lesser level of export potential existed for bovine meat and sugar. The absence of reliable data led the Commission to conclude that there was little scope for increased quantities of wheat and greater study was required before a conclusion could be reached on vegetable oil and soybeans. The conclusion drawn from this, although recognized as both partial and general, was that:[88]

> Effective protection against unforeseen surges in imports as a result of [the least developed countries] revising their productive capacity can only be provided by an adequate safeguard mechanism. If the granting of preferences to [the least developed countries] is on an autonomous basis, such a mechanism, would as a matter of course be built into the preference package.

It is clear that the Community will not repeat the 'mistake' it made with respect to the negotiation of the concession on manioc. It is also clear that the Community does not envisage the unrestrained growth of imports from all the least developed countries. Improvements in the rules of origin for the non-ACP least developed countries are offered as one means of improving the market access of these countries. What is not offered is the extension of the trade treatment afforded to be equivalent to that offered to the ACP least developed countries under the Lomé Convention. Although a package of measures has been agreed, major changes will have to wait until the expiration of the Lomé Convention in 2000 and the further evolution of the Community's CAP and development cooperation policy.[89]

The gradual integration of development cooperation concerns into the domestic policies of the Community, as advocated by the 1971 Commission memorandum, seems not to have occurred if the experience of the CAP is anything to go by. The inclusion of Article 178 by the Treaty on European Union has likewise not increased the ability of the Community to offer genuine concessions to developing countries. The Agreement on Agriculture is unlikely to change this conclusion. As the Community expands eastwards in the next decade, concerns with budgetary expenditure will continue to be a primary feature. The need to avoid the social and economic repercussions of enlargement rather

---

[87] Above n. 85, p. 29. The eight products are coffee, cocoa beans, tea, pepper, groundnuts, palm kernels, palm oil and copra.

[88] *Ibid.*, p. 30.

[89] See Regulation 602/98 (OJ 1998 L 80/1) extending the coverage of Regulations 3281/94 and 1256/96 concerning Community schemes of generalized tariff preferences for the benefit of least developed countries.

than the improvement of the position of developing countries will continue to dominate Community thinking on agriculture. A policy which has had a negative impact on developing countries is therefore likely to continue, and further reforms will again be motivated by internal rather than external factors. The coherence advocated by the Treaty on European Union will not be realized for some time, so the problem of coordination addressed by Article 178 will remain unresolved.

CHAPTER SIX

Structural policy

6.1 Introduction

A strict interpretation of the objectives set for the CAP in Article 33(1) would suggest a connection between the first two paragraphs, which implies that the CAP would be a type of regional structural policy. Article 33(2) adds weight to this implication by requiring the particular nature of agricultural activity to be taken into account in the working out of the policy. Support for such an interpretation can also be found in the jurisprudence of the Court.[1] However, the policy as it developed emphasized the importance of a markets and prices policy rather than a structural policy. This was in keeping with the conclusions of the 1958 Stresa Conference, which stressed the importance of a common price policy over the need to reform the structure of European agriculture.[2] As a consequence structural policy was slow to develop.

This chapter will trace the development of that policy from its inception to its current status as nearly an equal partner with the markets and prices policy. In this development, the scope of the policy has expanded from being concerned with farm modernization and farming in less favoured areas to include such matters as regional policy and the protection of the environment. The current position of near equality between the two aspects of the CAP is largely a result of the 1992 reform of the CAP, and the reforms agreed at the Berlin European Council will promote greater equality between the two aspects. It is therefore possible that at some stage in the future, the mechanisms of the CAP will truly reflect the objectives set for it in 1957.

---

[1] Case 297/82 *De Samvirkande Danske Landboforeninger* [1983] ECR 3299, p. 3317. See also Opinion of Advocate General Capotorti in Cases 114, 116 and 119–20/76 *Behla-Mühle* [1977] ECR 1211, p. 1229.
[2] JO 1958 291, Resolution of the Stresa Conference.

6.2. Early developments

It is not the case that structural policy was ignored during the transitional period, but merely that it was not considered as important as the markets and prices policy. In 1962, a Standing Committee on Agricultural Structures was established by a Decision which set the three principles for the future of the policy which was recognized as an integral part of the CAP; the three principles were, close coordination between the markets and prices policy and the structural policy, harmonization between structural policy and regional policy, and the primary responsibility for structural policy to lie with the Member States.[3] In 1964, Regulation 17/64, which split the EAGGF into two sections, confirmed that the Guidance Section would fund the measures needed to implement the structural policy.[4] According to Article 11, these included:

(a) the adaptation and improvement of conditions of production in agriculture;
(b) the adaptation and guidance of agricultural production;
(c) the adaptation and improvement of the marketing of agricultural products;
(d) the development of outlets for agricultural products.

Funding by the Community, in the form of capital subsidies and limited to no more than 25% of the total cost, was given as a priority to projects which were part of a system of comprehensive measures 'aimed at encouraging the harmonious development of the overall economy of the region where such projects will be carried out'.[5] In this way structural policy would, as the 1962 Decision recognized, be tied to regional policy. All projects, according to Article 14, had to 'contribute to the improvement of the social and economic conditions of persons engaged in agriculture'. Application for assistance were submitted to the Commission after approval by the Member States, thus confirming the third principle identified in 1962. After the end of the transitional period, Regulation 729/70 confirmed that the Guidance Section would finance common measures adopted to achieve the objectives set out in Article 33(1)(a).[6] However, by this stage proposals had already been made for a more active type of structural policy – one which would seek to promote the first principle identified in the 1962 Decision.

Describing the existing policy as 'a few facile measures', the proposals

---

[3] JO 1962 2892.   [4] JO 1964 586.   [5] Ibid., Article 15.
[6] JO 1970 L94/13, Article 1.

argued that farmers should be given a range of opportunities to enable them to determine their own future:[7] 'The bases for such a policy cannot be rigid patterns, laws and rules. The wide regional differences call for a greater measure of flexibility with regard both to the establishment and the implementation of the policy to be pursued.'

The proposals, which were the work of the then Commissioner for Agriculture, Mansholt, envisaged a reduction in the number of persons engaged in agriculture, in part through the creation of larger, more economic farms and by taking land out of production. The resulting change to the structure of agriculture within the Community would be reinforced by changes to the existing price policy to one more closely related to demand. A connection was made, as it had been in the 1962 Decision on the principles of structural policy, between the markets and prices policy and the structural policy, and the proposals emphasized the need for close co-ordination between the two policies. The proposals concluded by noting that there was no more time to lose.

This sentiment was not shared by the Council, however, which considered the price aspects of the plan to be unacceptable. In addition, there was a dispute over whether structural policy was an area of specific Community responsibility, or whether the role of the Community was one of coordinating the various structural policies of the Member States. The opinion of some Member States, that the Community had no power other than promoting coordination, seemed to be confirmed by the 1962 Decision establishing the three basic principles of structural policy, which noted that the primary responsibility for structural policy lay with the Member States. Such an opinion, however, has no basis in the Treaty provisions dealing with agriculture. Structures are specifically mentioned in Articles 33 and 34, and so an argument that Community involvement in the CAP was restricted to markets and prices policy could not be sustained. The problem was resolved by the 1971 Council Resolution on the new orientation of the CAP; and as for the measures to implement the proposed structural aspects of the plan, these did not emerge until 1972.[8]

Three measures were introduced in 1972. Directive 72/159 on the modernization of farms was designed to help farmers on low incomes.[9] Under the Directive, a six-year development plan was drawn up so that farmers, who practised farming as their main occupation and who possessed adequate occupational skills and competence, would achieve an

---

[7] EC Bull. Supp 1/69, *Memorandum on the Reform of Agriculture in the EEC*, p. 6.
[8] See Council Resolution on the new orientation of the CAP, JO 1971 C 52/7.
[9] JO 1972 L 96/1.

income comparable to the average for non-agricultural workers in the region. It was left to the Member States to define the expression 'a farmer practising farming as his main occupation'.[10] Under Directive 72/160 on measures to encourage the cessation of farming, payments could be made to farmers aged between 55 and 65 who left farming.[11] The land freed up as a result, if it was not used by farmers benefiting from Directive 72/159, was to be withdrawn from production, although it could be used for afforestation, recreation or public health. The final directive, Directive 72/161, provided for socio-economic guidance and training for farmers as part of an effort to raise their level of occupational skills.[12] A further Directive was added in 1975, Directive 75/268 on mountain and hill farming and farming in less favoured areas, containing measures which were designed to ensure the continuation of farming and thus a minimum population in these areas as well as conserving the countryside.[13] Although measures under this Directive could have fallen within the definition of 'common measures' used in Directive 72/159, it acted as evidence of an increasing concern with regional problems within the Community. A series of measures adopted between 1979 and 1981 is further evidence of the increasing regionalization of the structural policy.[14]

In 1985, the three 1972 Directives and the aid provisions of Directive 75/268 were replaced by Regulation 797/85 on improving the efficiency of agricultural structures.[15] Under the Regulation, investment aid was granted to farmers who practised farming as their main occupation, whose income levels were below average for non-agricultural workers in the region and who submitted an investment plan, for example involving the reduction of costs. Community contributions to farmers in less favoured areas, as defined by Directive 75/268 (45% of the costs of fixed asset investment and 30% of the costs of other investments), were 10% higher than Community contributions in other areas. The Regulation also continued the provisions of Directive 75/268 which allowed for an annual compensatory allowance to continue farming. Special aid under the Regulation was also payable to 'young' farmers. The purpose of this Regulation was changed by Regulation 1760/87, which introduced two schemes for the preservation of the countryside.[16] The schemes are conversion, that is, a switch from surplus to non-

---

[10] See discussion in 1.2.1 above.   [11] JO 1972 L 96/9.
[12] JO 1972 L 96/15. See also Directive 81/529 (OJ 1982 L 197/44) on the introduction of special training programmes to promote new activities relating to agricultural processing and marketing.
[13] OJ 1975 L 128/1.   [14] See discussion in 6.3, 'Regional Policy'.
[15] OJ 1985 L 93/1.   [16] OJ 1987 L 167/1.

surplus products, and extensification, an output reduction of at least 20% without any increase in other production capacity. The environmental dimension of Regulation 797/85 was also strengthened as a result of a new Article 19, which provided for the development of aid schemes for areas which, considering the need to preserve the countryside/ environment, were deemed to be 'particularly sensitive'.

Further extensions to the scope of structural policy would result from the February 1988 agreement of the Brussels European Council on the Community's future financing.[17] The extensification aspect of Regulation 1760/87 became part of a Community set-aside scheme where at least 20% of arable land would be taken out of production for at least five years in return for the payment of a premium, financed by both the Guidance and Guarantee Sections of the EAGGF, to the farmer.[18] A similar financing arrangement operated under Regulation 1096/88, which introduced a Community scheme to promote the cessation of farming through early retirement.[19] To promote greater economic and social cohesion as advocated by the Brussels European Council, the existing structural funds were reformed and Guidance Section funds would be allocated to two of the five objectives established by this reform. So, just as the original Directives had responded to new concerns of a regional nature, structural policy would have to respond to new and wider concerns over the environment and the need to promote greater economic and social cohesion. The 1990s would witness further adaptations to the scope of structural policy, thus emphasizing its increasing importance.

6.3 Regional policy

Directive 75/268 represented the beginning of the adaptation of structural policy to reflect regional concerns. Reference should also be made to Regulation 1360/78, which was designed to encourage the formation of producer groups and associations of such groups for certain products in Italy, Belgium, southern France and the French overseas departments.[20]

---

[17] Bull. EC 6-1987, points I.1.1 to I.1.9. See also Bull. EC 2-1988, I.1.1, Budgetary Discipline and Budget Management.

[18] Regulation 1094/88 (OJ 1988 L 106/28). See also Regulation 4115/88 (OJ 1988 L 361/13). As for the powers of the Member States in this area, see Case C-190/91 *Lante* [1993] ECR I-67 and Case C-255/95 *Agri and Agricola Venta* [1997] ECR I-25.

[19] OJ 1988 L 110/1.

[20] OJ 1978 L 166/1. The geographical scope of the Regulation was extended to Greece by Regulation 3086/81 (OJ 1981 L 310/3) and to Spain and Portugal by Regulation 2224/86 (OJ 1986 L 194/4).

The Regulation encouraged the formation of producer groups at a time when such groups were weak and, subject to certain conditions, the Member States were allowed to grant aid, financed in part by the EAGGF, to such groups following their recognition to facilitate the operations listed in the Regulation.[21] As for the conditions, producer groups had to contribute to the objectives of Article 33, for example, by laying down common rules for the production and marketing of goods. Despite the fact that aid could only be granted to producers for a period of five years, aid to producer groups and associations under the Regulation continued to be offered.[22] However, despite the realization that such aid is essential to the fulfilment of the objectives of Article 33(1) of the Treaty, as from 1 January 2000 it will no longer be financed from the Guidance Section of the EAGGF. Regulation 1257/99 makes it clear that aid will continue to be given to producer groups but that this will be in the context of the common organizations of the market rather than as part of a regionally orientated structural policy.[23]

The example provided by Regulation 1360/78 was followed in 1979 with the adoption of a series of measures, referred to as the Mediterranean package, designed to improve structures in Italy and southern France.[24] Building on this package, a series of pilot actions forming an Integrated Mediterranean Programme was adopted in 1984, which eventually led to a Regulation on such programmes which concentrated on rural development measures and involved funding from sources other than the Guidance Section.[25] As a result of the original Mediterranean package, specific programmes for regions other than the Mediterranean areas were also adopted, covering areas such as the West of Ireland and Northern Ireland.[26] The final group of measures adopted around this time were referred to as Integrated Development Programmes, which, like the later Integrated Mediterranean Programme, extended beyond the improvement of agricultural structures to aid with the development of tourism, crafts and other activities.[27] It is worth noting that these measures were also adopted as Regulations rather than Directives,

---

[21] See also Regulation 2083/80 (OJ 1980 L 203/5) establishing various minimum conditions which the producer groups had to satisfy.

[22] For example, it was continued by Regulation 1760/87 (above n. 16). See also Regulation 3669/93 (OJ 1993 L 338/26). See also Regulation 952/97 (OJ 1997 L 142/30).

[23] OJ 1999 L 160/80.

[24] For example, Regulations 269/79 and 270/79 (OJ 1979 L 38/1 and 6).

[25] Regulation 2088/85 (OJ 1985 L 197/1). As for the pilot studies, see Decisions 84/70 to 84/82, OJ 1984 L 44.

[26] See, for example, Regulations 1942/81 and 1943/81 (OJ 1981 L 197/17 and 23).

[27] See, for example, Regulations 1939/81 to 1941/81 (OJ 1981 L 197/6, 9 and 13).

pointing to the increasing importance of the regional dimension of the structural policy.

One further set of measures which seeks to develop the regional dimension is Regulations 2081/92 and 2082/92.[28] The latter Regulation allows certificates to be issued indicating the specific character of agricultural products and foodstuffs. In essence the certificates will allow for the reproduction of the Community symbol on such products, indicating that they are a traditional speciality. Regulation 2081/92 established a Community framework with respect to protected designations of origin and protected geographical descriptions. With respect to designations of origin, the particular product must possess the quality or characteristics which are exclusive to a particular geographical environment, within which the production, processing and preparation of the product occur. As for protected geographical descriptions, the product must possess a specific quality, reputation or characteristic which is attributable to a particular geographical area. In contrast with designations of origin, these products may be produced and/or processed and/or prepared within this particular geographical area. Producers or processors may apply for registration of their products, which is decided on by the Commission.[29] A recent amendment to the lists prepared by the Commission on the registration of designations of origin and of geographical indicators brings to nearly 500 the number of agricultural and food products covered by this Regulation.[30]

By virtue of amendments introduced by the Single European Act, Article 158 of the Treaty now requires the Community to 'develop and pursue actions leading to the strengthening of its economic and social cohesion' as part of the efforts to promote overall harmonious development within the Community. Such actions would be designed to lead to the reduction of disparities between development levels of various regions and less favoured areas, including rural areas.[31] Impetus to the development of these actions would be given as a result of the agreement reached at the 1988 Brussels European Council to adopt a guideline for agricultural expenditure allowing greater resources to be devoted to the Structural Funds (the Guidance Section of the EAGGF, the European Social Fund and the European Regional Development Fund). The drive

---

[28] OJ 1992 L 208/1 and 9. On the former Regulation, see Cases C-321/94 to C-324/94 *Pistre* [1997] ECR I-2343 and Joined Cases C-129/97 and C-130/97 *Chiciak and Fol* [1998] ECR I-3315.

[29] See Regulation 1107/96 OJ 1996 L 148/1. See also Regulations 2400/96 (OJ 1996 L 327/11) and 2139/98 (OJ 1998 L 270/7).

[30] Regulation 644/98 (OJ 1998 L 87/8).

[31] See, with respect to rural areas, COM (88) 371, *The Future of Rural Society*.

towards greater economic and social cohesion, as required by the Single European Act and endorsed by the 1988 Brussels European Council, would be enhanced by the reform of these funds effected by Regulation 2052/88.[32]

Of the five objectives chosen by the Regulation for concentrated funding, Guidance Section funds would be allocated to two objectives: Objective 1 (the development and structural adjustment of the regions whose development is lagging behind); and Objective 5 ((a) to speed up the adjustment of agricultural structures and (b) to promote the development of rural areas, in both cases with a view to the reform of the CAP). A further objective was added as a result of the 1995 enlargement of the Community. Objective 6 provided for special structural instruments for sparsely populated areas and areas where climate conditions were very difficult. Further detail on the measures which could be financed by the Guidance Section under these objectives was laid down in Regulation 4256/88, which, for example, indicated a range of measures to be financed or co-financed under Objective 5(a); these merely represented a list of existing measures financed under the structural policy.[33] Since 1994, Objective 5(a) measures were integrated into programmes established under Objective 1.

The majority of Objective 1 regions within the Community were in fact rural areas where agriculture and forestry constituted the main land use and the primary source of income and employment. The aim of the resulting integrated development programmes was to diversify agriculture and extend the range of activities which could generate income and employment. As for contributing to measures under Objective 1 (and Objective 5(b)), reference must be made to Regulation 951/97 on improving the processing and marketing conditions for agricultural products.[34] Aid for such purposes, which has always formed part of the Guidance Section,[35] in the form of investment subsidies was intended to

[32] OJ 1988 L 185/9 as amended by Regulation 3193/94 (OJ 1994 L 337/11). See also the implementing regulations, Regulations 4253/88 and 4256/88 (OJ 1988 L 374/1 and 25). For a discussion of the 1988 reform, see Lowe, P., 'The Reform of the Community's Structural Funds' (1988) 25 CMLRev 503.

[33] OJ 1988 L 374/25 as amended by Regulation 2085/93 (OJ 1993 L 193/44). See also Decision 94/836 (OJ 1994 L 352/12) approving the single programming document for Community structural measures for improving the processing and marketing conditions for agricultural products in the United Kingdom in respect of Objective 5(a) (1994–99).

[34] OJ 1997 L 142/22.

[35] See Article 11, Regulation 17/64 (above n. 4), Regulation 355/77 (OJ 1977 L 51/1) which replaced this particular aspect of Article 11 and Regulation 866/90 (OJ 1990 L 91/1) as amended by Regulation 3669/93 (above n. 22) and Regulation 2843/94 (OJ 1994 L 302/1). See also Decision 90/342 (OJ 1990 L 163/71) on the selection criteria to be adopted for investments under the Regulation and Case T-478/93 *Wafer Zoo* [1995] ECR II-1479.

support measures forming part of a programme which would lead to lasting improvements in the production, processing and marketing of agricultural products.[36] Such improvements might arise as a result of, for example, developing storage facilities, rationalizing existing storage facilities or improving marketing channels. Such programmes had to offer adequate guarantees that they would be profitable and offer producers an adequate and continuing share in any economic benefits which accrued.[37] In contrast with previous regulations on this topic, Regulation 951/97 gave greater emphasis to the need to contribute to the adjustment of various agricultural sectors which are faced with new situations as a result of the ongoing process of reform of the CAP.[38]

Other measures to be financed in Objective 1 areas could arise under Regulation 950/97.[39] This Regulation, the successor to Regulation 2328/91[40] and Directive 75/268, listed four objectives for funding: to contribute to market equilibrium; to improve the efficiency of farms; to offset the effects of natural handicaps; and to contribute to safeguarding the environment. The particular measures to be part-financed by the Community included those relating to investment in agricultural holdings to help realize the objective of Article 33, the establishment of young farmers and vocational training projects associated with these measures. Continuing the scheme established by Directive 75/268, the Regulation allowed for aid schemes to be introduced by the Member States, which could include compensatory allowances to encourage farming and to raise farming income in less favoured areas. These were defined as including:[41]

> ... mountain areas, in which farming is necessary to protect the countryside, particularly for reasons of protection against erosion or in order to meet leisure needs; they shall also include other areas where the maintenance of a minimum population or the conservation of the countryside are not assured.

As for the protection of the environment, the Regulation allowed for investment schemes to be introduced which would protect and improve the environment; such state aids for investments were generally allowed,

---

[36] Aid is not granted under the Regulation if the project is covered by another 'common measure'. See Case 107/80 *Adorno* [1981] ECR 1469 for a discussion of this provision in Regulation 355/77.

[37] Above n. 34, Article 12.   [38] *Ibid.*, Article 1(2)(f).

[39] OJ 1997 L 142/1. See also Regulation 2331/98 (OJ 1998 L 291/10) the most recent amendment to this regulation.

[40] OJ 1991 L 218/1. On the interpretation of this Regulation and Directive 75/268, see Joined Cases C-9/97 and C-118/97 *Jokela and Pitkäranta* [1998] ECR (unreported; 22 October 1998).

[41] Above n. 39, Article 22.

provided that they did not entail an increase in production capacity.[42] Although the Regulation repeated the requirement that to qualify for Community investment aid, a farmer must normally practise farming as his or her main occupation, the requirement of devoting at least 50% of his or her time to farming did not apply to investment aid for activities designed to safeguard the environment and maintain the countryside.

As a result of the 1993 amendment of Regulation 2052/88, assistance from the EAGGF Guidance Section must help to safeguard the environment and preserve the countryside.[43] The environment also featured as one of the seven development priorities under Objective 5(b) measures.[44] Other priorities included the diversification of the primary sector, the development of non-agricultural sectors and tourism, the development of human resources, and the development and renovation of villages. The broad range of measures supported under these development priorities is also supported through the LEADER programme, first introduced in 1991, which assists rural associations and local governments in rural areas in the design and implementation of small-scale projects which constitute an integrated local development strategy.[45] The current programme, LEADER II, is based on three priorities for which funding will be available to support:

(a) innovative projects which can be transferred and which demonstrate new approaches to rural development;
(b) exchanges of experience and the transfer of know-how; and
(c) cross-border cooperation projects.

The programme represents an innovative approach to the problem of reducing the disparities between levels of various regions and less favoured areas, and points to the gradual transformation of the regional aspect of structural policy into a genuine rural development policy.

Such a development was foreshadowed by a 1996 Conference organized by the Commission to consider the current and future challenges facing rural areas in the Community. The Conference, held in Cork, Ireland, pointed out that 80% of the territory of the Community was rural and 25% of its population lived in such areas, hence the need to promote the sustainable development of such areas. It was also recognized in the resulting Declaration that:[46]

---

[42] *Ibid.*, Article 12(2)–(4).   [43] Regulation 2081/93 (OJ 1993 L 193/5), Article 3.
[44] The areas qualifying for Objective 5(b) funding are listed in Decision 94/197 (OJ 1994 L 36/1).
[45] See LEADER Notice, OJ 1991 C 73/33.
[46] Bull. EU 11–1996, point 1.3.95. The text of the Declaration is also available on the EU's website (europa.eu.int) at comm/dg06/rur/cork_en.htm.

... the Common Agricultural Policy will have to adapt to new realities and challenges in terms of consumer demand and preferences, international trade developments and the EU's next enlargement; that the shift from price support to direct support will continue; that the CAP and the agricultural sector will have to adjust accordingly, and that farmers must be helped in the adjustment process, and be given clear indicators for the future.

Clear indicators would emerge from making a new start in rural development through the adoption of a ten-point programme for a more transparent and effective rural development policy. The policy advocated by the Conference would make sustainable rural development a fundamental principle of all Community action, while recognizing that the policy must respect the principle of subsidiarity, especially in its management. Greater resources, through a single programme which was coherent and transparent, would be needed to achieve sustainable rural development which was recognized to be multi-disciplinary in concept and multi-sectoral in application. The need to preserve and improve the quality of the rural environment would be achieved by requiring its integration into all Community policies that would affect rural development.

One of the ten points identified in the Cork Declaration, simplification of existing legislation, was taken up by the Commission in its 1998 proposal for a new Community Regulation on Aid for Rural Development which eventually led to Regulation 1257/99.[47] The Regulation provides a single legal framework for a reformed rural development policy covering all the rural areas of the Community. Specific reference is made to the objective set out in Article 158 for a common policy of economic and social cohesion, and the Regulation will contribute to this by promoting rural development in those areas whose development is lagging behind. As for the rural development measures which will attract Community funding, these include those which have traditionally been financed by the Community, such as those identified in Regulations 4256/88, 950/97 and 951/97.

Regulation 1257/99, like the Cork Declaration, recognizes that rural development is wider than agricultural development and that agricultural development must occur alongside other regional developments if it is to be sustainable. Furthermore, the Regulation recognizes that there are limits to the scope of the Community's activities in this arena. While it can establish common rules, for example by establishing limits to the

---

[47] COM (98) 158 and above, n. 23.

aid granted by each Member State to ensure that competition within the internal market is not distorted, its role is subsidiary to that of the Member States. This has been recognized within the LEADER programme, and the Regulation emphasizes that the seven-year rural developments plans must be drawn up at the most appropriate level and, whenever possible, integrated into a single plan for each Member State.

6.4 The environment

At the 1972 Summit Meeting of the Heads of State and of Government of the Member States, it was recognized that there was more to the Community than economics. This led to an increasing emphasis on the regional problems of the Community, as evidenced by Directive 75/268 for example. In time this concern would be reflected in changes to the Treaty; in this particular case to the insertion of Article 158 on economic and social cohesion, a principle which was subsequently established as an objective of the Community by the Treaty on European Union. A similar pattern emerges with respect to the environment. In 1972 the Community adopted its first Environmental Action Programme, which was developed and enhanced by further programmes throughout the remainder of the 1970s and early 1980s. A legal basis for such a Community environmental policy was given by the Single European Act and confirmed by the Treaty on European Union.

According to Article 174 this policy would seek to preserve, protect and improve the quality of the environment, protect human health, promote international measures to deal with regional or global environmental problems and promote a prudent and rational utilization of natural resources. Article 174 continues:

> Community policy on the environment shall aim at a high level of protection taking into account the diversity of situations in the various regions of the Community. It shall be based on the precautionary principle and on the principles that preventive action should be taken, that environmental damage should as a priority be rectified at source and that the polluter should pay.

The status of environmental policy will be further enhanced as a result of amendments introduced by the Treaty of Amsterdam which provide that to promote sustainable development 'environmental protection requirements must be integrated into the definition and implementation' of all Community policies and activities mentioned in Article 3.

It is trite to remark that a policy designed to preserve, protect and improve the quality of the environment and to promote a prudent and rational utilization of natural resources would have an impact on agriculture and *vice versa*. Indeed, it is beyond dispute that agriculture has contributed, through for example intensive production methods, to various environmental problems, such as water and air pollution and the loss of bio-diversity.[48] It was for this reason that agriculture was one of the five target sectors of the fifth Environmental Action Programme.[49] As to the impact of the operation of the CAP on the environment, this raises a more difficult set of questions which lead to the conclusion that:[50]

> ... there is a *prima facie* case that high support prices, the particular balance of supports between products and some of the structural support measures under the CAP have had damaging effects on the rural environment. This damage has mostly resulted from an over-expansion and over-intensification of agriculture.

It must be noted that over-expansion and over-intensification of agriculture might also have arisen even if the CAP had not existed. It must also be realized that the CAP does have some beneficial effects on the environment, for example, through the operation of Directive 75/268 and, more generally, measures funded for the Objective 1 and 5(b) regions to promote economic and social cohesion in the Community. The point to be made in conclusion is that while the CAP and the Community's environmental policy have different objectives, which may be difficult to reconcile, the need to promote sustainable agriculture makes it essential to preserve the environment and points to an increasing role of environmental objectives within the CAP.

This found expression in the 1992 reforms of the CAP, which introduced environmental concerns into the operation of various common organizations of the market and a range of accompanying measures in addition to the existing agricultural structural measures. With respect to the reforms of the various common organizations, it is possible to point to a number of examples.[51] In the cereals sector, reference has already been made to various set-aside schemes under which farmers received compensation, in part financed by the Community, for the loss of

---

[48] For further discussion see Stanners, D. and Bourdeau, P. (eds), *Europe's Environment – The Dobris Assessment* (European Environment Agency, Luxembourg, 1995).

[49] *Towards Sustainability: A European Community Programme of Policy and Action in relation to the Environment and Sustainable Development* (European Commission, Brussels, 1993).

[50] Report of an Expert Group, *Towards a Common Agricultural and Rural Policy for Europe*, Chapter 3.3.3, 'Environmentally damaging effect of CAP', available on the europa website, europa.eu.int/en/comm/dg06/publi/buck_en.

[51] For further details see 3.2.

income, subject to a maximum amount per hectare. In the common organization of the market in beef and veal, a number of premiums, the most important of these being the suckler cow premium, have been introduced. Environmental considerations are relevant in the payment of this premium, which is limited according to the application of a 'density factor' established on the basis of the number of 'livestock units' per hectare of forage for the animals for which the application for a premium has been made.

As for the accompanying measures, three measures were adopted as part of the 1992 reform package. The first measure, Regulation 2079/92, continued the Community scheme introduced in 1988 to promote the cessation of farming through early retirement.[52] Environmental considerations were to the fore in the second measure adopted, Regulation 2080/92, which introduced a Community aid scheme for forestry measures.[53] Under the Regulation financial aid was granted as a contribution to the costs of afforestation, the maintenance of forests, investments for the improvement of farm woodlands and the income lost as a result of taking land out of production to be converted to forest. The most important of the three measures was Regulation 2078/92, which established a framework for Community aid, financed by the Guarantee Section, for schemes, devised by the Member States, which contributed to agricultural income diversification and rural development and which had a positive impact on the environment.[54]

As for the range of measures which could be funded, farmers received aid if they undertook, for example, to reduce substantially the use of fertilizers and/or plant protection products, or to maintain the reductions already made, or to introduce or continue with organic farming. In this regard Directive 91/676 aims at reducing water pollution caused by nitrates from agricultural sources.[55] In relation to plant protection products, given the potential threat to human health and the environment as a result of these products, the Community has adopted a series of directives on them. For example, Directive 91/414 provides that plant protection products can be placed on the market and used only after an examination which demonstrates that when properly used such products do not have harmful effects on human health or unacceptable effects on the environment.[56] This directive complements Directive 79/117, which

[52] OJ 1992 L 215/91. [53] OJ 1992 L 215/96.
[54] OJ 1992 L 215/85. See also Regulation 746/96 (OJ 1996 L 102/19).
[55] OJ 1991 L 375/1.
[56] OJ 1991 L 230/1. Directive 94/43 (OJ 1994 L 277/31) implementing Annex VI of this Directive was annulled by the Court in Case C-303/94 *Parliament v Council* [1996] ECR I-2943.

prohibits the placing of certain plant protection products containing certain active substances on the market,[57] and a series of directives which lay down maximum residue levels in most food crops.[58] As for organic farming, Regulation 2092/91 established a harmonized framework for the labelling, production and control of agricultural products bearing a mark indicating that organic production methods had been used.[59] This Regulation is intended to provide a Community framework to meet increasing consumer demand for products grown under conditions which provide for limited, if not zero, use of fertilizers and pesticides. To meet this demand, the Regulation lays down the minimum requirements which must be complied with for a product to bear a label indicating that it was grown organically. Aid can be granted under a number of Community measures, in addition to Regulation 2078/92, to encourage farmers to re-orientate their existing production practices to organic farming.[60]

Outside this category, the Regulation also funded schemes which use other farming practices which are compatible with the protection of the environment and natural resources and which maintain the countryside and the natural landscape. As for the other aid schemes under this Regulation, funding was available to support the reduction in the number of livestock units per forage area, the upkeep of abandoned farmland or woodlands and a long-term set-aside scheme. In contrast to other schemes which can be funded under the Regulation, which involved a five-year commitment by the farmer, the long-term set-aside scheme involves a 20-year commitment. During this period the land must be used for environmental purposes, such as the establishment of a natural park. Regulation 950/97 gave some idea why funding for such measures came from the Guarantee Section rather than the Guidance Section. According to its preamble, the need for reform of the CAP had given rise to a new context in which that policy must operate. It continues:[61]

> whereas in this context, structural policy must be used to help farmers adapt to this new situation and to cushion the effect that the new markets and price policy is likely to have on agricultural incomes in particular.

[57] OJ 1979 L 33/36.

[58] See, for example, Directive 76/895 (OJ 1976 L 340/26), Directive 90/642 (OJ 1990 L 350/71) and Directive 98/82 (OJ 1998 L 290/25).

[59] OJ 1991 L 198/1 and see also Regulation 2083/92 (OJ 1992 L 208/15). See Case C-156/93 *Parliament v Commission* [1995] ECR I-2019, where the Court rejected a challenge to the Commission regulation implementing the general regulation.

[60] Indeed Regulation 3669/93 (above n. 22) introduced organic farming as one of the priority areas for which investment aids are available under Regulation 866/90.

[61] Above n. 39, recital 10.

Interestingly, Regulation 950/97 was one of the regulations relating to the more general agricultural structural measures. Reference has already been made to this Regulation, which had as one of its objectives a contribution to safeguarding the environment, and to the 1993 amendment of Regulation 2052/88 under which assistance from the EAGGF Guidance Section must help to safeguard the environment and preserve the countryside.[62] Article 3 of Regulation 951/97 required the Member State, when presenting a regional structural plan, to indicate:

> the arrangements made to associate the competent environmental authorities designated by the Member States in the preparation and implementation of the operations measures laid down in the plan and to ensure compliance with Community rules concerning the environment.

It has also been noted above that the environment featured as one of the seven development priorities under Objective 5(b) measures.

Just as provisions of agricultural policy have an environmental dimension, various environmental policies have an agricultural dimension. For example, Directive 92/43 on the conservation of natural habitats allows for the creation of Special Conservation Areas.[63] Within such conservation areas, the Member States are to establish a management plan, which can be integrated with other development plans, if necessary, to ensure the conservation of species, flora and fauna. Co-financing is available to the Member States under the various structural funds and the new financial instrument created to contribute to the development and implementation of the Community's environmental policy and legislation, known as Life.[64] Measures within the Special Conservation Areas, and other aspects of the Directive, such as those on spatial development, will have an impact on agriculture. As for other environmental policies which may have an impact on agriculture, reference may be made to Directive 85/337 which lays down rules for the assessment of environmental effects of public and private projects.[65] Annex II of the Directive lists a number of agricultural projects for which an environmental impact study may be conducted when the Member States consider that it is required by the characteristics of the project. Such a study must be conducted for agricultural projects listed in Annex II if

---

[62] See discussion in 6.3, above.

[63] OJ 1992 L 206/7. The programme is designed to establish a coherent European ecological network, to be called Natura 2000.

[64] Regulation 1973/92 (OJ 1992 L 206/1) as amended by Regulation 1404/96 (OJ 1996 L 181/1).

[65] OJ 1985 L 175/40.

they receive their funding from the structural funds under Objectives 1 and 5(b).

The above discussion has illustrated the extent to which environmental considerations are being gradually incorporated within the definition of agricultural policy. The effects of these reforms on the environment have been described by the Commission in the Agenda 2000 document as 'mixed'.[66] The status of some of these measures as 'accompanying measures' indicated that the primary concern is, as was noted above, the preservation of farmers' income rather than pursuing environmental goals as an essential element of agricultural reform. After noting the symbolic importance of the absence of an environmental aim from Article 33, Ockenden and Franklin continue:[67]

> As environmental difficulties have emerged, the EU has attempted to tackle them in a relatively imaginative way, although never addressing (until 1992) the central problem of price support; but the response has remained reactive, rather than to turn the environment into a central feature of agricultural policy.

As noted above, the status of environmental policy will be further enhanced as a result of the Treaty of Amsterdam, which added a provision that to promote sustainable development 'environmental protection requirements must be integrated into the definition and implementation' of all Community policies and activities mentioned in Article 3.[68] This implies that greater efforts than have been made in the past will have to be made in the future to integrate environmental considerations into the operation of the CAP.

This conclusion has been recognized by the decision of the Parliament and the Council on the integration of environmental considerations into other policies.[69] In relation to agriculture, the Decision sets the priority objectives of the Community to be:[70]

---

[66] COM (97) 2000, Part 1, Chapter III.1. As for the impact of the Fifth Environmental Action Programme, see also the Interim Review of the programme, COM (94) 453 and the Progress Report, COM (95) 624.

[67] *European Agriculture: Making the CAP Fit the Future* (Pinters, London, 1995), p. 44.

[68] In this respect see Regulation 3281/94 (OJ 1994 L 348/1) and Regulation 1256/96 (OJ 1996 L 160/1) allowing for the incorporation of environmental considerations into the Community's Generalized System of Preferences. See also Regulation 1154/98 applying the special incentives scheme for the environment in these regulations. For discussion, see Waer, P. and Driessen, B., 'The New European Union Generalised System of Preferences – A Workable Compromise for the EU but a better Deal for Developing Countries' (1995) 29 JWT (No. 4) 97; Peers, S., 'Reform of the European Community's Generalised System of Preferences – A Missed Opportunity' (1995) 29 JWT (No. 6) 79; and Driessen, B., 'On Very Sensitive Cauliflowers and the (P)Re-Cooked EU Agricultural Generalised Scheme of Preferences' (1996) 30 JWT (No. 6) 169.

[69] Decision 2179/98 (OJ 1998 L 275/1).   [70] *Ibid.*, Article 2(1)(a).

... better to integrate market, rural development and environmental policies with a view to securing sustainable agriculture, notably in the
framework of the reform process launched by the Commission's Agenda
2000 proposals by:
- integrating environmental considerations into agricultural policy making and taking appropriate steps to ensure that specific environmental
  objectives are achieved pursuant to the process of the reform of the common agricultural policy;
- considering the scope for the incorporation of additional environmental
  considerations into agricultural policies.

In addition to these objectives, the Decision goes on to specify others.
These include the promotion of sustainable farming, a comprehensive
approach to rural development and a more integrated strategy for reducing the risks to human health and the environment arising from the use
of pesticides and plant protection products. In its response to the
Decision, the Commission, after reviewing the proposals made for
the reform of the CAP, expresses its confidence that, once adopted, the
reformed CAP will lead to more sustainable forms of agriculture and
rural development in the Community; the Commission's confidence can
be assessed by examining Regulation 1257/99.[71] The Regulation incor-
porates the accompanying measures adopted in the 1992 reform of the
CAP and it will now be the primary instrument supporting these measures, which have been supplemented by the scheme for less-favoured
areas and areas with environmental restrictions. The Regulation will
also lend support for agricultural production methods which are
designed to protect the environment. Such support requires the farmer to
give at least a five-year agri-environmental commitment which will
involve more than the application of usual good farming practices.

6.5 Agenda 2000

A start has already been made on the integration of environmental protection requirements into the definition and implementation of the CAP.
However, further measures need to be taken. The Agenda 2000 document envisages action on two fronts: internally, the process of
incorporating environmental concerns into the operation of the CAP
will continue; and externally, the Commission advocates the need to
begin international trade negotiations on new issues, such as environmental standards in agriculture.[72]

---

[71] *Ibid.*, p. 12 and above, n. 23.   [72] Above n. 66, Part 1, Chapter III.2.

The predecessor to the WTO, the GATT, had devoted considerable attention to the question of the relationship between environmental standards and international trade law, through for example, the work of the GATT Group on Environmental Measures and International Trade.[73] A further aspect of the GATT concern with the environment arose from Articles XX(b) and (g) GATT, which allowed exceptions for measures necessary to protect human, animal or plant life and health and for measures relating to the conservation of natural resources if accompanied by equivalent restrictions in domestic production or consumption.[74] This concern with the environment is forcefully restated in the preamble to the WTO Agreement which recognizes that in the conduct of international trade there is a need:[75]

> ... while allowing optimal use of the world's resources in accordance with the objective of sustainable development, [for] seeking to protect and preserve the environment and to enhance the means for doing so in a manner consistent with their respective needs and concerns at their different levels of development.

Reference to this statement was also found in the Final Act of the Uruguay Round, which included a Decision on Trade and Environment providing for the establishment of a Committee in this area.

The mandate of the Committee on Trade and Environment includes making recommendations for changes to the rules of international trade to ensure the positive interaction between trade and environmental measures and the avoidance of protectionist trade measures. The work of the Committee has involved an examination of the relationship between WTO provisions and trade measures adopted under a number of multilateral environmental agreements, such as the Convention on International Trade in Endangered Species of Wild Flora and Fauna. In addition to the work of this Committee, it must be pointed out that various agreements concluded during the Uruguay Round include provisions relating to environmental considerations, usually in the form

---

[73] See BISD 40/S 75. For discussion of GATT and the environment, see Foy, G., 'Towards Extension of the GATT Standards Code to Production Process' (1992) 26 JWT 121; Sorsa, J., 'GATT and Environment' (1992) 15 *World Economy* 115; Thomas, C. and Tereposky, C., 'The Evolving Relationship between Trade and Environmental Regulation' (1993) 27 JWT (No. 4) 23; and Weimann, J., 'Green Protectionism: A Threat to Third World Exports?' in P. Van Dijk and S. Sideri (eds), *Multilateralism versus Regionalism: Trade Issues after the Uruguay Round* (Cass, 1996).

[74] See, for example, BISD 37/S 200 Report on Thai restrictions on the importation of internal taxes on cigarettes and BISD 35/S 98 Report on Canadian Measures affecting exports of unprocessed herring and salmon. See also, Charnovitz, S., 'Exploring the Environmental Exceptions: GATT Article XX' (1991) 25 JWT (No. 5) 37.

[75] Reproduced in OJ 1994 L 336/3.

of exception clauses.[76] In relation to agriculture, environmental considerations have also been included within the scope of the Agreement on
Agriculture.[77] As part of the agreement reducing the level of support
offered to farmers through domestic support policies, a figure, known as
the Aggregate Measurement of Support (AMS), must be calculated.
There are a number of specific policies which need not be included
within the commitment to reduce the total level of support.[78]

The policies, the so-called 'green box policies', that will be excluded
from the reduction commitment include: structural adjustment assistance provided through producer retirement programmes, resource
retirement programmes and investment aids; payments under environmental programmes; and payments under regional assistance
programmes. Annex 2(1) of the Agreement on Agriculture states:

> Domestic support policies for which exemption from the reduction com-
> mitments is claimed shall meet the fundamental requirement that they have
> no, or at most minimal, trade distortion effects or effects on production.
> Accordingly all policies for which exemption is claimed shall conform to
> the following basic criteria:
>
> (i) the support in question shall be provided through a publicly-funded
>   government programme (including government revenue foregone) not
>   involving transfers from consumers; and,
> (ii) the support in question shall not have the effect of providing price
>   support to producers.

If excluded, it is up to the member to ensure that such policies remain
consistent with the requirements of Annex 2.[79]

The examples cited above of green box policies are a feature of the
existing agricultural structural policy. Under Regulation 1257/99 structural adjustment assistance is provided through producer retirement
programmes; structural adjustment assistance provided through resource
retirement programmes is provided for under the various set-aside
schemes. Structural adjustment assistance provided through investment
aids can be made under this Regulation, and payments under regional
assistance programmes are also provided. It is for the Community to
ensure that such policies have no, or at most minimal, trade distortion

---

[76] For example, Article 2(2) of the Agreement on Technical Barriers to Trade and Article
3(2) of the Agreement on Sanitary and Phytosanitary Measures. The texts of these
agreements are reproduced in OJ 1994 L 336/86 and 40 respectively.
[77] For further discussion of this point see 7.4.2.
[78] OJ 1994 L 336/20, Annex 2, sections 2–13.
[79] *Ibid.*, Article 7(2)(a) provides that in the event that the measures do not meet the
requirements of Annex 2, they will be included in future calculations of the total AMS.

effects or effects on production and that the support they provide does not have the effect of giving price support to producers. The analysis offered above, including the rationale for some of these measures, would tend to suggest that further reforms of these measures are needed to ensure that the Community can benefit from their classification as 'green box' measures.

The question of further reform is addressed in the Agenda 2000 document. In relation to agri-environmental policy, the document notes:[80]

> In the coming years, a prominent role will be given to agri-environmental instruments to support a sustainable development of rural areas and respond to society's increasing demand for environmental services. The measures aimed at maintaining and enhancing the quality of the environment shall be reinforced and extended.

This prominent role will be assured by increased budgetary resources being allocated to these measures. However, it is clear from the discussion of the reform of the CAP in the Agenda 2000 document that these agri-environmental measures are complementary, or 'accompanying measures', to price support and production control measures. The primacy accorded to these latter measures confirms that the preservation of farmers' income rather than the pursuit of environmental goals remains the essential core of the CAP.

A similar conclusion emerges with respect to rural development policy, which Agenda 2000 recognized as being 'a juxtaposition of agricultural market policy, structural policy and environmental policy with rather complex instruments and lacking overall coherence'.[81] The Commission has, as noted above, proposed a new Community Regulation on Aid for Rural Development in an attempt to promote greater coherence.[82] This would reduce the existing nine regulations under which rural development aid can be granted to one which would govern all rural development measures to be financed by the EAGGF. Under the proposal, the Guarantee Section would finance measures, such as the accompanying measures implemented as part of the 1992 reform of the CAP and aid to farmers in less favoured areas. All other measures, for example, farm modernization and diversification, would be financed by the Guidance Section. The new framework would provide for the decentralized application of existing measures in the regions as part of a contribution to economic and social cohesion within the Community.

---

[80] Above n. 66, Part 1, Chapter III.4.   [81] *Ibid.*, Part 1, Chapter III.1.
[82] See discussion in 6.3 above.

Under the proposed changes to the structural funds advocated by Agenda 2000, the existing Objectives 1 to 6 would be replaced by just three objectives as part of a more simplified, flexible and decentralized scheme.[83] Objective 1 areas would remain those which are facing serious difficulties in terms of income, employment, productive system and infrastructure. Areas falling below 75% of the Community's GDP, a criterion which would be strictly applied, would fall within Objective 1, an objective which would attract 66% of the structural funds. Funding under the new Objective 2 would be devoted to economic and social restructuring in areas, for example, undergoing economic change or in declining rural areas. As in Objective 1 areas, funding would be available to promote economic diversification and the promotion of human resources. For regions not covered under either Objective 1 or Objective 2, the promotion of human resources would be advanced through a common European framework funding for the adaptation and modernization of existing systems of education, training and employment. Activity in this area would complement activities conducted as part of the Community's new employment strategy. Like the proposed new Community Regulation on Aid for Rural Development, which would reduce the existing nine regulations under which rural development aid can be granted to one, existing Community initiatives would be reformed to promote just three fields of activity: rural development; human resources; and cross-border, transnational and interregional cooperation to promote harmonious and balanced spatial planning.

The phasing out of structural funds assistance for those areas which benefited under Objective 1 but which now exceed the 75% threshold, and the overall reduction of the population coverage of current funds from 51% to 35–40% under the proposals resulted in political objections to the proposed changes. This is despite the fact that under the proposed new financial perspective for the period 2000–2006, the existing Member States would actually receive more than they did under the 1993–99 financial perspective.[84]

As for the outcome of the negotiations on the Agenda 2000 reform package, the political agreement on reforms reached by the Agriculture Council in March 1999 indicated that there was broad agreement on the proposals advanced by the Commission. In relation to rural development policy, the Council endorsed the Commission's proposals for a more coherent and sustainable rural development policy which would create a stronger agricultural and forestry sector which would be more competitive and respectful of the environment and the rural heritage.

[83] Above n. 66, Part 1, Chapter II.2.   [84] COM (98) 164.

The agreement was largely endorsed by the European Council. One aspect of the latter objective was agreement on another major feature of the Agenda 2000 reform package – structural operations.[85] As recommended by the Commission, the number of Objective areas was reduced to three. Objective 1 areas, which would be allocated 74% of the available funds, would promote the development and structural adjustment of those regions whose *per capita* GDP fell below 75% of the Community average. Just short of 13% of available structural funds would be used to support the economic and social conversion of those areas facing structural difficulties, defined as Objective 2 areas, which includes declining rural areas. Lastly, Objective 3 would lend support, in the form of just over 12% of the available structural funds, to the adaptation and modernization of policies and systems of education, employment and training outside Objective 1 areas. Furthermore, the number of Community initiatives in the field of structural policy would be reduced to three, which include the INTERREG scheme on cross-border and interregional cooperation and the LEADER scheme on rural development. Additional funding for rural development would also be available under the agricultural aspect of the financial perspective, which indicates that financing for rural development and accompanying measures shall not exceed an average of 4,340 million euros over the period 2000–2006.

The analysis of the Agenda 2000 document as it relates to agri-environmental policy, regional policy and changes to the structural funds, and the outcome of the negotiations on that document suggest that more reform is needed for the Community to ensure that such policies have no, or at most minimal, trade distortion effects or effects on production and that the support they provide does not have the effect of giving price support to producers. Only when such reforms are complete will the Community benefit from the classification of these measures, as 'green box' measures, and at that time structural policy will enjoy a status equal to that currently enjoyed by the markets and prices policy.

---

[85] *Presidency Conclusions Berlin European Council*, Part I A. Heading 2 (Structural operations) (available on europa website). See also European Commission Directorate General of Agriculture Newsletter, *Berlin European Council: Agenda 2000, Conclusions of the Presidency* (Brussels, 1999). See also Regulations 1260–63/99 which incorporate these decisions into Community law (OJ 1999 L161).

CHAPTER SEVEN

The international dimension

7.1 Introduction

In the Working Party established in 1956 to examine the compatibility of the Treaty of Rome with the General Agreement on Tariffs and Trade (GATT), concern was expressed over the interpretation of the provisions of the Treaty dealing with agriculture. Several factors contributed to this concern, notably, the absence of a precise plan showing the application of these provisions and the wide area of discretion left to the Community institutions in this area. The major concern was that 'the particular measures envisaged by the Treaty carried a strong presumption of increased external barriers and a substitution of new internal barriers in place of existing tariffs and other measures'.[1] No firm conclusions were reached, however, and the Working Party merely recommended that the GATT should set up suitable machinery 'to follow and consider together with the six' the measures to be taken in the implementation of the CAP and the relationship between these measures and the provisions of the GATT.

Having failed to influence the development of the CAP through the Working Party report on the compatibility of the Treaty of Rome with Article XXIV, another indirect attempt was made to do so in the report of a Panel of Experts established to consider trends in international trade. The resulting report, better known as the Harberler Report, recognized that the domestic agricultural policies of the Contracting Parties were major factors in restraining the growth of international agricultural trade. Having identified the basic elements of these policies as being stabilization and/or protection, the Report went on to urge the GATT Contracting Parties that in the implementation of these elements, preference should be given to policies based on a system of deficiency

---

[1] Basic Instruments and Selected Documents (BISD) 6th Supplement (6/S) 71 (1958), p. 88.

payments rather than interventionism.[2] External protection was identified as a factor leading to instability in international trade.[3] By basing its
policy on interventionism and external protection, it was obvious that
the CAP would be a source of conflict between the Community and
other Contracting Parties.[4]

These early examples of the failure of the GATT to influence the
future development of the CAP were to be repeated in the years that followed in both the application of the GATT rules to the policy and in
multilateral efforts to promote freer and more orderly international
trade in agricultural products. With the advent of increased surpluses
and the consequent budgetary problems arising from such surpluses, a
concern which prompted action within the Community in 1988, action
would also be taken within the GATT. The Uruguay Round, launched in
1986, would lead to strengthened and more operationally effective
GATT rules and, more importantly, to the first Agreement on
Agriculture. Taken together these measures provide the framework for
the reform of domestic agricultural policies by increasing the market orientation of agricultural trade, leading to improved predictability and
stability in importing and exporting countries alike. This chapter will
trace the evolution of the Community's relationship with the GATT, and
now its successor, the World Trade Organization (WTO), before an
examination of the Agreement on Agriculture and its impact on the
Community. The chapter will end by looking forward to the next stage
of international agricultural trade reform set to begin in 2000.

7.2 The GATT and agriculture

In the history of the GATT as it relates to agriculture, a significant number of disputes involving the Community have arisen as a result of the
operation of the CAP; such disputes were usually in relation to quantitative restrictions and other import barriers (Article XI GATT) and the use
of export subsidies (Article XVI:3 GATT). As an example of a dispute
involving Article XI, one of the more illustrative was a complaint by
the United States (US) concerning the Community's arrangements for the
imports of certain processed fruits and vegetables.[5] The US requested the
establishment of a Panel in June 1976, but it took a number of months

---

[2] *Trends in International Trade* (GATT, Geneva, 1958), p. 102.
[3] *Ibid.*, pp. 67–68.
[4] See also the follow-up to the Harberler Report, in particular the work of Committee II,
BISD 8/S 121 (1960) and 10/S 135 (1962).
[5] BISD 25/S 68 (1979).

to agree membership of the Panel and its report did not emerge for another 27 months. When the Panel report was published, it was noticeable that considerable legal argument had gone into proving that the Community arrangements were a violation of the GATT.[6]

The arrangements at issue involved a minimum import price, an import licence, and a system of surety deposits for the import of tomato concentrates. The US complaint was that the establishment of a minimum import price violated paragraph 1 of Article XI, as did the other measures that restricted trade. The response of the Community was to admit that these measures did fall within Article XI:1 but were exempt from complaint by virtue of paragraph 2(c)(iii) of that Article. The Panel disagreed with the Community argument, pointing to the absence of a domestic limitation on the production of the fresh produce that would be rendered ineffective by the importation of the processed product as required by Article XI.[7] While this finding was consistent with GATT rules, it appeared that the Panel's ruling that the system of surety deposits was not a breach of Article II and VII GATT was incorrect.[8] Similar problems in establishing a Panel were encountered in the next US complaint against the Community relating to measures on animal feed proteins.[9]

The major reason for disputes against the Community has been the use by the CAP of export subsidies which come under Article XVI:3 GATT. This provides that no Contracting Party should acquire 'more than an equitable share of world trade' through the use of export subsidies. A number of complaints against the Community must be mentioned. Before this, it should be noted that Article XVI:3 gives rise to a significant number of problems, particularly in relation to the definition of the terms used. For example, what is 'more than an equitable share'?[10] Moreover, to be successful any complainant will have to show the existence of a causal connection between the grant of the subsidy and the acquisition of more than an equitable share of world trade. An effort was made during the Tokyo Round to deal with these problems. Article 10(2) of the Code on Subsidies and Countervailing Duties

---

[6] The report was 39 pages long, and it is noticeable that a complaint against Canadian quotas for eggs made in 1975 invoking Article XI did not attract the same degree of legal argument. BISD 23/S 91 (1977).

[7] Above n. 5, pp. 95–107.

[8] *Ibid.* The Panel concluded that the surety deposit scheme was permitted because it was limited to the cost of services rendered. Yet the service was neither rendered by a government nor charged by one.

[9] However, in this case the legal interpretation of the relevant GATT articles appears to be totally correct, BISD 25/S 49 (1979).

[10] See BISD 7/S 46 (1959), for a discussion of this point in the context of an Australian complaint about French exports of wheat flour.

defined 'equitable share' as including 'any case in which the effect of an export subsidy ... is to displace the exports of another signatory bearing in mind developments on world markets'.[11]

The conclusions of the Panel reports into the complaints made by Australia and Brazil, during the Tokyo Round, about export refunds on sugar granted by the Community illustrate the fact that this additional definition did not remedy the problems of Article XVI:3.[12] The Panels could not conclude that the Community had acquired more than an equitable share of world trade and, even if they could have, they would have struggled to demonstrate a causal connection between the increase in exports by the Community and the decline in exports of the complainants.[13] All that the Panels could conclude was that the system operated by the Community had depressed world sugar prices, indirectly causing prejudice to Australian and Brazilian interests.[14] Given the significance of the export subsidy system to the CAP, it could be suggested that this conclusion was politically acceptable to the Community as it maintained the integrity of the system while forcing it to engage in consultations on possible limitations of the system. Subsequent attempts by Australia and Brazil failed to eliminate the prejudice (or threat of prejudice) caused by the Community's export subsidy system.[15]

The argument presented by the Community in the Panels sought to exploit the problems inherent in Article XVI:3, especially the causation problem, and the Panels did not help to achieve a resolution of this problem owing to their failure to give a clear legal ruling.[16] This failure was to be regretted in a number of further complaints against the Community's export subsidy system. The first of these cases was brought by the US against the Community's export subsidy system for wheat flour, alleging a breach of the Tokyo Round Subsidies Code.[17] Evidence suggested that the Community had acquired more than an

---

[11] BISD 26/S 69 (1980).

[12] BISD 26/S 290 (1980) – Australian complaint; BISD 27/S 69 (1981) – Brazilian complaint. As the findings of both Panels are identical, further references relate only to the Australian complaint.

[13] *Ibid.*, p. 318. [14] *Ibid.*, p. 319

[15] See the reports of two Working Parties on the possibility of the Community limiting export subsidization, BISD 28/S 80 (1982) and 29/S 82 (1983).

[16] Similar problems of lack of clear legal interpretation also affected another Panel report at this time, BISD 27/S 98 (1981) Community Restrictions on Imports of Apples from Chile. This was a surprising result given that the restrictions at issue were similar to those in the tomato concentrates case, above n. 5.

[17] This constituted a 'breach' of the implied understanding between the US and the Community reached during the Tokyo Round that the former would not use the Subsidies Code to attack the CAP; see Hudec, R., '"Transcending the Ostensible": Some Reflections on the Nature of Litigation between Governments' (1987) 72 Minn L Rev 101 for discussion of this understanding.

equitable share of world trade as its market share had risen from 18% to 62% since the introduction of the CAP. However, the Panel could not reach a decision given the problems arising from the concept of 'more than an equitable share'. Adoption of the report, naturally advocated by the Community, was resisted by the US and it remained unadopted.[18]

Even greater problems arose in the pasta dispute.[19] The Community challenged the legal basis of the US claim arguing that it had misinterpreted the Subsidies Code. Eventually a Panel was established, but given the history of the dispute and the consequences of a negative outcome for the CAP, it was obvious that the Panel report would not be adopted.[20] The failure of either this report or the one discussed above to be adopted was mirrored in a further US complaint against the Community's system of production aids for canned fruit.[21]

The results in these cases, especially in the wheat flour and pasta cases, merely served to highlight the problems inherent in the concept of 'more than an equitable share' and the need for reform in this area. The 1985 GATT-sponsored Leutwiler Report concluded:[22]

> We believe this concept is economically misconceived, since it impliedly endorses market-sharing. It is also too vague and subjective to permit clear judgment on whether a subsidy is acceptable or not – as was shown by the result of a US complaint to the GATT about European exports of subsidized flour. A better test of legitimacy than that of equitable share is needed for subsidies on primary products.

While there is no doubting the accuracy of this sentiment, it could be argued that disputes were politically motivated in that they constituted a fundamental attack on the nature of the CAP which had escaped largely unscathed from the previous rounds of multilateral trade negotiations.[23] Irrespective of this, the net impact of these disputes was to cast great

---

[18] The response of the US is discussed in Echols, M., 'Just Friends: The US-EC Agricultural Export Subsidies Standoff', Proceedings of the 77th Annual Meeting of the American Society of International Law 119.

[19] See Coccia, M., 'Settlement of Disputes in GATT under the Subsidies Code: Two Panel Reports on Community Export Subsidies' (1986) 16 Georgia J Int'l and Comp L 1, and Phegan, C., 'GATT Article XVI:3: Export Subsidies and "Equitable Shares"' (1982) 16 JWTL 251.

[20] A bilateral agreement between the parties eventually settled the dispute, see OJ 1989 L 275/36.

[21] This was subject to later bilateral settlement in 1986, see GATT Focus No. 38, p. 1.

[22] Trade Policies for a Better Future (GATT, Geneva, 1985), p. 40.

[23] For example, a complaint was also made by the US against the Community export subsidy system for poultry exports. This, and a similar complaint against Brazil, was settled through consultations, see BISD 32/S 162 (1986). See Ames, G., and Centner, T., 'US Poultry Exports: Challenging European Community and Brazilian Poultry Subsidies' (1986) 1 Florida Int'l Law J 109.

doubt on the continuing relevance of the GATT to international agricultural trade, something which various rounds of multilateral trade negotiations had sought to promote.

7.3 Multilateral trade negotiations

The 'meagre success'[24] of the GATT in trade in agriculture products, in contrast, for example, to trade in industrial products, can be ascribed, in part, to the attitudes of the major Contracting Parties to GATT in attempts to regulate this area of international trade. There had been two important rounds of multilateral trade negotiations, the Kennedy and Tokyo Rounds, before the Contracting Parties were to be successful in the Uruguay Round.

7.3.1 The Kennedy and Tokyo Rounds

After the conclusion of the Dillon Round, directed primarily at the negotiation of compensatory adjustments under Article XXIV:6, arising from the creation of the Community, the Contracting Parties were soon to launch another round of multilateral trade negotiations. One of the prime factors behind this round was a change of emphasis in American agricultural trade policy which was reflected in the Kennedy Round Declaration, which listed as one of the objectives for the negotiations the need to provide for 'acceptable conditions of access to world markets for agricultural products'.[25] Agriculture would therefore be an integral part of multilateral trade negotiations for the first time; but not for the first time the Contracting Parties would fail to agree.

At the heart of the agricultural negotiations was a Community proposal, referred to as either Mansholt II or the *montant de soutien*, which had two elements.[26] The first element was the establishment of a mechanism through which the level of support provided by each Contracting Party to its agricultural producers could be measured; this would be done through comparing the guaranteed price given by Contracting Parties to their domestic producers and the price of the product on the international market. The second element of the proposal involved the binding of these levels of support which would then form the basis for

---

[24] See generally, Warley, T., 'Western Trade in Agricultural Products', in Shonfield, A. (ed.), *International Economic Relations of the Western World 1959–1971* (Sage, London, 1976), p. 287.

[25] BISD 12/S 36 (1964).

[26] Above n. 24, p. 383.

future negotiations on agriculture. The proposal suffered from a number of defects, most notably the failure to consider the protection afforded by tariffs and non-tariff barriers and the assumption that world prices represented the true cost of production, thereby ignoring the impact which domestic agricultural programmes had on the international market price. Although the proposal would have led to restrictions being imposed on domestic policies, notably in the area of export subsidies, the fact that the plan provided for limited trade expansion was one of the reasons which led to its rejection by other Contracting Parties.[27]

The significance of the proposal was that it represented an attempt to reach international agreement on agricultural policies. The poor reception of the plan by other Contracting Parties was due in part to the feeling that what was being proposed was a mechanism to ensure international acceptance of the Community's variable levy system at best, or the entire CAP at worst, as an effective means of protecting its domestic producers. The result of the Kennedy Round was that:[28]

> ... on the central issues nothing substantial had been accomplished. Apart from an enhanced understanding of the issues involved, the principal legacies were heightened friction between the two major protagonists (the US and the Community) and a polarization of views as to the basic conditions under which agricultural trade should be conducted.

In retrospect the failure of the Kennedy Round marked a major turning point for the GATT's treatment of agriculture, as in the years that followed the Community completed the implementation of the CAP. One consequence of this was that it would no longer be a net importer of agricultural products; the objectives set for the policy would be realized but the instruments of the policy would not be changed to reflect this. As a result the level of Community exports rose; and such exports usually occurred with the assistance of export subsidies, thus adding to the problems of regulating international trade in this area.

The Tokyo Round Declaration, reflecting the failures of the Kennedy Round, provided for 'an approach to negotiations which, while in line with the general objectives of the negotiations, should take account of the special characteristics and problems in this sector'.[29] Once again, no great progress was made. One reason for this was the limited mandate given to the Commission which stressed that the principles and mechanisms of the CAP should not be called into question, nor should they

---

[27] See Evans, J., *The Kennedy Round in American Trade Policy* (Harvard University Press, Cambridge, 1972), p. 210.
[28] Above n. 24, p. 377. [29] BISD 20/S 19 (1974).

constitute a matter for negotiation.[30] The approach dictated by the mandate emphasized the need to expand trade through the stabilization of markets. Such stability would be achieved through international agreements, either commodity agreements or orderly marketing arrangements, for what were referred to as 'main products', such as cereals, rice, sugar and milk products. The Community's espousal of stability as the main problem of international agricultural trade was not shared by others; the United States, for example, believed that the problem was one of establishing rules promoting greater efficiency in such trade. The resulting conflict between the 'main protagonists' was one of the reasons for the limited success of the Tokyo Round.[31]

7.3.2 The Uruguay Round

In relation to agriculture the Uruguay Round Declaration stated:[32]

> Contracting Parties agree that there is an urgent need to bring more discipline and predictability to world agricultural trade by correcting and preventing restrictions and distortions ... so as to reduce the uncertainty, imbalances and instability in world agricultural markets.
>
> Negotiations shall aim to achieve greater liberalization of trade in agriculture and bring all measures affecting import access and export competition under strengthened and more operationally effective GATT rules and disciplines, taking into account the general principles governing the negotiations, by:
>
> (i)   improving market access through, *inter alia*, the reduction of import barriers;
>
> (ii)   improving the competitive environment by increasing discipline on the use of all direct and indirect subsidies and other measures affecting directly or indirectly agricultural trade, including the phased reduction of their negative effects and dealing with their causes;
>
> (iii)   minimizing the adverse effects that sanitary and phytosanitary regulations and barriers can have on trade in agriculture, taking into account the relevant international agreements.

In order to achieve the objectives set, the negotiating group on agricul-

---

[30] See Harris, S., *EEC Trade Relations with the USA in Agricultural Products* (1977) and various contributions in Tracy, M. and Hodac, I. (eds), *Prospects for Agriculture in the EC* (De Tempel, Bruges, 1979).

[31] See, for example, the International Dairy Agreement (BISD 26/S 91 (1980)), the Arrangement on Bovine Meat (BISD 26/S 84) and, most importantly, the inclusion of agriculture within the scope of the Code on Subsidies (BISD 26/S 56).

[32] BISD 33/S 19, p. 24 (1987).

ture was to use the recommendations of the Committee on Trade in Agriculture which had been established in 1982 to find lasting solutions to the problems of trade in agricultural products.[33] The Uruguay Round Declaration and discussions built on the work of this Committee. Despite this, progress was not swift.

The initial negotiating position of the Community anticipated short-term action to ease the strain in certain markets, usually in the form of annual marketing undertakings, and longer-term action to reduce the level of internal support and external protection offered by domestic agricultural policies. The goal for the Community was managed trade or stability, yet for other Contracting Parties, notably the United States and the Cairns Group, the goal was efficiency.[34] Resolution of the differences between these contrasting negotiating positions and ongoing agricultural trade disputes between the Contracting Parties, notably between the Community and the US in the oilseeds sector, ensured that the negotiations would be protracted. By the mid-term review in Montreal in December 1988, the Contracting Parties were unable to reconcile the differences between the contrasting negotiating positions put forward. Despite the lack of progress, the review reaffirmed their commitment to the objectives set forth in the Uruguay Round Declaration. The review document, finally agreed in April 1989, set the end of 1990 as the date for agreement on the long-term reform programme and the implementation period.[35] Optimism that agreement could be reached by December was high, but the Ministerial meeting in Brussels resulted in stalemate.

Negotiations continued throughout 1991 with the hope that agreement could be reached by December of that year and the Round formally concluded in 1992. As it turned out, the negotiations continued throughout 1992 and well into 1993; the Uruguay Round negotiations were not formally concluded until April 1994.

7.4 The Agreement on Agriculture

The Uruguay Round was formally concluded by the Marrakech Declaration of 15 April 1994, adopted by the 124 governments and the Community that had participated in the negotiations. The opening

---

[33] BISD 29/S 16–17 (1983).

[34] For a discussion of the progress of negotiations, see Breen, J., 'Agriculture' in Stewart, T. (ed.) *The GATT Uruguay Round: A Negotiating History (1986–92)* (Kluwer, Deventer, 1993), Vol. 1, pp. 125–254.

[35] GATT Newsletter *Focus* No. 69 (May 1989), pp. 4–5. See also Hoekman, B., 'Agriculture and the Uruguay Round' (1989) 23 JWTL 83.

words of the Declaration state that: 'Ministers salute the historic achievement represented by the conclusion of the Round, which they believe will strengthen the world economy and lead to more trade, investment, employment and income growth throughout the world.'[36] In relation to agriculture, the Uruguay Round was a very historic achievement. Not only will there be strengthened and more operationally effective GATT rules, but there is also to be an Agreement on Agriculture that will shape the future content of the agricultural policies of the Contracting Parties. Indeed, the preamble to the Agreement on Agriculture recalls the objectives set for the negotiations by both the Uruguay Declaration and the mid-term review. What is envisaged is the adoption of specific commitments in the areas of market access, domestic support, and export competition. Pending the full implementation of these commitments, the Agreement provides for a 'peace clause' limiting the possibility of disputes.

7.4.1 Market access

The results of the market access negotiations, set out in Article 4(1) of the Agreement, were recorded in the national schedule of concessions annexed to the Uruguay Round Protocol that forms an integral part of the Final Act. In addition to the usual reductions in the levels of tariffs, there are also to be concessions on non-tariff measures. These latter concessions are the result of the adoption of the process of tariffication that applies to nearly all types of non-tariff barriers.[37] The average reduction for these tariffs over the duration of the agreement will reflect differential levels of development within the Contracting Parties; for developed Contracting Parties the average reduction is to be 36% over six years, whereas for developing Contracting Parties the average reduction is to be 24% to be implemented over a ten-year period. To reflect the comprehensive nature of the market access negotiations, all participating Contracting Parties are required to make minimum reductions on each tariff line. In reflection of their low level of development, the least developed Contracting Parties are not required to reduce their tariffs.

7.4.2 Domestic support

The centrepiece of the commitments in this area is the concept of the Aggregate Measurement of Support (AMS), which is defined in Article

---

[36] GATT *Focus* No. 107 (May 1994), p. 7.

[37] The process of tariffication is dealt with in the discussion of import levies in Chapter 5 above.

1(a) as 'the annual level of support, expressed in monetary terms, provided for an agricultural product in favour of the producers of the basic agricultural product or non product-specific support provided in favour of agricultural producers in general'. Annex 3 to the Agreement gives detailed guidance on the calculation of the AMS. According to the provisions of this Annex, the AMS is to be calculated on a product-specific basis for each product receiving any type of support that is not exempt from the reduction commitment. Further guidelines indicate that what is being attempted is the calculation of all those financial factors that influence the decision of a farmer to produce a certain product.[38] The reference period for the calculation of the external reference price, which is a significant factor in the calculation of market price support, is the period from 1986 to 1988.

Having calculated the AMS, the next step is to calculate the total AMS, as there are a number of specific policies which need not be included within the commitment to reduce the total AMS. Annex 2(1) states:

> Domestic support policies for which exemption from the reduction commitments is claimed shall meet the fundamental requirement that they have no, or at most minimal, trade distortion effects or effects on production. Accordingly all policies for which exemption is claimed shall conform to the following basic criteria:
>
> (i)   the support in question shall be provided through a publicly-funded government programme (including government revenue foregone) not involving transfers from consumers; and,
> (ii) the support in question shall not have the effect of providing price support to producers.

The Annex goes on to list 12 specific types of policies, the so-called 'green box policies', that will be excluded from the reduction commitment.[39] If excluded, it is up to the member to ensure that such policies

---

[38] For example, the following factors are listed in Annex 3: subsidies which include both budgetary outlays and revenue forgone by governments or their agents; specific agricultural levies or fees paid by producers are to be deducted from the AMS; the AMS will be calculated as close as practicable to the point of first sale of the product concerned. Agreement on Agriculture, Pt III, Annex 3, sections 2, 4 and 7. The text of the Agreement is reproduced in OJ 1994 L 336/22.

[39] *Ibid.*, Annex 2, sections 2–13. The 12 categories are: general services (for example research); public stockholding for food security purposes; domestic food aid; direct payments to producers; decoupled income support; government financial participation in income insurance and income safety-net programmes; payments for relief from natural disasters; structural adjustment assistance provided through producer retirement programmes; structural adjustment provided through resource retirement programmes; structural adjustment assistance provided through investment aids; payments under environmental programmes; and payments under regional assistance programmes.

remain consistent with the requirements of Annex 2; in the event that they do not, they will be included in future calculations of the total AMS.[40] Further exclusions from the commitment can be found in Articles 6(4), the *de minimis* provision, and 6(5), direct payments under production limiting programmes. In a related Article, domestic support measures that fully conform to the provisions of Annex 2 are non-actionable for the purposes of countervailing duties, exempt from actions based on Article XVI of the GATT and part III of the Subsidies Agreement, and exempt from actions based on Article II of the GATT.[41] Any consultations or disputes about these provisions are to be settled using the new dispute-settlement procedure.[42]

The commitment of the members of the Agreement is to reduce the product-specific and non product-specific support that does not qualify for exemption by 20% during the implementation period. A member will comply with the reduction commitment when in a particular year the level of domestic support provided to agricultural producers does not exceed the commitment specified in that member's schedule. Reflecting the differential treatment accorded to developing countries, their reduction commitment is set at 13.3% with no reduction being necessary for the least developed countries. Developing countries also benefit in that investment subsidies and other agricultural input subsidies forming part of agricultural and rural development policies will be excluded from the calculation of the total AMS.

7.4.3 Export subsidies

Whereas the approach to domestic support is to outline those measures to be exempt from the reduction commitment, in relation to export subsidies the approach is to list those export subsidies subject to reduction commitments.[43] The export subsidy commitments undertaken by the members of the agreement may relate to budgetary outlay and export quantity. For developed country members the commitment is to reduce the budgetary outlays of the export subsidies and the quantities benefiting from such subsidies, over the implementation period covered, to a level 36% and 21% below the levels in the 1986–1990 base period. To respect the principle of differential treatment for developing countries,

---

[40] *Ibid.*, Article 7(2)(a).

[41] *Ibid.*, Article 13(1). A similar exception is provided in Article 13(2) for those domestic support measures that have been exempted under Articles 6(4) and 6(5).

[42] *Ibid.*, Article 19.

[43] The commitment of the parties in this area are dealt with in the discussion of export subsidies in Chapter 5 above.

the equivalent percentage reductions are to 24% and 14% over a ten-year period. As in other commitments under the Agreement, the least developed country members are not required to undertake reduction commitments. Additional differential treatment is provided for these countries as a number of prohibited export subsidies are exempt from the reduction commitment provided that such subsidies are not applied in a manner that would circumvent the reduction commitment.[44]

7.4.4 Other issues

Throughout the Agreement special and differential treatment is accorded to developing countries, and even more favourable treatment to the least-developed countries.[45] The special treatment accorded to the least-developed countries is further enhanced by the decision on measures concerning the possible effects of the reform programme on least-developed and net food-importing developing countries. The decision recognizes that the implementation of the reform package in agriculture may have negative effects on these countries in relation to the supply of food imports on reasonable terms and conditions. These negative effects may be ameliorated through the provision of food aid, aid for agricultural development, and the possibility of assistance from the IMF and World Bank. The Committee on Agriculture, which is established by Article 17 of the Agreement on Agriculture, is responsible for monitoring the follow-up to this decision.[46] According to Article 18, the Committee on Agriculture will review the progress in the implementation of the commitments undertaken on the basis of notification submitted by members and any documentation requested by the WTO. Within this process members will have an opportunity to raise matters relevant to the implementation of the reform programme.

To complete the package on agriculture, a number of other issues should be noted. The first of these is found in Article 14 of the Agreement on Agriculture, which urges the members to give effect to the Agreement on Sanitary and Phytosanitary Measures (SPS), which applies to measures applied, *inter alia*:[47]

(a) to protect animal or plant life or health within the territory of the Member from risks arising from the entry, establishment or spread of pests, diseases or disease-carrying or disease-causing organisms;

---

[44] Above n. 38, Article 9(4).   [45] *Ibid.*, Article 15.
[46] *Ibid.*, Articles 16(2) and 17.
[47] Annex A, paragraph 1, SPS Agreement. The text of the SPS Agreement is reproduced in OJ 1994 L 336/40.

(b) to protect human or animal life within the territory of the Member from risks arising from additives, contaminants, toxins or disease-causing organisms in foods, beverages or feedstuffs; ...

According to Article 1(1), the SPS Agreement is concerned with SPS measures 'which may, directly or indirectly, affect international trade', and such measures must be 'developed and applied' in accordance with the provisions of the Agreement. Paragraph 1 of Annex A gives an extremely broad definition of measures, including, for example, standards produced by non-governmental bodies.

The exact scope of the obligations of the members under the Agreement would be amply demonstrated in the hormones dispute, in which Canada and the US complained that various Community measures were inconsistent with Articles 2, 3 and 5 of the SPS Agreement which deal respectively with the basic rights and obligations of members under the Agreement, the objective of harmonization of sanitary measures on the basis of international standards, and the obligation of risk assessment and the determination and application by members of the appropriate level of protection. The Community measures which were at issue were a series of directives which prohibited the import of meat and meat products derived from cattle which had been treated with a series of growth promoting hormones.[48] The prohibition was not total. For example, Directive 81/602 allowed for the relevant hormones to be used for therapeutic or zootechnical purposes if administered by a veterinarian or under a veterinarian's responsibility. With the failure of consultations between the parties, a Panel was established which delivered its report in August 1997.[49] Dissatisfaction with the Panel reports led the Community and both Canada and the United States to file notices of appeal, and the resulting Appellate Body report (which overturned some of the findings of the initial Panel report) was issued in January 1998.[50]

The United States and Canada claimed that the measures adopted by the Community were a breach of Articles 2, 3 and 5 of the SPS Agreement. In particular, they breached Article 2(2), as they were neither based on scientific principles nor maintained with sufficient scientific evidence, and Article 2(3), as they were more trade-restrictive than was necessary to achieve the appropriate level of protection and amounted to arbitrary and unjustified discrimination between the members to the Agreement. As for the alleged breach of Article 3 of the SPS Agreement,

---

[48] In particular Directive 81/602 (OJ 1981 L 222/32), Directive 88/146 (OJ 1988 L 70/16) and Directive 88/299 (OJ 1988 L 128/36). See also Directive 96/22 (OJ 1996 L 125/3).
[49] WT/DS26/R/USA and WT/DS48/R/CAN.   [50] WT/DS26/AB/R and WT/DS48/AB/R.

it was claimed that the measures were not based on relevant international standards as required by Article 3(1) and that there was no justification for the departure from these standards as required by Article 3(3). Lastly, in terms of Article 5, it was alleged that the measures breached paragraph 1 as they were not based on an assessment of risk as required by that paragraph, were not based on scientific principles as required by paragraph 6 and could not be justified as provisional measures under paragraph 7.

The approach of the Community to these claims was to argue that there was no breach of the provisions of the SPS Agreement. Under Article 2(2) of that Agreement, a member is required to base its measures on scientific principles after a risk assessment has been performed to establish the scientific basis for action. As this had been done, the Community argued that there could be no ground for complaint. Moreover, the Community had sought to achieve a level of protection higher than that recommended by the *Codex Alimentarius* Commission.[51] The resulting high level of protection, based on the precautionary principle, could not be attacked under the SPS Agreement, which related only to the question of whether the measures had been adopted in conformity with that Agreement and not to the level of protection which the Agreement recognized was a matter for each member to determine on the scientific evidence which formed the basis of the measures.

The Panel ruling, and later the Appellate Body ruling, was represented as a victory for both the Community and the complainants. For the Community, the legitimacy of the measures had been upheld to the extent that the SPS Agreement allowed for a higher level of sanitary protection than prevailing international standards. For the complainants, the particular measures were declared to be contrary to the SPS Agreement, in part because there had been no proper risk assessment, hence there was no rational relationship between that risk assessment and the SPS measures. This absence was used by the Community to argue that the period to be allowed for implementation of the reports should be 39 months – two years for a risk assessment to be conducted and 15 months for the necessary legislative action which would follow this assessment. For the complainants, this period could not be considered a 'reasonable period of time' within the meaning of the Dispute Settlement Understanding. The resulting arbitration set the period for

---

[51] By virtue of Annex A, paragraph 3 of the SPS Agreement, the international standards on which members are required to base their measures under Article 3 are those of the *Codex Alimentarius* for food safety.

implementation at 15 months, from February 1998 when the Appellate Body report was adopted, on the basis that that report had declared the Community measures not to be based on a risk assessment in accordance with the provisions of the SPS Agreement.[52]

7.4.5 Impact on the CAP

That the WTO can affect elements of the CAP, despite the existence of a peace clause covering the main elements of the Agreement on Agriculture, had already been demonstrated before the ruling of the Panel and the Appellate Body in the hormone dispute. The evidence had also emerged as a result of the Panel and Appellate Body report in the banana dispute. The common organization of the market in fresh bananas came into force in July 1993,[53] and in the establishment of the trading system the Community had tried to reconcile a number of diverging interests, while seeking to ensure that the system was consistent with international trade law.[54] The import regime allowed for the continuation of traditional levels of ACP banana exports to the Community while setting a quota for Latin American producers.[55] For the latter group of countries, special arrangements were made for Colombia, Costa Rica, Nicaragua and Venezuela as a result of the Banana Framework Agreement concluded during the Uruguay Round.[56] Imports of bananas, irrespective of source, would be subject to various licensing procedures.

The new regime was applauded by ACP producers as it allowed for the continuation of their traditional exports to the Community. However, the Latin American producers were very critical of the regime and a complaint was made to the GATT, which resulted in an increase in the quotas for 1994 and 1995 for Latin American and non-traditional ACP exporters.[57] However, this did not put an end to the dispute and a further complaint was made by Ecuador, Guatemala, Honduras, Mexico and the US to the WTO in February 1996. Consultations between the complainants and the Community were held in March, and in April the complainants requested the establishment of a Panel. The final report of

---

[52] WT/DS26/15, para. 37.   [53] Regulation 404/93 (OJ 1993 L 47/1).
[54] COM (92) 359 Proposal for a Council Regulation on the common organization of the market in bananas, p. 5.
[55] The initial quota was at 2 million tonnes (Article 18(1)). See also Regulation 478/95 (OJ 1995 L 49/93).
[56] See Regulation 3224/94 (OJ 1994 L 337/72).
[57] GATT *Focus* No. 97 (March 1993) pp. 2–3. For latter developments, see Nos 98, 100–103, and 108.

the Panel was issued in April 1997 [58] and the Appellate Body issued its report in September 1997, in which, by and large, it endorsed the findings of the Panel.[59]

As for the substance of the case, the Panel decided that the Community's import regime for bananas was inconsistent with Articles I:1, III:4, X:3 and XIII:1 of the GATT, Article 1(3) of the Licensing Agreement and Articles II and XVII of the General Agreement on Trade in Services. As a result the benefits which the complainants had expected to receive had been nullified or impaired. The Community had argued that the banana regime was consistent with the GATT and other agreements, and if the Panel found it to be inconsistent then such inconsistencies would be covered by the Lomé waiver. The Panel did not entirely dismiss this latter claim but it did decide that there were limits to the applicability of the waiver.[60] In essence the waiver applied to preferential tariff treatment only, so, by allocating tariff quota shares in excess of the best-ever levels of ACP banana exports to the Community, it had gone beyond what was allowed by the waiver.[61] As a consequence of this, aspects of the banana regime were subject to the rules of the GATT and other agreements. So, for example, the Panel and the Appellate Body concluded that the Community had acted inconsistently with Article XIII GATT dealing with the administration of tariff quotas, which requires a member to treat all imports in a similar manner, by drawing a distinction between various types of imported bananas – traditional ACP bananas, non-traditional ACP bananas, BFA bananas and others.[62] The Lomé waiver excused Community action only in granting tariff quotas to specific traditional ACP banana exporters which were not in excess of their pre-1991 best-ever exports to the Community.[63]

In January 1998, one year before it had to comply with the WTO rulings,[64] the Commission began the process of responding to the challenge posed by these rulings on its banana import regime.[65] In July 1998, the Council enacted Regulation 1637/98 which changed the common organization of the market in bananas as from 1 January 1999.[66] Under the Regulation the GATT-bound tariff quota of 2.2 million tonnes will be maintained and the tariff rate will be 75 ECU per tonne; this will be reduced to zero for non-traditional ACP imports. In addition to this quota, an autonomous tariff quota of 353,000 tonnes will also be opened with the same tariff rate being applied. Quota allocations have

---

[58] WT/DS27/Rep. [59] WT/DS27/AB/R. [60] Above n. 58, para. 7.97.
[61] *Ibid.*, paras 7.131–41.
[62] *Ibid.*, para. 7.90. (For the ruling of the Appellate Body, see above n. 59, paras 158–62.)
[63] *Ibid.*, paras 7.103 and 110. [64] See WT/DS27/15. [65] COM (98) 5.
[66] OJ 1998 L 210/28.

been made to all substantial banana suppliers.[67] The quantity of traditional ACP bananas imports at zero duty is set at 875,000 tonnes; quantities beyond this tariff quota will benefit from a preferential tariff. A new licence system has also been introduced to allow a right to import in 1999 to all operators who have imported during the reference period 1994–96, and excluding all those who merely traded in licences.[68] The licensing system overall, which was the subject of severe criticism in both the Panel and Appellate Body reports, is made more transparent.

Although removing some aspects of the existing regime which were found objectionable by the Panel and the Appellate Body, doubts as to the compatibility of the new regime with international trade law remained, especially as the regime appeared to continue the discrimination condemned by the WTO. This appeared to be limited now to the allocation of quantities to the traditional ACP exporters of bananas. Problems with the new regime led to a threat of retaliation by the US in November 1998, using section 301 of the 1984 Trade Act.[69] (A threat which is inconsistent with more than one of the provisions of the Dispute Settlement Understanding.[70]) The question of the level of retaliation was referred to arbitration by the Community who disagreed with the level suggested by the US of some US $520 million. In the examination of the consistency of the new regime with the WTO rules, the arbitration panel concluded that the new regime remained inconsistent with various rules of the GATT and GATS. As a result there was a continuation of the nullification or impairment of the benefits which the US had expected to receive under the WTO, which the arbitration panel estimated to be US $ 191.4 million.[71]

In making the changes to the banana regime, it seems that the Community has been torn between the demands of the WTO rulings and the needs of the ACP countries. Although the WTO rulings had interpreted the Lomé waiver restrictively, the approach of the Community is designed to honour the commitments of Protocol 5 of the Lomé Convention. A solution which offered only a preferential tariff to the ACP may have required a higher tariff for dollar-zone and non-tradi-

---

[67] For example, Ecuador (26.17%), Costa Rica (25.61%), Colombia (23.03%) and Panama (15.76%). The transferability of country quotas permissible under the previous regime is no longer possible.

[68] Regulation 2362/98, OJ 1998 L 293/332.

[69] *Financial Times*, 11 November 1998, pp. 1 and 6. See generally Bayard, T. and Elliott, K., *Reciprocity and Retaliation in US Trade Policy* (IIE, Washington, 1994).

[70] In particular, Article 21(5), which provides that in the event of a dispute concerning the implementation of a WTO ruling, the WTO dispute settlement procedures are to apply, and Article 23, which prohibits unilateral determinations by WTO members.

[71] WT/DS27/ARB, Part VIII.

tional ACP banana suppliers. Such a solution would also have been inconsistent with the demands of the WTO rulings. Beyond the dispute about bananas, the Community had already begun the process of changing the CAP to accord with the Agreement on Agriculture through the introduction of amendments to various common organizations of the market by Regulation 3290/94.[72] The common organization of the market in cereals was amended, for example, through the addition of a new title on imports and exports. This recognized that cereals would be a sector where the Community would avail itself of the possibilities of special safeguard measures offered by Article 5 of the Agreement on Agriculture.[73] Further provisions recognize that the Community has assumed obligations with respect to market access and export subsidies under the Agreement on Agriculture.[74]

At the more general level under the Agreement, for the Community, the average reduction for tariffs over the duration of the Agreement will be 36%, and for export subsidies there is a commitment to reduce the budgetary outlays on, and the quantities benefiting from, such subsidies to a level 36% and 21% respectively below the levels in the 1986–1990 base period. In a study of the implementation of the Agreement on Agriculture within the Community, Thomson points out that the implementation of the Agreement's provisions on domestic support and market access has been carried out 'with less than maximum rigour', but that the export subsidy reduction commitments are likely to constrain future behaviour.[75] As for the overall impact of the Agreement on the immediate prospects of reform of the CAP, Thomson concludes:[76]

> So far, then, there seems little in [the Agreement on Agriculture] to enforce rapid or radical CAP reform. Given the exemptions, and the prospects for stronger world markets than appeared likely a few years ago, there seems enough scope in the Agreement itself, to enable the Commission to avoid even changing the CAP on this account, except in relatively minor administrative ways, at least until well into the next decade ...

This conclusion seems to be vindicated through an examination of the

---

[72] OJ 1994 L 349/105. See also Regulation 1340/98 OJ 1998 L 184/1.
[73] *Ibid.*, Annex 1, amending Article 11 of Regulation 1766/92 (OJ 1992 L 181/21).
[74] *Ibid.*, Articles 12 and 13 respectively. See also Scott, J., 'Tragic Triumph: Agricultural Trade, the Common Agricultural Policy and the Uruguay Round' in Emiliou, N. and O'Keefe, D. (eds), *The European Union and World Trade Law: After the GATT Uruguay Round* (Wiley, 1996), pp. 165–80 who discusses the impact of the Agreement on the cereals sector.
[75] 'The CAP and the WTO after the Uruguay Round Agreement on Agriculture' (1996) 1 EFA Rev 169.
[76] *Ibid.*, p. 183.

notifications of the Community to the Agreement's Committee on Agriculture in relation to its market access and export subsidy commitments and special safeguard measures for the year 1995/96.[77] These reveal that in very few cases were the tariff quotas opened by the Community fully utilized, that the export subsidies granted fell well short of the commitments with respect to expenditure and quantities, and that the volume-based special safeguard measures were not invoked in 1995/96.

7.5 The future of agricultural trade reform

It is unlikely that a similar assessment will be possible after the forthcoming round of agricultural trade negotiations given the end of the peace clause, likely agreement on greater tariff reductions and further reductions in the values and volumes of subsidized exports. Article 20 of the Agreement on Agriculture recognizes that:

> ... the long-term objective of substantial progressive reductions in support and protection resulting in fundamental reform is an ongoing process, Members agree that negotiations for continuing the process will be initiated one year before the end of the implementation period.

The negotiations will consider the experience and effects of the reduction commitments, non-trade concerns, and special and differential treatment accorded to developing countries. Other factors to be included in these negotiations involve a consideration of what further commitments are necessary to achieve the long-term objective of establishing a fair and market-orientated agricultural trading system. The Agreement on Agriculture is the start of the process of reform, and Article 20 makes it clear that this Agreement is merely the first step in a long-term process.

In the Agenda 2000 document, the Commission indicated that the Community would be confronted with a number of problems in agriculture over the coming years.[78] The successor to the Uruguay Round was identified as one of these problems. In addition to the areas outlined in Article 20 of the Agreement on Agriculture, the Commission considered that negotiations on a range of new issues, such as environmental and social standards and consumer protection, should begin. The Commission concluded:[79]

---

[77] See Committee on Agriculture documents G/AG/N/EEC 3–6. See also Regulation 3066/95, OJ 1995 L 328/31 (on the opening of various Community tariff quotas for certain agricultural products) and Regulation 2435/98, OJ 1998 L 303/1.
[78] Agenda 2000, Part 1, Chapter 3.2.   [79] Ibid., Chapter 3.3.

In order to help European agriculture take advantage of the expected positive world market developments, further reform of the CAP must improve the competitiveness of Union agriculture on both domestic and external markets. Greater market orientation will facilitate the progressive integration of new Member States and will help prepare the Union for the next WTO Round. It will also help the Union to reinforce its position as a major world exporter.

For the Commission, achieving this goal would involve a 'deepening and extending' of reform through a further package of reforms aimed at converting the primary support mechanism of the CAP from price support to direct payments.

On 18 March 1998, more detailed proposals for the reform of the CAP were published by the Commission, which were intended to translate the reforms advocated in the Agenda 2000 document into legal texts.[80] What is problematic about the Agenda 2000 document and the 18 March proposals is their failure to address properly the international dimension of the reform process. The discussion of price support and production controls ignores the likely impact of future tariff reductions and export subsidy reductions. Equally, in terms of direct support, there are no proposals for the abolition of this form of 'compensation'. Under Article 13 of the Uruguay Agreement on Agriculture, the so-called peace clause, the 1992 reform measures were classified as 'blue box measures' and so not subject to reduction commitments.[81] However, the peace clause expires in 2003 and, if such measures continue in their present form, they are likely to be challenged in the forthcoming WTO negotiations.

To avoid a successful challenge such payments must be production neutral and must be related to the pursuit of a legitimate public policy objective to qualify as what the Agreement on Agriculture refers to as 'green box measures'.[82] Annex 2 of the Agreement on Agriculture lists 12 specific types of policies, the so-called 'green box policies', that will be excluded from the commitment to reduce the AMS. If excluded, it is up to the member to ensure that such policies remain consistent with the requirements of Annex 2; in the event that they do not, they will be included in future calculations of the total AMS.[83] The most obvious legitimate public policy objective is the protection of the environment. Yet the Agenda 2000 document and the 18 March proposals continue to emphasize the primacy of price support and production control measures; the environment (rural development) is seen as complementary to these measures rather than as an equal priority for the CAP.

---

[80] See the EU's website, europa.eu.int/en/comm/dg06/ag2000/agprop/mpt-en.htm for details.
[81] Above n. 38, Articles 6 and 5(a). [82] *Ibid.*, Annex 2 (1). [83] *Ibid.*, Article 7(2)(a).

The discussion of direct support ignores the need to convert blue box measures into green box measures, so as to allow for the continuation of these measures. The Agenda 2000 document and the 18 March proposals, therefore, do not fully address the need to convert the primary instruments of the CAP into green box measures. This is a surprising omission given the Commission's insistence that the next round of trade negotiations encompass such matters as environmental and labour standards.[84] As a possible explanation of this omission, the Commission may have been more interested in ensuring that its proposals for the further reform of the policy are accepted, especially given the impending enlargement of the Community to include major agricultural producers in Central and Eastern Europe.

In the aftermath of the publication of the Commission proposals considerable discussion occurred between the Member States on the scope of the reform of the CAP. In preparation for the European Council in Berlin in March 1999, the Council eventually reached a political agreement on a compromise package of reforms.[85] Overall, although less ambitious than the original proposals of the Commission, the political agreement on reforms represented an attempt by the Council to continue with the reform process initiated by the MacSharry reforms. Although various changes were made to the political agreement at the Berlin European Council, the overall package represents an important milestone for the Community.[86] However, by ignoring the problems identified above with the proposals, the international trade negotiations set to begin in late 1999 will be made more difficult. This is especially the case as the European Council recognized that the decisions adopted regarding reform will 'constitute essential elements in defining the Commission's negotiating mandate for the future multilateral trade negotiations at the WTO'.[87]

---

[84] For discussion of GATT and the environment, see 6.5. For a discussion of social clauses in international trade, see Barnard, C., 'The External Dimension of Community Social Policy: the Ugly Duckling of External Relations' in Emiliou, N., and O'Keefe, D. (eds), *The European Union and World Trade Law* (Wiley, 1996); Charnovitz, S., 'The World Trade Organization and Social Issues' (1994) 28 JWTL (No. 5) 17; Mandel, H., 'In Pursuit of the Missing Link: International Workers Rights and International Trade' (1989) 27 *Columbia Journal of Transnational Law* 442; and Waer, P., 'Social Clauses in International Trade – The Debate in the EU' (1996) 30 JWTL (No. 4) 25.

[85] See European Commission Directorate General of Agriculture Newsletter, *Agriculture Council: Political Agreement on CAP Reform* (Brussels, 1999).

[86] *Presidency Conclusions Berlin European Council*, Part IA. Heading 1 (Agriculture) 4 (available on europa website). See also European Commission Directorate General of Agriculture Newsletter, *Berlin European Council: Agenda 2000, Conclusions of the Presidency* (Brussels, 1999). See also Regulations 125/99, 1253–59/99 (OJ 1999 L 160) and 1260–63/99 (OJ 1999 L 161).

[87] *Ibid.*, Heading 1 (Agriculture) 4.2.

CHAPTER EIGHT

The future of the Common Agricultural Policy

8.1 Introduction

The long-term outlook for agriculture as outlined in the Agenda 2000 document indicated that the Community would be confronted with a number of problems.[1] Firstly, the outlook for the existing policy was described as 'not very promising' as structural surpluses would begin to re-emerge for a number of products. The traditional means of dealing with such problems, increased use of export subsidies, would no longer be available to the Community as a result of the commitments made in the context of the Uruguay Round. The successor to this round was identified as a second problem for the Community. According to Article 20 of the Agreement on Agriculture, negotiations for a further package of reforms would begin in 1999. This would continue the process of improving market access, reducing direct budgetary support and implementing further decreases in the levels of export subsidization which represents the core of the Uruguay Round commitments of the parties in the area of agriculture. In addition, negotiations on a range of new issues, such as environmental and social standards and consumer protection, would begin. Lastly, during the period of these negotiations, accession negotiations would be conducted with the applicant countries of Central and Eastern Europe and Cyprus. The resulting accession of these countries to the Community would necessitate an adaptation of the existing CAP. This was the third problem.

This chapter will specifically address two of these particular problems, the enlargement of the Community and the internal adaptation of the existing policy. The ongoing process of international reform has already been dealt with, as has the incorporation of environmental standards into international trade law. However, before moving on to a

[1] Agenda 2000 (COM (97) 2000), Part 1, Chapter 3.2.

discussion of enlargement and the adaptation of existing policy, past attempts to reform the CAP will be examined.

8.2 Past reforms of the CAP

The fundamental nature of the CAP has not changed since the inception of the policy. Although the range of measures available under the policy has increased significantly, the core of the policy remains the three principles of common prices, common financing and Community preference. Even though a fourth principle, producer responsibility, has been added over the years, it has not yet assumed an overall level of importance equivalent to the three core principles. The original principles were designed to meet the situation where Europe was still a net importer of agricultural products. The support of farm incomes through internal price arrangements, and the partial or total exclusion of imports for certain products as a result of increased protection at the frontiers of the Community, ensured that the policy met the problems it was initially designed to deal with. However, once this situation had been reached, the instruments of the policy were not changed.

As a result surpluses appeared in a number of areas, with a consequent negative impact on prices, and trade relations with third countries deteriorated with increases in the level of Community-subsidized exports and continuing restrictions on imports. Reform of the policy was inevitable. Such reform, according to the Commission in 1980, would have to reconcile four main objectives:[2]

(1) to maintain the positive aspects achieved, i.e. consumer security of supply, income of farmers, free trade and the contribution of farming to external trade;

(2) to set up mechanisms whereby the budgetary consequences of production surpluses may be held in check. This could be achieved by adjustment of market organizations to introduce the principle of co-responsibility or producer participation;

(3) to ensure better regional distribution of the benefits derived by farmers from the CAP; this would entail a radical readjustment of structural policy aimed at the reduction of regional disparities; and,

(4) to organize the financing of the CAP on sound foundations which will not cause disputes in future between Member States.

[2] COM (80) 800, *Reflections on the Common Agricultural Policy.*

Gradual reforms were introduced throughout the 1980s, and to a limited extent they met the objectives set by the Commission in the above statement. For example, on the institution of mechanisms to check the budgetary consequences of surplus production, it is possible to point to the introduction of milk quotas in 1984.[3] Further confirmation of the emergence of a fourth principle, producer responsibility, would emerge in 1986 and 1987 as limits were imposed on market support for cereals and milk products. In 1988 further stabilization measures were introduced in all market organizations and, also in 1988, the European Council agreed to place an overall ceiling on agricultural expenditure, linking it to trends in the Community's GDP. Reform of structural policy later in 1988 constituted an attempt to ensure a better regional distribution of the benefits derived from the CAP.

These reforms represented the beginning of a process of continuing reform of the CAP, but the most significant set of reforms to date emerged in 1992 with the so-called 'MacSharry reforms'. In essence these reforms were two-fold. Firstly, there was a three-year reduction in the level of prices in the arable crops and beef sectors. The purpose of such a reduction was to bring the level of Community prices closer to those on the world market, so improving the competitiveness of Community production. The negative impact of such a prices reduction on the income of farmers was mitigated by the introduction of compensatory payments, which in the case of certain arable crops was based on the withdrawal of land from production – referred to as the set-aside premium – the premium being linked to past production. Likewise in the beef sector, compensatory payments were introduced and were made payable on the basis of a reduction of the stocking rate per hectare. The second set of reforms built on the compensatory payments by introducing a range of accompanying measures, such as the granting of aid to farmers to encourage the protection of the environment, the landscape and natural resources. These latter reforms would be built on as a consequence of the reference in the Maastricht Treaty to rural areas in the context of the economic and social cohesion of the Community, and would also allow the Community to build on the 1988 reforms of the structural funds which had encouraged integrated rural development.

As for an assessment of these reforms, it must be pointed out that they

---

[3] See Avery, G., 'The Common Agricultural Policy: A Turning Point' (1984) 21 CMLRev 481.

were limited to cereals, oilseeds and the dairy and beef sectors. These were areas in which the budgetary and international trade problems had become most acute; other areas, such as sugar, were excluded as such problems had not arisen. So the 1992 reforms were not a wholesale reform of the CAP but rather a response to both internal and external problems, thus raising some doubt as to what was likely to happen in other sectors of the policy in the years that would follow, where the problems were not so prominent. As was usual, the Commission's reform proposals were more dramatic than the end result; the original proposals had called for a 40% reduction in cereal prices but the final figure was 29%. Having said this, agreement on such a large cut did represent a significant shift in the attitudes of the Member States and a symbol of the future direction of the CAP. As for the nature of the symbol, it was clear, especially with regard to the conditions attached to the set-aside provisions, that the burden of financing agricultural expenditure was being shifted from the consumer to the taxpayer. One commentator concluded:[4]

> [The reforms] have failed to address the fundamentally objectionable features of the CAP and they have introduced a new and unwelcome policy instrument into the CAP's operations. They have not addressed the distortions the CAP creates, they leave decision making capacity in the hands of institutions that have demonstrated their incapacity to make good decisions, and they even appear unlikely to have solved the budgetary problems that first put reform on the EC agenda.

In its assessment of the MacSharry reforms, the Agenda 2000 document noted a considerable improvement of market balances and continuing improvements in average agricultural incomes; but the reforms had mixed effects on the environment and had led to increased budgetary expenditure in the sectors affected by them. The reforms were characterized as insufficient to meet the new demands confronting the CAP in the years to come.

8.3 The CAP and enlargement

Of these new demands confronting the CAP in the years to come, one of the most significant will be the enlargement of the Community to

---

[4] Atkin, M., *Snouts in the Trough* (Woodhead Publishing, 1993), p. 146.

include the countries of Central and Eastern Europe and Cyprus. According to the Agenda 2000 document:[5]

> Extension of the Common Agricultural Policy (CAP) in its present form to the acceding countries would create difficulties. Given the existing price gaps between candidate countries and generally substantially higher CAP prices, and despite prospects for some narrowing of these gaps by the dates of accession, even gradual introduction of CAP prices would tend to stimulate surplus production ..., thus adding to projected surpluses.

Such surpluses could not be disposed of by means of export subsidization, given the new rules for international agricultural trade. Moreover, extension of the existing CAP to the countries of Central and Eastern Europe would add around 11 billion ECU *per annum* to the Community budget. The resulting cash injections would create income disparities and social distortions in the rural areas of these countries. So, the prospect of further enlargement would have prompted the reform of the CAP even without the emergence of problems in the existing policy.

There is no doubting the importance of the agricultural sector to the applicant countries in Central and Eastern Europe, even with the problems caused by the transition to a market economy. This is amply demonstrated by looking at the contribution of agriculture to each of the applicant countries' Gross Domestic Product (GDP) and to the percentage of the population employed in agriculture, and comparing these figures with the equivalent figures for the existing Community. While for the Community the contribution of agriculture to the Community's GDP amounts to just 2.4%, for the applicant countries the figures range from 4.3% in the case of Slovenia to 7.2% for Hungary.[6] A similar picture emerges with respect to agricultural employment: for the Community this figure represents just 5%, whereas the range for the applicant countries is from 6.3% in the case of the Czech Republic to 27% for Poland. These figures can be contrasted with the equivalent figures produced in 1994 by the Commission which demonstrate an overall greater dependence on agriculture and illustrate the depth of the problems of the transition to a market economy.[7]

---

[5] Above n. 1, Impact Study, Chapter 1.4.

[6] Figures obtained from COM (97) 2000, 2001, 2002, 2006, 2009 and 2010. See also *Special Accession Programme for Agriculture and Rural Development*, available on DG VI's website europa. eu.int/comm/dg06/index.htm.

[7] COM (94) 361 *Follow-up to Commission Communication on 'The Europe Agreements and Beyond: A Strategy to Prepare the Countries of Central and Eastern Europe for Accession'*, Annex III reveals the figures for the Czech Republic to be 8.5% and 9.9%, for Hungary 15% and 10%, for Poland 7.3% and 28.1% and for the Community 2.8% and 5.8%. No figures were given for Estonia and Slovenia at that time.

Although the structure of agricultural production varies between each of the applicant countries, a distinction can be drawn between Hungary and Poland, on the one hand, and the remaining three applicants. In the case of Hungary, it is a net exporter of agricultural products covered by the CAP and its agricultural policy is export-orientated.[8] Hungary's main crop is cereals, of which 15% is exported, followed by oilseeds. It is self-sufficient in sugar and in years of high production it exports sugar. It also exports a large variety of fruit and vegetables and is a traditional exporter of wine. It is also a traditional exporter of dairy products, and although production has declined in the meat sector, it continues to export pigmeat. Poland is also an exporter of pigmeat, along with fresh and processed fruit and vegetables (in particular potatoes), and is considered self-sufficient for the main CAP products.[9] In contrast to these two countries, Estonia, the Czech Republic and Slovenia are net importers of agricultural products.[10] The application of the main instruments of the CAP to these countries could lead to an overall improvement in their level of self-sufficiency for a range of products and, in some cases, to exports of any resulting surplus production.

As for the agricultural policies currently being followed by these countries, Hungary has moved towards an agricultural policy which gives direct market support for a range of products through guaranteed prices within maximum quantities. These prices are lower than Community support prices, although wholesale prices are closer to Community prices for several products. For a further range of products indirect market support is available and stability in the market is maintained through external trade measures.[11] Similar mechanisms have been introduced in Poland for major commodities, and although these are similar to the instruments of the CAP, market and support prices are, as in Hungary, significantly lower than the equivalent Community prices.[12] For example, the intervention price for wheat was only 79% of the Community intervention price in 1995–96, and the beef prices were 46% of the 1995 Community price. A significant element of the Polish agricultural budget is devoted to the social security system for farmers. Great efforts are also being made to introduce a range of rural, structural and environmental measures to promote a more modern and competitive rural sector.

As for the adaptation of existing policies by these countries to meet the demands of the existing CAP, all the countries will bring with them a

[8] COM (97) 2001, pp. 64–5.   [9] COM (97) 2002, pp. 67–8.
[10] COM (97) 2006, pp. 67–8, 2009, pp. 65–6 and 2010, pp. 73–4.
[11] Above n. 8, pp. 65–7.   [12] Above n. 9, pp. 68–71.

range of common problems to be resolved.[13] Farm productivity falls well below existing Community levels, although this problem is not so acute in Hungary which is recognized as being the most competitive of the applicant countries. The process of land reform is causing some problems – for example, violent demonstrations occurred in 1997 in Hungary against a proposed law allowing businesses, including foreign-owned businesses, to own agricultural land.[14] Similar problems arise in the other applicant countries – for example, in Poland, where the process of collectivization was never completed but where 50% of farms have less than five hectares and where the privatization process has been hampered by the lack of investment capital.[15] Each of the countries will have to make greater efforts to ensure the implementation and enforcement of veterinary and phytosanitary requirements which meet existing Community standards.[16] Existing administrative structures will also have to be strengthened to ensure the ability of each of the applicant countries to implement and enforce the policy instruments of the CAP.

At the more specific level, Hungary is progressively adapting its policies to the CAP, but greater progress will be needed in certain sectors, notably, pigmeat, dairy quotas and cereals.[17] Equivalent problems exist in all the applicant countries, especially Poland.[18] To a greater extent than is the case with Hungary, if the problems of Polish agriculture are remedied, they will allow it to become a significant exporter of products for which the Community is already self-sufficient or an important exporter. Given the almost total absence of product support policies in Estonia, there will need to be a fundamental reform of Estonian agricultural policy to meet the demands of membership of the Community.[19] The situation in the Czech Republic and Slovenia is only slightly better, with market regulations existing for only a few essential products, with price levels significantly lower than those of the Community. In both countries, the focus of agricultural policy has not been market support; rather, in the case of the Czech Republic, increasing attention has been devoted in recent years to rural development and environmental policies[20] and, in the case of Slovenia, to the achievement of sustainable rural development in the less-favoured hilly and mountainous regions of the country, through income support rather than support prices.[21]

---

[13] See, for example, above n. 8, p. 69.
[14] *Financial Times*, 9 December 1997, 'Survey on Hungary', p. 6.
[15] Above n. 9, p. 68.
[16] See, for example, the dispute concerning imports of Polish milk into the Community arising from hygiene problems in industrial milk premises, *Financial Times*, 1 December 1997, p. 7.
[17] Above n. 8, pp. 67–9.   [18] Above n. 9, pp. 71–4.   [19] COM (97) 2006, p. 69.
[20] COM (97) 2009, p. 66.   [21] COM (97) 2010, p. 74.

In each of the current and prospective assessments of the future development of the agricultural policies of the applicant countries, the Commission acknowledged that:[22]

> It is difficult to foresee at this stage how agricultural support prices in [the applicant country] will develop in the period before accession; this will depend on a number of factors including the domestic economy, the situation in export markets, and the development of price support levels in the Union.

However, it is possible to identify a number of constraints on the development of agricultural policy in each of the applicant countries over the next few years. In the case of the Czech Republic, Hungary, Poland and Slovenia, membership of the Central European Free Trade Area entails progressive agricultural market liberalization with the goal of achieving complete market integration by the end of 1999. The countries have also made commitments under the Uruguay Round Agreement on Agriculture. For example, Hungary established a number of minimum access quotas for a wide range of products, it set a maximum level for the Aggregate Measurement of Support it will grant (about 10% of existing production value) and set a limit to export subsidization for its main products.[23] A similar range of commitments was made by Poland, the Czech Republic and Slovenia. As noted above, in all cases the overall level of support falls well below that of the Community, and so it would be difficult to imagine a scenario in which the commitments under the WTO Agreement on Agriculture could be reviewed upwards as part of their accession to the Community.[24]

As a further constraint, all of the countries have concluded Europe Agreements with the Community, as part of the two-pronged approach to prepare these countries for accession.[25] The agreements give a limited range of agricultural concessions to these countries, which have been characterized by the Commission as leading to improvements in the level of access for these countries. It is ironic that the day before the Commission published its proposals for reform, ministers agreed to suspend preferential import tariffs on Czech pigmeat, poultry and fruit juice exports in retaliation against the introduction of Czech restrictions on

---

[22] Above n. 9, p. 68. [23] Above n. 8, pp. 66–7.

[24] The figure for the Producer Subsidy Equivalent (PSE) for the Community was calculated by the OECD to be 49% in 1995; the equivalent figures for the applicant countries are Hungary – 16%, Poland – 21%, Estonia – 3%, Czech Republic – 14%, and no figure was given for Slovenia.

[25] COM (94) 329, *The Europe Agreements and Beyond: A Strategy to Prepare the Countries of Central and Eastern Europe for Accession*, and COM (94) 361 (above n. 7).

the import of Community apples.[26] This particular action lends some support to other evaluations of the impact of the Europe Agreements which are not as positive as the Commission's.[27] Ockenden and Franklin note that:[28]

> The agricultural access provided by the association agreements is not generous, thanks to the influence of farmers' lobbies and finance ministries. However, by offering only restricted access to the distorted prices of the CAP, the EU may not only have saved itself money but also have curtailed the corrosive effect of the wrong prices.

This may have been a benefit to the Community, but it must also be considered a benefit to the applicant countries. To have moved towards the adoption of the instruments of the CAP would have been, and to some extent continues to be, both economically and politically unrealistic. Instead, the applicant countries are attempting to resolve a number of problems in the agricultural sector, mainly social, structural and environmental, to promote a more modern and competitive rural sector. In terms of the objectives of the CAP, the focus of agricultural policy is not market or producer support as in Article 33(1), but rural development as in Article 33(2).

The second part of the preparation for these countries is the adoption of the pre-accession Regulation which will address the priority needs of agriculture and rural development in each of the applicant countries. In Regulation 622/98, a long list of 'indispensable' pre-accession measures is given with a view to allowing the applicant countries to adapt to what is described as 'a rather complex Community "acquis" in this area'. Community expenditure on the agricultural pre-accession instrument was set at 520 million euros by the European Council meeting in Berlin in March 1999.[29]

8.4 Agenda 2000 and the existing policy

As the Agenda 2000 document noted, the Community will be faced with three distinct but interrelated problems: adaptation of the existing policy

---

[26] *Financial Times*, 18 March 1998, p. 36.

[27] See, for example, House of Lords Select Committee on the EC, *The Implications for Agriculture of the Europe Agreements*, Paper 57–I (1994).

[28] *European Agriculture: Making the CAP Fit the Future* (RIIA/Pinters, London, 1995), p. 81.

[29] *Presidency Conclusions Berlin European Council*, Part IA (Presentation of the financial perspective in the context of enlargement) (Heading 7). Available on europa website.

to maintain the Community's position in world trade; an element of that adaptation will involve the re-negotiation of existing international commitments and the negotiation of new commitments; and, lastly, the adoption of this new policy, accompanied by consequential reforms, by the six applicant countries on their accession to the Community. Any one of these problems represents a significant challenge to the Community, but the combined solution to these three problems may indicate that the new CAP which will emerge will be fundamentally different from the CAP which existed at the time of the first enlargement, some 30 years earlier. This will involve a 'deepening and extending' of reform through a further package of reforms aimed at converting the primary support mechanism of the CAP from price support to direct payments.

The initial Commission thinking on the nature of the reforms needed in the CAP was outlined in the Agenda 2000 document. It would involve a continuation of the process of reducing support prices for those agricultural products which were expected to generate surpluses in the years to come such as cereals and beef. The existing quota scheme for milk would continue until 2006, with a 10% reduction in the level of support prices over this period. This was a surprising recommendation given the acknowledgement by the Commission that dairy farmers should not be given the impression that the current system would last forever. No proposals were made for the future of the dairy regime beyond 2006, thereby adding a degree of uncertainty to the long-term prospects of this sector. Moreover, no reference was made in the section of the paper on new reforms to measures which would lead to the eventual elimination of the existing quota system in the sugar sector. With respect to direct income support, the Commission acknowledged that there would be an individual ceiling for such payments, allowing Member States, under commonly agreed rules, to supplement these payments. The model used in the most recent enlargement of the Community to include Austria, Finland and Sweden may therefore be extended to all the Member States.[30]

In addition to the conversion of the CAP from a system of price support to a system of direct income payments, the new CAP would also have to agree a more aggressive rural policy. This was needed not only to implement a more coherent policy to tackle the social and economic problems of rural areas, but also to reinforce and enhance the existing environmental aspects of these areas and the CAP. This latter aspect of

[30] See Articles 138–144, Act of Accession of Austria, Finland and Sweden, OJ 1994 C 241, pp. 45–7.

rural policy was seen as increasingly demanded by the citizens of the Union, who at the same time, in their capacity as consumers, were also demanding greater food safety and products which are both 'environmentally-friendly' and 'culturally-significant'. In addition to these objectives, the promotion of greater economic and social cohesion between the Member States would also be demanded by the new CAP. The first report of the Commission on economic and social cohesion pointed out that only five of the then 12 Member States received positive net transfers from the operation of the CAP; of the four cohesion countries, only Portugal was a net contributor to the Community's agricultural budget.[31]

On 18 March 1998, more detailed proposals for the reform of the CAP were published by the Commission, which were intended to translate the above reforms into legal texts.[32] For arable crops, there would be a new regulation which would, in part, confirm the future role of intervention as a safety net for farmers rather than as a guarantee of price stability. To reinforce this change, the intervention price would be reduced by 20% in one step. Beyond this the essential elements of the regime agreed in 1992 would continue. In the beef sector, the existing intervention scheme would be replaced with a private storage system, similar to that used in the pigmeat regime, to be introduced by 2002, by which stage the effective market support level for beef would have been reduced by 30%. To ensure a fair standard of living for the farmers affected by these changes, the direct payments introduced in 1992 would be increased. In the dairy sector, internal prices were to be reduced by 15% (in four stages), instead of the 10% suggested in the Agenda 2000 document, while there would be a 2% increase in the total reference quantity for milk under the existing quota scheme. Young farmers in all Member States would benefit from a 1% increase in the overall quota, with the remaining 1% to be allocated to farmers in mountainous areas, so not all Member States will benefit. Changes were also proposed to the premium paid to dairy farmers, involving the division of the farmer's quota by the average Community yield of milk per cow, with payments being based not on the number of cows they actually have but on the number they would have if they had an average yield – a virtual cow.[33]

---

[31] See COM (96) 542 final/2, pp. 59–66. The report does note that two of the poorest regions in Portugal were net beneficiaries of transfers under the CAP.

[32] See the EU's website, europa.eu.int/en/comm/dg06/ag2000/agprop/mpt-en.htm for details. This website also contains other publications outlining the reforms of various common organizations.

[33] See *Financial Times*, 4 March 1998, p. 3, 'Brussels offers farmers the virtual cow solution'.

The proposals recognized the diverse nature of the agricultural situation in the Member States by promoting a new division of functions between the Community and the Member States. For example, in the area of direct payments to producers, compensation would be provided in the form of national envelopes by the Community, with the Member States being responsible for the allocation of this money, subject to agreed criteria, to their agricultural producers. As examples of the agreed criteria, a degressive ceiling was proposed on the amount of direct aid that a farm can receive and Member States will be able to adjust the direct aids awarded on criteria they define relating to the number of workers employed on a farm. A similar decentralized approach was also to be taken in the area of rural development, where there would be a new legal framework as part of the process of the simplification of Community agricultural legislation.

The new framework provided for two groups of rural development measures, a kind of second pillar to the CAP. Those relating to less-favoured areas and the measures in the 1992 reform package, such as early retirement, and agri-environment measures would be co-financed by the Community through the EAGGF Guarantee Section for all regions of the Community. The second group of measures, relating to modernization and diversification, would be financed as part of the Community's efforts to promote greater economic and social cohesion in the Community in the newly defined Objective 1 and Objective 2 areas. (Measures in Objective 1 areas would be financed through the Guidance Section and measures in Objective 2 areas would be financed through the Guarantee Section.) Beyond these areas, rural development measures were to be financed across the Community from the Guarantee Section. As a further contribution to the simplification of existing agricultural legislation, a new regulation on the financing of the CAP was proposed.

In the aftermath of the publication of the Commission proposals, considerable discussion occurred between the Member States on the scope of the reform of the CAP. In preparation for the European Council in Berlin in March 1999, the Council eventually reached a political agreement on a compromise package of reforms.[34] As for the elements of the reform package, the intervention price for arable crops was to be cut by 20% in two steps starting in 2000/2001; to compensate farmers for the loss of income, direct payments were to be increased. With the return of intervention to the role of providing a safety net, seasonal price correc-

---

[34] See European Commission Directorate General of Agriculture Newsletter, *Agriculture Council: Political Agreement on CAP Reform* (Brussels, 1999).

tions were to be abolished, as would be the reference price system for oilseeds. In recognition of the Blair House agreement, limitations on oilseeds production would begin in the marketing year 2002/2003. As for other measures, compulsory set aside is to be retained with the basic rate to be set at 10% for the two marketing years beginning in 2000, but it will be reduced to 0% as from 2002; the system of voluntary set aside is to be maintained and improved. In the beef sector, the price reduction is also set at 20% to be achieved by three equal steps; when the final step is taken a basic price for private storage of beef will be established, as will a 'safety-net' intervention system. Once again, as compensation for the price reductions, payments under various premiums will be increased subject to various regional ceilings. As a measure to promote flexibility, various national envelopes are established allowing Member States to compensate producers for regional variations in production practices and conditions.

The political agreement on reforms to the arable crops and beef sector follows the proposals advocated by the Commission with certain important changes – notably, the price reduction in the arable crop sector is to be 20% over two years rather than the one year proposed, and price reduction in the beef sector is to be 20% rather than the 30% advocated. This pattern is repeated in the reforms agreed in the milk sector. Although the intervention price is to be reduced by 15%, as advocated by the Commission, the increase in quotas is set at 2.39% rather than 2%. The quota for most Member States is to be increased by 1.5% in three steps as from 2003, with provision for special quota increases for some Member States as from 2000. As for the future of the regime beyond 2006, discussions will begin in 2003. Once again, to compensate farmers for the price reductions a system of aids will be introduced which may be supplemented through agreed national envelopes.

As for measures applicable to all common organizations of the market, there was broad agreement within the Council on the proposals advanced by the Commission, although significantly the proposal to impose ceilings on direct payments was not endorsed. In relation to rural development policy, the Council endorsed the Commission's proposals for a more coherent and sustainable rural development policy, which would create a stronger agricultural and forestry sector which would be more competitive and respectful of the environment and the rural heritage. Overall, although less ambitious than the original proposals of the Commission, the political agreement on reforms represented an attempt by the Council to continue with the reform process initiated by the MacSharry reforms. However, the agreement still had to be endorsed by the European Council as it was only one part of the Agenda 2000 package of reforms. In welcoming the political agreement of the Council, the European Council commented that:[35]

> The content of this reform will ensure that agriculture is multifunctional, sustainable, competitive and spread throughout Europe, including regions with specific problems, that it is capable of maintaining the countryside, conserving nature and making a key contribution to the vitality of rural life, and that it responds to consumer concerns and demands as regards food quality and safety, environmental protection and the safeguarding of animal welfare.

Despite this welcome, various changes were made to the political agreement on reform.[36] For example, the agreed changes to the dairy regime, save those on quotas, were not to enter into force until the marketing year 2005/2006; and the intervention price for cereals, instead of being reduced by 20%, is to be reduced by 15% with the base rate of compulsory set aside to be fixed at 10% for all of the period 2000–2006. Beyond these changes, the Council and the Commission were requested to pursue additional savings, except in the areas of rural development and veterinary measures, to ensure that average annual agricultural expenditure over the period 2000–2006 does not exceed 40.5 billion euros. It was considered by the European Council that the reform of the CAP over this period along the lines agreed by the Council, as amended by the European Council, would lead to a reduction in expenditure over the period thus contributing to the overall objective of achieving a more equitable financial framework. One aspect of the latter objective was agreement on another major aspect of the Agenda 2000 reform package – structural operations.[37]

As part of improving the effectiveness of structural operations, thus promoting greater economic and social cohesion within the Community, the number of Objective Areas was reduced to three. Objective 1 areas, which would be allocated 74% of the available funds, would promote the development and structural adjustment of those regions whose *per capita* GDP fell below 75% of the Community average. Just short of 13% of available structural funds would be used to support the economic and social conversion of those areas facing structural difficulties, defined as Objective 2 areas, which includes declining rural areas. Lastly, Objective 3 would lend support, in the form of just over 12% of the

[35] *Presidency Conclusions Berlin European Council*, Part IA Heading 1 (Agriculture) 2 (available on europa website).
[36] *Ibid.*, 4. See also Regulations 1251/99 and 1253–59/99 (OJ 1999 L 160).
[37] *Ibid.*, Heading 2 (Structural Operations). See also Regulations 1260–63/99 (OJ 1999 L 161).

available structural funds, to the adaptation and modernization of policies and systems of education, employment and training outside Objective 1 areas. Furthermore, the number of Community initiatives in the field of structural policy would be reduced to three, which include the INTERREG scheme on cross-border and inter-regional cooperation and the LEADER scheme on rural development. Additional funding for rural development would also be available under the agricultural aspect of the financial perspective, which indicates that financing for rural development and accompanying measures shall not exceed an average of 4,340 million euros over the period 2000–2006.

The overall agreement on the Agenda 2000 package reached at the Berlin European Council undoubtedly represents an important milestone for the Community. The question to be asked is whether or not the reforms agreed will allow the Community to meet the problems identified in the Agenda 2000 document. With respect to the existing policy, the reforms do not go as far as advocated by the Commission. The traditional slippage between Commission proposals and Council agreement has recurred; indeed, this time the European Council added to the slippage. So problems with the existing policy are likely to re-emerge, assuming of course that the reforms agreed are adequate to allow some of the problems to disappear for a time. It is possible that new problems may also arise, for example in the area of the decentralization of payments under the CAP in the form of national envelopes. The size of these national envelopes in the beef sector will be 493 million euros and the envelopes will give the Member States the flexibility to compensate for regional production variations and conditions and to encourage extensive production. So a Member State may be able to adjust the direct aids awarded on criteria they define relating, for example, to the number of workers employed on a farm, and one consequence of this may be that distortions in competition will arise between the Member States which may threaten the integrity of the single market. It must be recognized at this point that the existence of various national quota schemes within the CAP is in effect an exception to the integrity of the single market.

As previously noted, the results of the reforms agreed at Berlin will make the international trade negotiations set to begin in early 2000 more difficult as the decisions adopted regarding reform will, as the European Council recognized, 'constitute essential elements in defining the Commission's negotiating mandate for the future multilateral trade negotiations at the WTO'.[38] In terms of direct support, there are no proposals for the abolition of this form of 'compensation' or for its

[38] *Ibid.*, Heading 1 (Agriculture) 4.2.

conversion into truly decoupled payments. Under Article 13 of the Uruguay Agreement on Agriculture, the peace clause, the 1992 reform measures were classified as blue box measures and so not subject to reduction commitments.[39] However, the peace clause expires in 2003, and if such measures continue in their present form, they are likely to be challenged in the forthcoming WTO negotiations. To avoid a successful challenge, such payments must be production neutral and must be related to the pursuit of a legitimate public policy objective to qualify as what the Agreement on Agriculture refers to as 'green box measures'.[40] Annex 2 of the Agreement on Agriculture lists 12 specific types of policies, the so-called 'green box' policies, that will be excluded from the commitment to reduce the AMS.[41] The most obvious legitimate public policy objective is the protection of the environment, hence the reference in the Agenda 2000 document to the beginning of international negotiations on new issues, such as environmental standards. The reform process, from the Agenda 2000 document to the conclusions of the Berlin European Council, continues to emphasize the primacy of price support and production control measures.

Lastly, in relation to enlargement there are two particular problems. Firstly, in relation to direct support, as there are no proposals for the abolition of this form of 'compensation' or for its conversion into truly decoupled payments, it is unthinkable that the acceding countries would agree not to have the same rights and duties with respect to agriculture as the existing Member States, but this raises the problem of these countries receiving 'compensation' for losses which they have not suffered. Secondly, by agreeing on lesser price reductions than proposed and by delaying in some cases the onset of those reductions, the agreement adds to the cost of enlarging the Community to include major agricultural producers in Central Europe without further reform to the CAP. The result may be that the working assumption of the accession of new Member States starting in 2002 may be overly optimistic, and this despite the appropriations made for agriculture in the context of accession.[42] The overall result may well be that rather than addressing the three problems identified in the Agenda 2000 document, the Community has merely postponed the adoption of realistic measures which would resolve these problems.

---

[39] Articles 6 and 5(a), Agreement on Agriculture, reproduced in OJ 1994 L 336/20.

[40] *Ibid.*, Annex 2, para. 1 of the Agreement on Agriculture. (For further discussion, see 6.5 above.)

[41] *Ibid.*, Annex 2, sections 2–13. The relationship between existing Community structural measures and these 12 categories is discussed at 6.5 above.

[42] *Ibid.*, Table B., 'Financial Framework for EU-21', which indicates the appropriations will rise from 1,600 million euros in 2002 to 3,400 million euros in 2006.

8.5 The future?

The international dimension points to the need to agree a realistic set of new objectives for the CAP. The existing objectives set for the CAP in Article 33(1) are:

(a) to increase agricultural productivity by promoting technical progress and by ensuring the rational development of agricultural production and the optimum utilization of the factors of production, in particular labour;
(b) thus to ensure a fair standard of living for the agricultural community, in particular by increasing the individual earnings of persons engaged in agriculture;
(c) to stabilize markets;
(d) to assure availability of supplies;
(e) to ensure supplies reach consumers at reasonable prices.

Further objectives, of a regional and social nature, are added by the second paragraph of Article 33. The end result is a series of objectives which are conflicting and not capable of reconciliation; despite the fact that this has been recognized for a long time, Article 33 has never been considered as an article in need of reform at the various Inter-Governmental Conferences.

To the list of objectives in Article 33, others have been added over the years, and the Commission now wishes to add an additional series of objectives. In essence, the Commission in the Agenda 2000 document is trying to rewrite the objectives set down in Article 33. Such a rewrite would set the objectives of the CAP as being:[43]

(a) to improve the Union's competitiveness through lower prices;
(b) to guarantee the safety and quality of food to consumers;
(c) to ensure stable incomes and a fair standard of living for the agricultural community;
(d) to make its production methods environmentally friendly and respect animal welfare;
(e) to integrate environmental goals into its instruments;
(f) to seek to create alternative income and employment opportunities for farmers and their families.

The obvious question to ask is: Is a reformed CAP the best way to

---

[43] See 'Agenda 2000 For a stronger and wider Union', part 4, 'Further reform of the Common Agricultural Policy', available on the EU's website europa.eu.int/comm/agenda2000/overview/en/agenda.htm.

achieve these objectives? For example, would environmental problems be resolved in a more effective and efficient manner through an enhanced environmental policy rather than through the environment being an element of a response to the problems arising from price support in the CAP?

In November 1995, the Directorate General for Agriculture invited a group of experts to analyze the inconsistencies and problems inherent in the existing CAP, and in this light to define a series of principles which would form the basis of a new integrated rural policy. The resulting report, known as the Buckwell Report, proposed that the existing CAP should be transformed into a Common Agricultural and Rural Policy for Europe (CARPE), the objective of which would be 'to ensure an economically efficient and environmentally sustainable agriculture and to stimulate the integrated development of the Union's rural areas'.[44] The three elements of the new policy – economic efficiency (through market stabilization), the environment (through environmental and cultural landscape payments) and rural development (through a series of incentives) – would, unlike the CAP, be equally balanced. The report makes it clear that the new policy, although revolutionary, will also be evolutionary, so allowing the policy to respond to new challenges as they emerge.

In relation to market stabilization, the goal will be to reduce the level of price support to world market levels, and the role of the Community will be to provide a safety net in the form of intervention. One of the advantages of this approach is that it would open the Community market to greater imports as the isolation of that market is ended. This would allow the Community to participate effectively in the next round of international trade negotiations on agriculture as the support which it provides would be decoupled.

One of the legitimate public policy objectives to qualify as what the Agreement on Agriculture refers to as 'green box policies', the protection of the environment, is the second aspect of the proposed CARPE. The environmental and cultural landscape payments are made for positive action taken by farmers, positive action being defined as the provision of services which impose any additional costs on farmers. The payments would be regionally based and there would be two levels of payments. The first level would be directed to farming systems providing high nature value; while the second level would concern specific environmental management practices, which involve intensive action to preserve or create significant environmental effects. The distinction between the two levels rests in the fact that level one is directed at farming whereas level

---

[44] See europa.eu.int/en/comm/dg06/publi/buck_en/index.htm, Chapter 6.1.

two is directed at the environment, although there would be some cross-fertilization between the two levels.

The environmental and cultural landscape programmes will form part of the third aspect of the proposed new policy, Rural Development Incentives. Rural development would remain wider than agricultural development and the approach would involve a continuation of the existing policy of promoting sustainable rural development. So the existing measures of assistance directed towards agricultural development would continue. Given the major changes involved in the transition from the CAP to the CARPE, the report recommended the transformation of the compensation payments introduced in the 1992 reform package into what is termed Transitional Adjustment Assistance. The three principles of such assistance are that it will be decoupled from production, be non-distorting to competition and that recipients should respect environmental conditions. The report concludes:[45]

> From its origins, when the CAP was most definitely part of the big European political and cultural compromise – assistance for agriculture to adjust, in return for an open market for industrial products – it has descended into [a] purely commodity approach. In this process it lost its sense of purpose. A bold new start towards a more integrated rural policy could reassert a constructive role for this important aspect of the European Union.

CARPE represents one bold new approach to the many problems facing the CAP over the years to come: problems with the existing policy; problems which may arise from the enlargement of the Community; and problems which may arise at the international level. Perhaps the Community should seize the opportunity presented by the approach advocated by the Buckwell Report rather than continuing with a policy which has clearly passed its sell-by date.

[45] *Ibid.*, Chapter 8.5.

Bibliography

Ames, G. and Centner, T., 'US Poultry Exports: Challenging European Community and Brazilian Poultry Subsidies' (1986) 1 Florida Int'l Law J 109

Atkin, M., *Snouts in the Trough* (Woodhead Publishing, 1993)

Avery, G., 'The Common Agricultural Policy: A Turning Point' (1984) 21 CMLRev 481

Barents, R., 'The System of Deposits in Community Agricultural Law: Efficiency v. Proportionality' (1985) 10 ELRev 239

Barents, R., *The Agricultural Law of the EC* (Kluwer, 1994)

Barnard, C., 'The External Dimension of Community Social Policy: the Ugly Duckling of External Relations' in Emiliou, N., and O'Keefe, D. (eds) *The European Union and World Trade Law* (Wiley, 1996)

Bayard, T. and Elliott, K., *Reciprocity and Retaliation in US Trade Policy* (IIE, 1994)

Braakman, G., 'Monetary Evolutions and the Common Agricultural Policy' (1978) 15 CMLRev 157

Breen, J., 'Agriculture' in Stewart, T. (ed.), *The GATT Uruguay Round: A Negotiating History (1986–92)* (Kluwer, 1993), Vol. 1

Buckwell, A. et al. *The Costs of the Common Agricultural Policy* (Croom Helm, 1982)

Camps, M., *Britain and the European Community 1955–63* (OUP, 1964)

Charnovitz, S., 'Exploring the Environmental Exceptions: GATT Article XX' (1991) 25 JWT (No. 5) 37

Charnovitz, S., 'The World Trade Organization and Social Issues' (1994) 28 JWTL (No. 5) 17

Coccia, M., 'Settlement of Disputes in GATT under the Subsidies Code: Two Panel Reports on Community Export Subsidies' (1986) 16 Georgia J Int'l and Comp L 1

Davenport, M., Hewitt, A. and Koning, A., *Europe's Preferred Partners? The Lomé Countries in World Trade* (ODI, 1995)

Driessen, B., 'On Very Sensitive Cauliflowers and the (P)Re-cooked EU Agricultural Generalised Scheme of Preferences' (1996) 30 JWT (No. 6) 169

Echols, M., 'Just Friends: The US-EC Agricultural Export Subsidies Standoff' Proceedings of the 77th Annual Meeting of the American Society of International Law 119

El-Agraa, A., *The Economics of the Common Market* (4th ed.) (Harvester Wheatsheaf, 1994)

Evans, J., *The Kennedy Round in American Trade Policy* (Harvard University Press, 1972)

Foy, G., 'Towards Extension of the GATT Standards Code to Production Process' (1992) 26 JWT 121

Francois, J., McDonald, B. and Nordström, H., *A User's Guide to Uruguay Round Assessments* (WTO Staff Working Paper RD-96-003)

GATT, *Trends in International Trade* (GATT, Geneva, 1958)

GATT, *Trade Policies for a Better Future* (GATT, Geneva, 1985)

Gilsdorf, P., 'The System of Monetary Compensatory Amounts from a Legal Standpoint' (1980) 5 ELRev 341 and 433

Grabbe, H. and Hughes, K., *Enlarging the EU Eastwards* (RIIA, 1998)

Grant, W., 'The Politics of the Green Pound 1974–79' (1981) 19 JCMS 313

Griffiths, R. and Girvin, B. (eds), *The Green Pool and the Origins of the Common Agricultural Policy* (Lothian Press, 1995)

Harris, S., *EEC Trade Relations with the USA in Agricultural Products* (CEAS, 1977)

Heidhues, T. et al., *Common Prices and Europe's Farm Policy* (TPRC, 1978)

Hertel, T., 'Agricultural Trade Liberalization and the Developing Countries: A Survey of the Models' in Goldin, I. and Knudsen, D. (eds), *Agricultural Trade Liberalization: Implications for Developing Countries* (OECD/World Bank, 1990)

Hoekman, B., 'Agriculture and the Uruguay Round' (1989) 23 JWTL 83

House of Lords Select Committee on the EC, *The Implications for Agriculture of the Europe Agreements*, Paper 57–I (1994)

Hudec, R., '"Transcending the Ostensible": Some Reflections on the Nature of Litigation between Governments' (1987) 72 Minn L Rev 101

Lowe, P., 'The Reform of the Community's Structural Funds' (1988) 25 CMLRev 503

Mandel, H., 'In Pursuit of the Missing Link: International Workers Rights and International Trade' (1989) 27 *Columbia Journal of Transnational Law* 442

Mansholt, S., 'Towards European Integration, Beginnings in Agriculture' (1952) 31 *Foreign Affairs* 112

Marsh, J. and Swanney, P., *Agriculture and the European Community* (Allen & Unwin, 1980)

Neville-Rolfe, E., *The Politics of Agriculture in the European Community* (European Centre for Political Studies, 1984)

Ockenden, J. and Franklin, M., *European Agriculture: Making the CAP Fit the Future* (Pinters, 1995)

Olmi, G., 'Common Organisation of Agricultural Markets at the Stage of the Single Market' (1967–68) 5 CMLRev 354

Page, S. and Davenport, M., *World Trade Reform: Do Developing Countries Gain or Lose?* (ODI, 1995)

Paulin, B. and Forman, J., 'The French Banana Story and its Implications' (1975) 12 CMLRev 399

Peers, S., 'Reform of the European Community's Generalised System of Preferences – A Missed Opportunity' (1995) 29 JWT (No. 6) 79

Phegan, C., 'GATT Article XVI:3: Export Subsidies and "Equitable Shares"', (1982) 16 JWTL 251.

Sack, J., 'The Commission's powers under the safeguard clauses of the common organizations of agricultural markets' (1983) 20 CMLRev 157

Scott, J., 'Tragic Triumph: Agricultural Trade, the Common Agricultural Policy and the Uruguay Round' in Emiliou, N. and O'Keefe, D. (eds), *The European Union and World Trade Law: After the GATT Uruguay Round* (Wiley, 1996)

Shaw, J., 'The effect of Article 46 EEC' (1984) 9 ELRev 284

Sorsa, J., 'GATT and Environment' (1992) 15 *World Economy* 115

Stanners, D. and Bourdeau, P. (eds), *Europe's Environment – The Dobris Assessment* (European Environment Agency, Luxembourg, 1995)

Strasser, D., *The Finances of Europe* (OOPEC, Luxembourg, 1981)

Strauss, R., 'The Economic Effects of Monetary Compensatory Amounts' (1983) JCMS 261

Thomas, C. and Tereposky, C., 'The Evolving Relationship between Trade and Environmental Regulation' (1993) 27 JWT (No. 4) 23

Thomson, K., 'The CAP and the WTO after the Uruguay Round Agreement on Agriculture' (1996) 1 EFA Rev 169

Tracy, M., *Agriculture in Western Europe: Challenge and Response (1880–1980)* (2nd ed.) (Granada, 1982)

Usher, J., 'Agricultural Markets: Their Price Systems and Financial Mechanisms' (1979) 4 ELRev 147

Usher, J., *Legal Aspects of Agriculture in the European Community* (OUP, 1988)

Vasey, M., 'The 1985 Farm Price Negotiations and the Reform of the Common Agricultural Policy' (1985) 22 CMLRev 649

Vasey, M., 'Decision-making in the Agricultural Council and the "Luxembourg" compromise' (1988) 25 CMLRev 725

Waer, P., 'Social Clauses in International Trade – The Debate in the EU' (1996) 30 JWTL (No. 4) 25

Waer, P. and Driessen, B., 'The New European Union Generalised System of Preferences – A Workable Compromise for the EU but a better Deal for Developing Countries' (1995) 29 JWT (No. 4) 97

Warley, T., 'Western Trade in Agricultural Products', in Shonfield, A. (ed.), *International Economic Relations of the Western World 1959–1971* (Sage, 1976)

Weimann, J., 'Green Protectionism: A Threat to Third World Exports?' in Van Dijk, P. and Sideri, S. (eds), *Multilateralism versus Regionalism: Trade Issues after the Uruguay Round* (Cass, 1996)

Wyatt, D., 'British Import Controls on Main Crop Potatoes' (1979) 4 ELRev 359

Spaak Report (Bruxelles, 1956)

COM (80) 800 *Reflections on the CAP*

Towards Sustainability: A European Community Programme of Policy and Action in Relation to the Environment and Sustainable Development (European Commission, Brussels, 1993)

COM (88) 371 *The Future of Rural Society*

COM (94) 329 *The Europe Agreements and Beyond: A Strategy to Prepare the Countries of Central and Eastern Europe for Accession*

COM(94) 361 *Follow-up to Commission Communication on the Europe Agreements and Beyond: A Strategy to Prepare the Countries of Central and Eastern Europe for Accession*

COM (96) 570 *Green Paper on relations between the European Union and the ACP countries in the eve of the 21st century: Challenges and options for a new partnership*

COM(97) 156 *Improving Market Access for Least Developed Countries*

COM (97) 477 *Mediterranean Concessions Impact Study*

COM(97) 537 *Guidelines for the negotiation of new cooperation agreements with the African, Caribbean and Pacific (ACP) countries*

Agenda 2000 (Brussels, 1997)

COM (98) 276 *Fight Against Fraud – Annual Report 1997*

Special Reports of the Court of Auditors

2/92 (OJ 1993 C 101/1) on export refunds

4/93 (OJ 1994 C 12/1) on the implementation of the quota system intended to control milk production

7/93 (OJ 1993 C 53/1) concerning controls of irregularities and fraud in the agricultural area

8/98 (OJ 1998 C 230/1) concerning the Commission departments responsible for fighting fraud, notably the Unit for the Coordination of Fraud Prevention (UCLAF)

europa.eu.int/comm/agenda2000/overview/en/agenda.htm
europa.eu.int/en/comm/dg06/publi/buck_en/index.htm

Index

Abbreviations used in the index are the same as those contained in the List of Abbreviations on page x